Status and Social Comparisons Among Adolescents

This insightful book examines the differences in the perception of social status and how they impact youth mental health and well-being. Looking at social status from a developmental perspective, the author explores the expansion of opportunities for social comparison and complex social hierarchies in modern society and amplified by social media use.

Focusing on how social status is ever-present across species in the animal world, the book begins by exploring the biology of social status, the biological mechanisms by which it affects health, and how it presents in the spaces in which children and adolescents live, e.g., schools, neighborhoods, and cultures. Case studies of adolescents interviewed about social status are included, as well as a final chapter detailing specific steps to help minimize the effects of hierarchies on health and ways to approach social status differences.

Bridging anthropological, economic, developmental, and psychological literature on children and adolescent social hierarchies, this book is an invaluable guide for parents, educators, and clinicians such as school counselors, psychologists, pediatricians, pediatric psychiatrists, and other healthcare providers to better understand and support youth's behavior. This will also be of interest for students studying Adolescent Health and Adolescent Development.

Carol Vidal is a child and adolescent psychiatrist and Assistant Professor of Psychiatry and Behavioral Sciences at the Johns Hopkins University, School of Medicine. She currently works clinically in a school-based mental health program located in Baltimore City Schools where she evaluates and treats adolescents with behavioral and depressive disorders. Her research interest lies in the intersection between the social environment and addictions, depression, and intentional injuries in adolescents.

Status and Social Comparisons Among Adolescents

Popularity in the Age of Social Media

Carol Vidal

Routledge
Taylor & Francis Group

NEW YORK AND LONDON

Designed cover image: getty images @ robypangy

First published 2025
by Routledge
4 Park Square, Milton Park, Abingdon, Oxon OX14 4RN

and by Routledge
605 Third Avenue, New York, NY 10158

Routledge is an imprint of the Taylor & Francis Group, an informa business

British Library Cataloguing-in-Publication Data
A catalogue record for this book is available from the British Library

Library of Congress Cataloging-in-Publication Data
Names: Vidal, Carol, author.
Title: Status and social comparisons among adolescents:
popularity in the age of social media / Carol Vidal.
Description: Abingdon, Oxon; New York, NY: Routledge, 2025. |
Includes bibliographical references and index.
Identifiers: LCCN 2024035745 (print) | LCCN 2024035746 (ebook) |
ISBN 9781032880365 (hardback) | ISBN 9781032880341 (paperback) |
ISBN 9781003535942 (ebook)
Subjects: LCSH: Social status. | Peer pressure in adolescence | Social media—
Psychological aspects. | Adolescent psychology. | Youth development.
Classification: LCC HQ799.2.P44 V53 2025 (print) |
LCC HQ799.2.P44 (ebook) | DDC 303.3/27—dc23/eng/20240830
LC record available at https://lccn.loc.gov/2024035745
LC ebook record available at https://lccn.loc.gov/2024035746

ISBN: 9781032880365 (hbk)
ISBN: 9781032880341 (pbk)
ISBN: 9781003535942 (ebk)

DOI: 10.4324/9781003535942

Typeset in Times New Roman
by codeMantra

Contents

Preface

Social status runs deep in our genes and behaviors, from those of our very first ancestors to those of today's humans. It plays a role in the dynamics between men and women; in the lives of our predecessors, and those of our children; in tribal tensions and in the latest international war; in small communities and in our office spaces. Our species, like any other primate species, lives in a constant state of tension between collaboration and dominance. The omnipresence of hierarchies in animal life goes beyond humans and primates, onto any species that shares a space and depends on others for survival. And often also, among species, like between a dog and a human. Those with higher status are able to dominate, reproduce more, and access more resources than those of lower status. And yet, in the midst of all of this evidence, many of us manage to live our lives thinking that the imposition of dominance and status dynamics are human aberrations, that they are only concerns of the morally inferior and those who are too ambitious, that they are absent from our relationships.

As a medical student, a friend shared with me the book *The Naked Ape*. We talked about it for hours at a metro exit on our way back from university, surprised at seeing how similar humans were to apes. But even then, my perception of the world was still one in which we naturally did not try to overpower anyone else unless we were forced to by the circumstances, because we were humans, not just apes. The strikingly similar motivations we share with other primates have only become more evident to me with time. Humans, like non-human primates, are seekers of status. That is our motivation. And we live in worlds of status differences. That is our reality.

Growing up I was exposed to differences in status within my family and community. Lucky enough to have been born to a family that had achieved a relatively comfortable financial status, I also spent summers on the street outside my mom's family business, playing with children from other working families. Some of us were forbidden from walking beyond our block to the 'park' with the benches where people who injected heroin gathered. When I entered university, my social circle expanded beyond my neighborhood and my small school. I met children of wealthier parents who had little pressure to earn an income immediately, and could afford to study medicine, a longer and more expensive path than the regular university experience. I also met students who did have that financial pressure. I was, like most children, slowly introduced to these status differences in the world. Once I woke up to them, the need to gage the environment became ever-present. I mock it, ignore it, and resist it, but it is there. The quest to keep up with others grew when I became an immigrant. In a strange environment, where we have to relearn everything seemingly much faster than those who have been here before, keeping up with the Joneses has more to do with survival than with wanting to one-up others.

As a child psychiatrist in the U.S., I have also had an open window into the stress caused by social status differences. Baltimore, my second home, has had me fascinated from the very beginning, as a display of raw human nature, with all the beautiful and all the ugly. In the middle of one of the wealthiest states in the country, Baltimore hosts big business owners, Nobel Prize winners, scientists who have made magnificent discoveries in infectious diseases and brain health, and surgeons who make miracles happen daily, classic writers, nationally renowned lawyers, famous activists, actors, and musicians. At the same time, it experiences excruciating violence in communities and schools, allowing guns in the hands of children who should be reading Harry Potter but are handling drug businesses like professionals to feed their families or keep the lights on, and potholes, hopelessness, and lack of future opportunities for some, in the midst of abundant opportunities for others. Living in Baltimore is a constant asking yourself: why can I live this comfortably when others are struggling so intensely? Nowhere are these discrepancies more evident than in the lives of Baltimore's children. They are down to earth, very aware of disparities, many-years-old souls in young bodies, no non-sense people, who can see through others like no one else because they are very much in touch with human's basic motivations.

This is the reason why, when I started working here, I spent much of my time trying to understand what was going through the minds of these children. What was it like to grow up in what seemed a very unequal and unjust environment? And more, what happens when you live in this environment, but you can look at the rest of the world from the device you hold in your hand all day and every day? Ten years ago, several factors conflated together: an economic crisis, an increase in violence, and the popularization of smartphones among children. I wanted to know what these changes did to children, so I asked them.

Population-based interventions focused on large numbers of people instead of one person at a time, such as vaccination and lead poisoning prevention, have saved many lives and decreased morbidity. Yet, we continue to invest heavily on medical interventions while often ignoring societal drivers of mental health outcomes in our most vulnerable population: children and adolescents. We are experiencing a crisis in pediatric mental health in the West. There have been rising levels of anxiety, depression, and suicide over the past two decades. At the same time, we have seen the limitations of the effects of the psychopharmacological interventions that became widespread during the 1980s with the introduction of Prozac, and more accepted and popular among pediatric populations in the 2000s. Biological and genetic changes do not explain the rapid increase in reports of depression in children and adolescents; societal changes and pressures are much more likely to have had a role in these changes. In the clinical setting, we mostly focus on the temperament and symptoms of patients who come to see us with mental health complaints, often paying less attention to contextual factors that may have a broader effect on the person's clinical presentation and illness trajectory. If we want to expand the interventions we provide and be more effective in managing mental health, we need to understand better how these social aspects affect health. One aspect of the social environment that encompasses psychosocial stressors and social disadvantage and impacts mental health is one's perceived social status.

This book explores social status and its relationship with mental health in children and adolescents. I review biological and anthropological factors of social status to emphasize that it is ever present and so innate in humans that any attempt to deny it will be a failure and lost opportunity. I discuss how this search for status is amplified in social media through social comparisons. While the adult literature makes a distinction between subjective and objective social status (e.g., income, employment, education), the focus of the book is on young populations, in which this differentiation becomes less important, and relative deprivation or low socio-economic status are just one aspect of how young children and adolescents see themselves in the social hierarchy. The terms are used interchangeably to give the reader a bird's eye view of this colossal topic. For more details, or a more subtle differentiation between definitions, I recommend the reader visit the reference section that lists key scientific publications on these topics.

Finally, while I bring up politics, intertwined with policy, this book tries to stay away from political positions. Economic and social inequalities are strongly linked to policy, and we would not be able to fully understand these inequalities without taking a look at how historical and current societal structures and policies have created them, or without understanding the tradeoffs of the different positions. Children care little about political parties other than what they hear from their parents, or now TikTok. Their politics at the local level, in the playground, the virtual friend group chat, or the school hallways are too intense for them to worry about progressive and conservative parties. And yet, they are victims or victors of the policies and practices adults implement in every facet of their lives. We are ultimately responsible for creating the environments in which children can achieve their full potential through healthy lives.

Acknowledgments

I want to thank the adolescents and parents in Baltimore who continue to trust me enough to share their thoughts and feelings every day. Without them, I would not only not stay abreast with the always-changing English language, but would not want to do this work. It is hard work. They make it worth it.

I want to also give thanks to Anny Kezar and the therapists and psychiatrists at the Johns Hopkins School-based program in Baltimore City Schools. They are the Robin Hoods of our Era. They could choose comfortable jobs in an office close to the water cooler, the coffee pot, and well-equipped bathrooms, and instead they choose a job in which they have none of those, and sometimes not even an office. But yet, day after day, they go to schools, find a space, and see students confronting situations most adults could never even imagine.

To Molly Selby, my editor, for believing this book should be published, and for the support she has given me through the process.

To Larry Wissow, who encouraged me to pursue my interest in this topic, and also suggested that I write a book about it, a long time ago, during a walk after a conference in Manhattan.

To Carl Latkin, an impressive mentor, who has understood more than anyone I know that mental health, like all health, cannot in any way be separated from our environments.

To the faculty, students, and colleagues at Universitat Autònoma de Barcelona, Drexel University, University of Maryland, and Johns Hopkins University who taught me what I know about medicine, public health, and child development.

To the American Academy of Child and Adolescent Psychiatry (AACAP). While the book does not focus solely on the research they funded, the organization took the chance to fund my proposal for a project on social status in adolescents that started me on this path a decade ago. Even though psychiatrists are often perceived by the public as solely 'pill prescribers,' AACAP's understanding and support of pediatric psychiatry remains comprehensive.

To Wilbur, my dog, proof that interspecies friendships exist, even with marked status differences. He has quietly laid next to my office chair for hours waiting for his daily walk. I could not have asked for a better companion.

To my brother Marc, and my sister Paula, my parents, Maribel and Miguel Angel, and grandparents, Carolina and Juan, and to my friends. They have taught me the most essential thing about a good life. That no matter what your status is, how much or how little respect you get, and how successful or not you are, if you are lucky, you will have people who will unconditionally love and support you.

To Zoë and Daphne who have me constantly in awe and are my inspiration. And to their friends. The car rides from and to soccer practice and the pool have allowed me to take a peek into this new generation of children, often misunderstood in their quest to live a social life between the world adults understand, and the one of which we can only get a glimpse.

Lastly, thanks to Flav. Not everyone gets to have a partner who will endure late night conversations about random topics like status, mental health, and child development, in exchange for hearing about history, space, plants, and future dystopian societies, all to end up talking about politics. His passion to keep me on my toes always makes life exciting.

1 Biology of social status, from animals to humans

From insects to primates

Nature is filled with examples of dominance and submission. The destiny of all species depends a great deal on how much stronger, faster, or bigger they are compared to those around them. Nature can be cruel and the consequences of being dominated can be deadly. It is clear that domination happens between species, but much of the social stress related to hierarchies actually happens within species.

Social hierarchies are part of nature. Insects, like ants and bees, have some of the most complex and well-run hierarchical systems. They belong to groups to survive as a species in a world where it would be impossible to make it as an individual organism, but where the group work ensures their survival. Even the types of bees that are relatively solitary and build and provide only for their own nests, still aggregate in groups. In the colonies, not everyone reproduces. Most of the individuals actually don't, but they help raise the offspring of those who do reproduce. For example, honey bees have a queen bee who will reproduce, and then other male (drones) and female (workers) individuals who will not. The tasks of the workers change over their lifetime and are dynamic. Moving from the center of the hive to the outskirts as they grow older, the workers' tasks change from tending to the queen and cleaning and feeding the brood to receiving and storing supplies (nectar and pollen), and finally guarding the hive and foraging towards the end of their lifetime. Their jobs will change depending on the needs and the composition of the hive's population. For example, if many older bees are killed by pesticides, younger bees will move their position to the outer parts of the hive.[1] These hierarchies are reminiscent of human dynamics and motions of soldiers in a war, or a coordinated dance.

To maintain hierarchies, animals, from insects to primates, will sometimes need to resort to aggression. Just like verbal aggression is often used to keep war soldiers functioning efficiently, at least in movies, aggression happens among the members within animal species. Those higher in the hierarchy have more access to resources, tend to reproduce more successfully, and tend to dominate those who are lower in the hierarchy. The subordinates, or those of lower rank, have less opportunities to maintain their fitness due to having less access to resources, and sometimes do not reproduce at all, like in the case of worker bees. Afterall, raising offspring is

DOI: 10.4324/9781003535942-1

costly to the group, because individuals will prefer to tend to the needs of their own offspring once they have them, rather than the needs of the group as a whole.

Some species of ants, like the Diacamma, have a queen that does not engage in games of dominance, but keeps aggression in the colony under control by its mere presence. In the absence of the queen, the workers will display more aggressive behaviors to compete over male reproduction. This happens because the most dominant workers do lay eggs and see the opportunity to reproduce when the queen is not there. There are even worker police ants, which display different behaviors than the aggression that takes place between nest workers. Aggression in the world of ants involves biting and jerking. Worker policing involves multiple individuals immobilizing a victim by attacking it at the same time.[2] The similarities between ant and humans' behavior are mesmerizing. But there are also obvious differences, as we will see.

Between food rewards, rodents have provided essential information on the stress processes such as what happens when the stress is so overwhelming that it causes the animal to be depressed or anxious; how the body, including the brain, reacts to stress; and how animals interact within social structures. These studies have shown that changes in hierarchies, and repeated aggression from other more dominant rats, are associated with changes in the neuroendocrine system, ranging from increases in corticosterone in the blood to changes in serotonin, oxytocin, and other hormones and peptides, and that the changes related to stress translate into behaviors, such as social avoidance.[3]

Theoretical models are used to guide research and allow us to test and explain phenomena in science. The model of *learned helplessness* was described through the experiments conducted by Maier and Seligman with dogs, and later replicated with other animal species. In the experiments, the dogs were prevented from escaping continued electric shocks. These dogs eventually lost the motivation to avoid the shocks, moved less, and avoided social interactions. In other words, they became 'depressed' or what depression would look like in a dog. These experiments, translated into the human world, link stress to depression.[4] Another model, the *social defeat model*, applies to social rank more directly and is another model for human depression. It explains how being defeated (or victimized, or dominated) by another individual causes stress. One experiment consists of placing the rat in an enclosed space with a bigger animal that is aggressive against the confined animal. Just imagine for a moment, being in a jail cell with a much bigger, aggressive, and stronger person. It would be stressful. Then the animal is placed in another cage by itself, but still being able to see the aggressor. The lower-rank animal shows the same signs of stress or animal depression, including an increase in stress hormones. Not only being victimized, but also watching another rat being victimized caused a similar effect. This finding about experiencing versus witnessing aggression or violence is relevant for children who may witness violence in their homes and communities, and something to consider when we think about humans' psyche in a world where images of violence are so prevalent and widespread, and where it is so difficult to prevent children's exposure to these images through social media.

Non-human primates and stress

Non-human primates are other often-studied mammals, especially in their natural habitat. A well-known expert in the field of non-human primate stress processes is Robert Sapolsky who has conducted interesting studies with baboons. These studies with baboons examine not only their hormone levels depending on their place in the group as either a dominant or a subordinate member, but also how different structures and times affect the dynamics of biological markers and observed behavior.[5]

While we tend to know, at least intuitively, how humans are ranked, animal ranking may be less obvious to the common observer, and researchers have had to develop particular ways to assess animal rank based on their behaviors and features. Animal rank can be deducted from interactions between pairs, for example, during fights or avoidant behaviors. You can easily see that in a visit to the gorilla, or the chimpanzee section in the zoo. You will find the bigger animals moving around without care, and sometimes freely moving into the space of a younger or smaller animal, while this younger or smaller animal quickly moves away to a less desired space or at least not the initially chosen one. If the lower-ranking animal resists this move, a fight may start that this wishful animal will likely lose. Other times, it is the tracking of the sight or the lack of eye contact with some group members what denotes the spot in the hierarchy. Subordinate members of the group have harder and more stressful lives in general. They have less support from others in the group, less control over what will happen to them, and less capacity to displace their frustration onto lower-ranking members of the group, as there may be few or none, if you happen to be the animal at the very bottom. Subordinate animals will also have less access to food and be less likely to reproduce for that reason. They may also be more likely to be attacked by predators as they are less protected by their own.

Living in this world of stress can cause changes to one's neuroendocrine system and consequently one's body functioning. The two main changes that take place when the stress system is activated are changes in catecholamines (norepinephrine or noradrenaline, and adrenaline or epinephrine) and changes in the hypothalamus-pituitary-adrenal (HPA) system. The changes in catecholamines happen right away and for short periods of time, as they are meant to get the body ready to fight or flight. In humans, for example, these hormones are involved in shutting down our digestive system, so we don't have to bother going to the bathroom when running away from (or freezing in front of) a bear, or when taking an exam. They also act as neurotransmitters in the brain causing us to focus intensely on our goal, much like when people with attention deficit hyperactivity disorder (ADHD) take a stimulant medication, and sometimes shutting down our ability to see things with perspective. Another set of hormones, glucocorticoids are regulated by the HPA system and are meant to help when the body is attacked by a stressor. The stressor can be an infection. For example, in the presence of an infection agent, glucocorticoids will start a reaction of inflammation so that white cells mobilize to fight this infection. The same would happen if the insult was internally generated in one's body.

These are the hormones that have been used to study stress in baboons because their changes are perceptible for up to 1–2 minutes. Studies on many mammals, from rodents to rabbits, to pigs, and monkeys show that subordinate individuals exposed to more stress due to their lower rank present higher peripheral levels of these stress hormones, in a pattern similar to that experienced by humans with depression.

The problem with corticosteroids being elevated, and especially when they are elevated all the time, like in rats that are enclosed in a space with other bullying, more aggressive rats, is that our bodies are not designed to withstand constant levels of stress. They are designed to respond to brief insults or stressors. Once the stressor disappears, our organism returns to its baseline or a state of equilibrium in which these hormones are lower again. In the face of chronic and persistent elevated levels of these hormones, our organs are functioning abnormally, and can be damaged. Blood pressure will increase damaging the cardiovascular system, blood levels of 'bad cholesterol' like LDL, and fat like triglycerides will also increase, while 'good cholesterol' like HDL will be lower. The damaged vessels will not function as expected and will not irrigate the organs well, including the heart, which won't get enough blood and oxygen, causing muscular damage. In this case, the cardiovascular problems are not related to an unhealthy diet or lack of exercise. As a matter of fact, experiments with monkeys have shown that macaques of lower rank had more cardiovascular disease than those of higher rank, even while eating the same diet.

Stress related to rank affects not only the cardiovascular system, but also the hormones involved in reproduction. For that reason, animals of lower rank will experience hormone level changes that will cause them to have more miscarriages, and to have their puberty delayed, rendering them less fertile. This effect has been shown in macaque females with higher corticoid levels that also happened to be more frequently the receiving victims of aggression perpetrated by dominant individuals and that had less contact and grooming. They also had less ovulation cycles.[6] In species like the Tamarin and marmosets, only dominant females ovulate. The subordinate females do not have higher glucocorticoid levels, and are not getting picked on, but are still of lower rank and sterile. Their function is to help care for the older sister's offspring,[7] much like the childless human younger sister who becomes the beloved and caring aunt. Subordinate male rodents also have lower levels of sex hormones; in their case, they show lower testosterone levels. An interesting thing happens in some non-human primates, though. Among wild baboons, lower-rank individuals will have decreased testosterone levels without these hormone levels having an effect on their reproductive ability. Males in this species are very skilled at reproducing regardless of the circumstances.

Rank also affects the immune system. This is largely due to the immunosuppressant properties of corticosteroids, meaning that they weaken our defense system. This is the reason why treatment with corticosteroids, often given to treat inflammation, requires a slow process of introduction and weaning to avoid a negative reaction in all organ systems. Stressors seem to make people more vulnerable to certain mild viral infections, like colds. It is also not uncommon for people with an underlying infection like herpes simplex to develop symptoms in times of stress. There is sufficient evidence across species to affirm that these reactions are due to the suppression of the immune system, but this does not necessarily lead to infection, at least not in a uniform way across species.

However, as mentioned before, subordination does not always equal stress. In many cooperative species, subordinates do not necessarily have higher levels of cortisol. What affects stress hormones is not necessarily the individual's rank, but what the rank means to said individual. If two things happen: (1) the higher-ranking individuals harasses the lower-ranked ones and (2) the lower-ranking individual lacks outlets for coping, then the stress may overwhelm the organism. Without harassment and with stress outlets, the story may be much different. For example, in troops of baboons that displayed lower levels of aggression, and more cooperation and support, subordination was not linked to stress.

Social rank from animals to humans

Human behavior shows fragments of the behaviors of many of these animal species. Humans navigate many different environments in which the dynamics and dimensions of rank are varied. For that reason, we can see ourselves reflected in many of the examples of animals in the wild or in captivity and it is easy to translate the findings of these animal studies to our human experience. Imagine a person working day after day in an office environment with a benevolent and considerate boss. That would not be stressful. It would be rewarding. Now imagine that boss is controlling and abusive, makes unreasonable demands, and never rewards the worker for their good work. In that case, it would be nice to have an outlet, like going out for a run or a drink after work, or playing in a band with colleagues. That could help keep your stress hormones down. Now, imagine you are a child constantly being harassed by peers who are bigger or stronger with no way to avoid them as you share a school with closed doors. In that case, the child has no outlet, and the stress hormones may be high, possibly contributing to the child's depression in this environment of social defeat.

Children live in the word as subordinates; they depend on adults for almost everything. But many parents and other adults in children's lives do a good job of giving them control, or at least perceived control. Giving children choices can be a way to help them feel they have control. The choice can be controlled by the adults, but it is nonetheless a choice. For children with more difficult-to-manage temperaments or who are more oppositional, finding a mid-way, negotiating, and giving choice becomes essential so that the relationship with adults does not turn into a hostile one that ends up in disengagement and ultimately worse behaviors.[8]

In all these situations, there are individuals of higher and lower status in the social rank, but the environments in which they live can be very different. These environments will determine if the hierarchies are more dynamic or more stable. In communities with more stability, there will be less stress as the hierarchies are already established and the members don't have to fight to establish themselves in a social rank position. The dominant individuals will be less stressed because they are the boss and can decide how things run. In unstable communities, the bosses become stressed because the infighting among lower-ranking members threatens their position of dominance, and their stress hormones levels will go up. These dynamics are easy to see when political instability threatens the position of the ruling class, causing them to be stressed.

In the wild, instability happens when some of the members die or migrate, whereas in captive groups, it happens in the first months of a group forming, much like middle-school humans anxiously scanning their new social environment at the beginning of the school year. Interestingly, stress will also be lower among those ranked immediately below from those who are dominant. The dominant ones may lose their position, while those so close below are just advancing.

In social rank studies, animals are labeled with numbers or number of matches won and lost. This system is a close reminder of rankings in human sports. Changing hormone levels have actually been studied in tennis players, in addition to wrestlers and other sportsmen. Testosterone levels in college tennis players appear to change after losing or winning a match.[9] While winning or losing does not affect the levels of cortisol, being higher up in the tennis ranking is associated with lower cortisol levels. Cortisol levels are also higher before than after the match regardless of ranking. Testosterone provides an orientation to competition, as higher levels create more impetus in trying to maintain a certain interpersonal status. When the person wins a match, testosterone rises. When the person moves down in status, testosterone drops. However, if the win is too close, everyone's testosterone drops. This is in part because if the person does not feel they deserve to win, they consequently do not experience the elated mood of the win. In essence, mood mediates the relationship between winning and the rise in testosterone. Additionally, if testosterone was high after a win, it remained higher before the next match, which was thought to contribute to winning (and losing) streaks. For all students, testosterone increased before the match in preparation for the competition. Picture King Kong pounding its chest before the battle. An interesting finding was that as the season progressed, cortisol levels in all members, regardless of ranking, decreased. As a player became more familiar with the matches, they felt less stressed. The basis of therapy for anxiety is exposure to the cause of fear or anxiety. Over time, exposure decreases the anxiety caused by that object or activity. In children, we include exposure in almost every intervention, be that school avoidance, social anxiety, and even habit-forming, because changing a habit can also cause anxiety. Only by trying and seeing that the world does not end with the changed behavior will the child continue the newly learned behavior.

Humans' bodies, as those of other animals, have evolved to respond to our environment by self-selecting for a system that allows us to react to threats quickly and then return to a baseline level when the threat is gone. This system is our neuroendocrine system. It releases catecholamines and glucocorticoids into our blood and affects all other bodily systems, activating our bodies to fight, flight, or freeze. While we don't encounter too many animals in our daily lives who would want to attack us for food, we are asked to do public presentations, meet with our bosses, respond to emergencies, or to an angry customer, all of which can set off this cascade of neuropeptide and hormone release starting in the brain and finishing in the peripheral glands that works in a feedback loop. Sometimes, the system is triggered by things that have not happened yet, but that we imagine will happen, like having to go into a new school as a student. And sometimes, things that happened in the past, like reminders of traumatic events, set this system off. The threat, real or imaginary, is important to activate this system. The system is key for life; if impaired, our bodies do not function well.

Psychological stress in social rank

Both physical and psychosocial stressors activate these neural and endocrine systems and inhibit other systems to allow us to respond to stressors. Initial activation happens by the stimulation of the sympathetic nervous system with the release of epinephrine (adrenaline) and norepinephrine (noradrenaline) from the adrenal glands. Minutes later, glucocorticoids are released from the adrenal glands following an endocrine cascade that starts in the hypothalamus. While these adaptations are necessary and positive to survive the initial stressor, they can be pathogenic if they are chronic and the individual does not have a chance to return to a state of homeostasis, potentially damaging all body systems. Whether an organism becomes overwhelmed with that stress will depend on how big the stressor is, how much the organism can adapt, and whether the organism can use coping mechanisms to overcome the stressor and its effects.[5]

Psychological stress, or the stress caused by the anticipation of an imagined threat, is greater when it is less predictable, when there is a lack of sense of control, when there are no outlets for frustration, when the stressor is interpreted in a negative way, and when the stressed organism has no social support. Studies with rodents have shown that when they are warned with a bell about an upcoming but intermittent electric shock, the shock is less likely to trigger a stress reaction that when the rat is not warned, because they can predict it. Rats that are trained to press a lever to avoid an electric shock also experience less stress than when the lever is disconnected and the shock cannot be avoided, because they have more control. Likewise, rats that can munch on food or exercise in a running wheel also tend to be less stressed when receiving shocks because they have an outlet. As humans, we also experience situations in which we lack control, or with an absence of warnings, outlets or support, or we interpret situations in ways that cause more stress.[5]

One example of how this knowledge can be applied for good is in in well-run pediatric healthcare settings with well-trained or experienced staff. Knowing that for any ill or even healthy child who needs to visit a clinic or a hospital, the visit can be stressful, and can even cause 'medical trauma,' and knowing that there are ways to prevent this stress, many healthcare settings try to mitigate it. The perfect example is the well-child yearly visit with a good pediatrician. The pediatrician will give information to the child about all the steps to be taken during the session. The doctor will say something like 'I am now going to use this tool to listen to your heart. Your heart is around this area. It may feel a little cold but it will just feel like that for a moment.' Sometimes the pediatrician will give the young patient the choice to listen to their own heart beating as well, if they wish. The pediatrician will then give a warning to the child that a vaccine is needed and why. When there is an explanation, the child can understand that it is not that the doctor enjoys inserting needles with viruses and bacteria in little kids' bodies, but that vaccines make the child's body stronger so they can fight bigger infections and that it will make them stay healthy. During the shot, the pediatrician will give the option to the parent to hold the child on their lap, or hold their hand, and hug them, allowing social support. The doctor or the nurse in the office may even offer a stress ball or a vibrating device to cause distraction, allowing for an outlet for frustration. Moreover, the child may get a choice of what color of Band-Aid they want, yellow or pink, one with a Batman or a Superman design. And to top it all, they will get a choice of a sticker or a lollipop on the way out of the office. Intended or not as a means to dampen stress, this works. At first, from the outside, this process may seem like a big theatrical American show. But it is important to understand that this 20-minute-long positive interaction of a child and professional staff in a clinical setting could set the stage for ongoing and even lifelong pleasant doctor visits, instead of traumatic ones. These visits will help prevent diseases and their progression, or at the very least, allow for the recommended screenings and vaccinations. A movement to provide trauma-informed care that seeks to avoid re-traumatization in healthcare settings follows this same philosophy of allowing choice, control, and support in a less hierarchical type of relationship between the provider and the patient.

The hypothalamus-pituitary-adrenal (HPA) axis and the brain

Sapolsky tried to answer questions about hierarchy and stress with his beautifully designed studies with primates, and has elegantly explained his findings in his many writings. Essentially, his studies with primates in their natural habitat examined their levels of stress hormones while studying their position in the hierarchy ladder. The use of physical force to impose social rank in primates causes stress and poorer health outcomes in those primates of lower hierarchical status as compared to those of higher status. These studies have also shown differences by primate species and by structure of the hierarchy, with those who are higher in the status hierarchy in unstable societies, and those who are subordinates in stable societies presenting more stress than those of lower status in unstable societies or those who are dominant primates in stable societies.[5]

In humans, chronic social stress affects the HPA axis,[10] which may induce depression and other medical conditions. Studies in human environments such as the workplace have confirmed the health benefits of being higher versus lower in the social rank among humans. People in the military[11] also showed that those of higher rank had lower resting state levels of cortisol and less anxiety than subordinates. However, having high cortisol and high anxiety were not related to each other, meaning that other hormones (noradrenergic system) were likely involved in the increase of anxiety. Furthermore, this decrease in anxiety and cortisol levels only happened if the person on top felt a sense of control. Interestingly, those who were supervising many people and had more authority felt a higher sense of control. But those who had to manage those subordinates directly actually experienced more stress. This is reminiscent of American administrators in universities, where there is a Provost who essentially manages the faculty and daily affairs of the university, and a President whose job, while still overseeing the university, is more ceremonial and oriented towards the outside of the institution, without the headaches of having to supervise disgruntled employees and other day-to-day issues involved in running the institution. This may also explain why chiefs of staff in the U.S. President's office last for an average of a little over 18 months in their job, while Presidents, despite angering half of the population on a regular basis, consistently run for a second four-year term.

Differences in rank are associated with brain function beyond catecholamines and the HPA axis. Other neurotransmitters are associated with rank-related processes. Serotonin, a neurotransmitter involved in anxiety, depression and suicide, and which receptors we target when we use the antidepressants called selective serotoninergic receptor inhibitors (SSRIs), also changes with rank. The serotonin transporter gene moderates the association between personal socio-economic status and how responsive is one's central nervous serotonergic system. Adult men and women were challenged to observe their responsiveness to an agent that releases serotonin (fenfluramine) and showed that serotonergic responsivity was predicted by the interaction of serotonin transporter genotype and socio-economic status measured as income and years of education. Those with lower socio-economic status had less sensitivity to the agent releasing serotonin, but only if they had at least one "short" allele of the gene that translated into a serotonin transporter.[12]

Given the complexity and multifaceted behaviors related to processing one's and other individuals' social status, multiple brain areas will be involved. For example, areas like the posterior superior temporal sulcus will be involved in visual perception, which plays a role in perceiving gaze direction, mouth movements, and facial expressions. The inferior intra-parietal sulcus is implicated in judgments about magnitude and number processing and may have a role in calculating rank orders. When presented with higher-status individuals, areas implicated in emotion regulation like limbic (amygdala and ventral anterior cingulate) and paralimbic areas (temporal pole and orbitofrontal cortex) and those involved in reward processing, like the ventral striatum, seem to react. Lesions to these areas involved in emotion regulation have also been associated with a loss of status in monkeys, who become unable to react to the social status of others. And finally, differences in the volume of these areas are also associated with how fast we learn about other people's status.

Some of the differences in brain activity by region correlate with status but not with network size, showing that there are neurobiological correlates that are specific to social rank and independent of other types of social behavior. Lower socio-economic status has also been associated with reduced grey matter volume in the anterior cingulate cortex across individuals. Having a parent of lower socio-economic status also predicted greater reactivity to angry faces in the amygdala of young adults in a functional neuroimaging study. Different areas of the animal brain show differences in grey matter volume depending on social rank exclusively, and not on other social behaviors. Subordinate macaques presented higher grey matter volumes in the striatum, while those higher in the rank had higher grey matter volume in the amygdala. Grey matter volume in certain areas of the prefrontal cortex was also higher in those monkeys with higher status and broader social network. These brain areas are involved in the mentalizing network in humans. This network is involved in 'mentalizing,' or the ability to 'put yourself in others' shoes' or understand how others are feeling or thinking.[13] It does make sense that those who can better predict other people's actions would be more successful at maintaining a higher social status. However, other research based on behaviors in humans and not on imaging in animals, would suggest otherwise, and could be related to those of higher social status not needing to be so attuned to the needs of others to succeed.

As we have seen, in animals, differences in hormones and brain neurotransmitters can also predispose some primates to higher status. For example, lower levels of metabolites of the neurotransmitters serotonin and dopamine predispose to higher status, and higher testosterone is found in primates of higher status. It is thought that these differences in levels of neurotransmitters are associated with specific behaviors (e.g., impulsivity or aggression) and that these would affect status, but these different levels also change depending on the environment and group interactions (e.g., testosterone levels increase when the primate is successful in challenging a group member). We also know that the levels of aggression are higher in the absence of hierarchical structures, and once these are established, there is an increase in cooperation.

Signs of social status

But, how do animals, adult and young humans perceive these differences? What goes on in the brain that helps us see who is higher and lower than us in the status ladder?

Hierarchies have value for social groups and they are created quickly and spontaneously.[14] In order for these hierarchies to generate so easily, organisms need to have an innate and unconscious ability to detect status differences. For example, among monkeys, gaze aversion can be a cue that indicates lower status to other monkeys. Humans also rapidly organize in hierarchical structures as they can quickly attribute status based on observations of others.[15] Humans as young as adolescents and even small children are able to perceive status differences. Body size is one of the markers of status among primates. As mentioned, gaze aversion communicates subordination. Other behaviors such as open-mouth threats or hitting and biting can denote dominance in primates.

Social status also affects cognitive processes, or how people or animals make decisions. Both monkeys and humans have a preference for higher-status individuals.[16] This preference translates into selective attention towards these more popular individuals as well as gaze-following, meaning that one cannot help but look at these higher-status individuals. Monkeys will forgo sugary rewards if the alternative is to be able to watch higher-status individuals. This would be equivalent to missing dinner to watch the Oscars or the Cannes Festival if we only had the option to watch it live. Memory is also involved as we may remember faces of people paired with higher status more than people of lower status. Executive processes are also affected, which is relevant for children in school. Studies of people experimentally grouped in a lower-status classification perform worse in subsequent IQ tests. However, the association between cognitive functioning and social status is complex as those who achieve higher status may also be those able to perform better at baseline. Another area is the perception of competency and moral decisions. People of higher perceived social status may be less likely to understand other people's perspectives and more likely to make unethical decisions. However, these unethical decisions made by people of higher status are more likely to go unpunished than if they were of lower social status because of other people's perceptions of their social rank.

Status in adult and young humans

In humans, height and body size and higher testosterone are also associated with higher status. But one does not reach higher status exclusively through aggressive dominance. Another mechanism of achieving higher status is through prosocial behaviors, also called 'sociable dominance,' which involves making friends or creating beneficial affiliations. These two types of dominance, aggressive and social, are not mutually exclusive, and the ideal for status achieving individuals is a combination of both.

For humans, a way to achieve high status without physical dominance is achieving prestige by displaying skills or knowledge. In fact, those who attain high status through gaining prestige or sociable dominance are more likable or respected than those who attain it through traditional dominance. This fact is validated by the comments in qualitative studies conducted with adolescents, as later explained, where distinctions are made between those who are considered higher in the status ladder because they are 'nice' versus those who bully their way into dominance.[17] Finally, physical attractiveness is a trait that helps gain status both in colleges and in the workforce.

Status can also be perceived in others not only through body size and strength, but also through behaviors such as the body position that tends to be more expanded in those who show dominance and more locked in subordinates. In both artificial (manipulated for the purposes of research) and actual couples, members of the partnership tend to complement each other and show more synchrony and more positive views of their partner when the behaviors are more complementary. Put differently, couples in which the one in a more dominant position is presented with someone with an equally more submissive position will have more positive views of each other and better interactions. Other behaviors particular to humans, such as the language used, the type of eye contact when speaking versus when listening, the speaking style, including the level of politeness, speed, confidence, and enunciation, or voice pitch can also denote higher or lower status. More maturity and masculinity in the facial cues also convey higher status, even in females, with those with more masculine traits being perceived as of higher status. Expressing certain emotions, like anger and disgust, is also more strongly associated with perceived dominance, whereas expressions such as fear or sadness, or even happiness are not. Differences in socialization of emotional expression between men and women may contribute to this perception of masculinity as dominant. Factors like occupation and income, intelligence, popularity, prestige, and reputation also impact how others perceive one's social status.

Finally, one person's self-perception of their own status affects how the person is perceived by others. This is key in the work of therapists regarding their patients' self-esteem. One has to wonder if the massive success that cognitive-behavioral therapy has had in mental health treatment across disorders and behaviors is related to this fact. Cognitive-behavioral therapy was designed by Beck based on the basic principle that those who were depressed had an anomalous and negative perception of the world, the future, and themselves.[18] That is, when you are depressed, you feel like the future is dark, the world is in a bad condition, and you are unworthy of love and rewards. With therapy, the hope is that thoughts about this tripartite of a person's life will change. When therapy works, and one starts feeling better, distorted thoughts about oneself will change and the person will have more self-worth. This change will automatically alter how the person interacts with others and how others perceive the person. Additionally, the connections that are now of better quality will also help improve the person's mood.

Men with higher self-perceived dominance have more trouble identifying cues of dominance in faces of other men when compared to men who score lower in dominance.[14] This finding is not surprising as lower-status individuals have much more to lose if they miss cues of dominance and have to be, in a way, more alert to those cues. There is also higher activity in areas of the brain involved in the mentalizing network among those of lower status, both subjective and objective. As mentioned, mentalization refers to one's ability to understand other people and one's own mental states, intentions, and affects. It may be affected in those with autism spectrum disorder but also in those with personality disorders and attachment problems, such as people suffering from borderline personality disorder. Mentalization-based therapy was developed in the 1990s and has now been established as an evidence-based type of treatment for borderline personality disorder, but also for other disorders such as addictions, antisocial personality disorders, and depression to improve the ability of those affected to regulate their emotions by focusing on own's mental state, differentiating it from other people's mental states, and understanding how mental states change behaviors.

Humans use social rank judgments as a mechanism to assess their social status in their group of reference. The difference between the environment in non-human primates and the very complex environments which humans navigate make for situations where a person could be higher up in social status in one environment and lower in social status in another.[5] Understanding the effects of social status in humans requires examining not only their relationships with complex and diverse environments, but also their stage of development. In youth, similar findings suggest changes in cortisol level varying by gender and position depending on the area in which youth compare themselves to their peers. For example, in a study conducted in a Scottish school, girls with lower academic scores and high peer ranking both presented higher morning cortisol levels, whereas among boys, low ranking in sports was associated with higher cortisol levels.[19] Meanwhile, socio-economic status, which has traditionally been used as a measure of social rank in adults, had no effect on the students' cortisol levels. These findings suggest that status relationships with stress are complex and dependent on the individual's age.

These also depend on the environment. For example, one aspect that changes hierarchy dynamics is the size of the group. In smaller groups, it is easier to recognize each other and who is higher and who is lower in the hierarchy. In larger groups, individuals have not engaged in 'tournaments' to assess who wins and loses in a dyadic match. Children make a big jump from elementary to bigger middle schools where status games are the prime activity, and can be a challenge to overcome for many children.

Chronic stress and trauma

Social status in humans is linked to stress levels and relevant to health. Indicators of status are measurable at the individual level, community and societal levels. These indicators include not only biological mediators of risk for disease but also unhealthy behaviors adopted by the individual and its proximal and distal contacts, risk factors for psychological and medical conditions, and markers of pathophysiology, like hypertension that put people at risk for clinical conditions. These indicators combine to contribute to health disparities. Health disparities that track a socio-economic gradient can be measured from early to later periods of life. The pathways that proximally link dimensions of social status position to observable health disparities over the life course also extend from genetic to environmental levels of analysis and are related to stress.

Chronic levels of corticoids, as when people receive corticoid for treatment for a few days, can have behavioral effects caused by changes in the expansion of amygdala's dendrites, which are the parts of our neurons, or brain cells, that extend from the body of the neurons like branches connecting with other neurons. The amygdala is the part of the brain involved in the fear response and its activation starts the cascade of hormones that will eventually end in higher stress hormones in the blood. It is also called the reptile brain, because it is the one that will react to create a flight or fight response if not stopped by the higher-functioning parts of the brain that evolved later in the history of evolution of the human brain. This latter, more evolved, part of the brain, the frontal lobe, is the one that will regulate this fear response when things are working well. Acute administration of corticoids has been shown to expand amygdala dendrites and increase anxiety 12 days after treatment in a study conducted with rats. Chronic administration of corticoids had a similar effect.[20] There were individual variations among rodents in their response to predator stress. For example, in an experiment in which rats were exposed to a cat without protection for ten minutes in an enclosed room, the rats differed in how they reacted and how their neurons changed. This considerably traumatic event for a rat, although none were hurt during these exposures, showed that some rats presented low levels of anxiety while others were more anxious, when presented with the same stressor. The well-adapted rats had shorter dendrites than the stressed rats, suggesting that those with shorter dendrites were less prone to experience anxiety, or more resilient to stress or trauma. This explains also why anxiety runs in some families.

This study's results are more important now than ever. From 1995 to 1997, the Adverse Childhood Experiences (ACE) study[21] revealed findings that would condition much of today's work in medicine and psychology. These findings have also now been adapted and extended to influence every single discipline in life, from education to the workplace. The study reviewed the health outcomes of people receiving treatment at Kaiser Permanente and the Center for Disease Control and Prevention. It essentially revealed that the more adverse or traumatic experiences one was exposed to as a child, the worse health outcomes as an adult. These health outcomes were not just mental health and substance use outcomes, which we can intuitively guess would be affected, but also a greater likelihood of cardiovascular disease, cancer, sexually transmitted diseases, and even a shorter lifespan. The study was conducted on mostly White Americans of middle- and upper-income class, which suggests that other populations may have had even higher number of ACEs. Over time, coincidental or not, the diagnostic classifications in psychiatry both in the U.S. and Europe have evolved to being more inclusive of traumatic experiences. The standard diagnostic label for a traumatic experience is post-traumatic stress disorder (PTSD). This diagnosis was initially defined to describe symptoms of veterans of war in the 1970s. It later evolved to include also other domestic and community-level traumatic experiences. In the 1990s, the introduction of complex or toxic trauma to describe ongoing trauma that the individual could not escape resonated with many victims and clinicians who saw populations in which a series of, and not just one, traumatic events were observed, like in war zones. The concept has been watered down a little in recent times, especially with social media, and the popularization of the word 'trauma' to mean anything that is distressing. The reality is that not all stressors are traumas, and not everyone who experiences trauma will develop symptoms of PTSD. This second point is important and brings us to the finding of the dendrites. There are people who, for biological reasons will be temperamentally more resilient, and will not suffer from experiencing the same events as others who will suffer.

Finally, animals also vary in their reactions to stress. Those that have ongoing behaviors disrupted easily by novelty, that have trouble distinguishing neutral from threat (or have a bias towards threat), or that tend to lack effective coping outlets for stress have a 'hot reactor' personality type. This is similar to a profile type in humans in which neutral stimuli are interpreted as threatening. These individuals have higher glucocorticoid levels and increased risk for cardiovascular disorders. These differences rise from developmental and genetic influences. In sum, we all experience stress differently, and the levels of stress vary. Social stress, in part due to social rank differences, varies depending on biological, developmental, and environmental differences and can affect health.

2 Evolution of status in human history

Early societies

Angus Deaton,[1] Nobel Prize winner, argues that today's humans are shaped by having spent nearly all of our existence as a species living in hunting and gathering societies. Because these societies tended to be nomadic and did not store food, wealth accumulation was non-existent, and the culture did not encourage hierarchies, nor leaders or rulers with power over others. Furthermore, ladder-climbers and those wanting to distinguish themselves from others were often ridiculed or killed.[2] The inability to store food and the instability of the environment promoted sharing and exchanging within the group. Over time, individuals and groups that were better at sharing succeeded and survived, and as Deaton remarked, humans evolved into a species hardwired to share and oriented towards fairness.[1] These hunter-gathering societies were not ideal, with unpoliced internal violence and violence with other groups, but are thought to have been more equal than later societies.

As foraging food became more difficult, successful humans adapted by introducing farming and agriculture.[3] Settled agriculture allowed for food storage, property ownership, and the development of towns and a ruling class, which led to inequality within communities. This system has persisted for the past 10 milenia; that is, for a very brief part of human history. By contrast, life in hunter-gathering societies constitute over 90% of human's existence, with many of these societies persisting well into the 20th century. Many recent social structure changes have taken place within the past 250 years, which have contributed to a swelling of social inequalities. Because as humans, we have adapted and are biologically wired to share and live in equal societies, attempting to adjust to today's societies could go against our own nature and contribute to stress and health problems, including mental health problems.

What archeology tells us about equality in hunter-gathering societies

According to Whiten and Erdal, one way to understand earlier societies is through archeological findings.[4] However, this method does not provide complete evidence of the way humans lived in the past. For example, we have evidence of the existence of weapons, but it is harder to garner evidence about gathering behaviors. For

DOI: 10.4324/9781003535942-2

that reason, anthropologists study societies that continue to maintain a similar style of hunting and gathering today. We now have enough collected evidence about this way of living. However, there are fewer of these societies as time passes, and it can also be challenging to make inferences about very early societies when our ancestors had smaller brains and simpler tools than those inhabiting similar societies of today. Between both of these approaches, however, we can get an approximate idea of how equal or not were those societies compared to our modern society.

There are tools used for butchery from around 1.8 millions of years ago and new evidence suggesting that stone toolmaking for meat may have actually started 3.4 millions of years ago, although it is unclear if these tools were used for hunting or only for scavenging on carcasses of prey killed by other carnivores. Hunting spears of about half a million years ago provide stronger evidence of active hunting. An example of how archeological findings alone may not tell the complete story is that current tropical societies that live on hunting and foraging engage in both plant and animal prey consumption, and not just meat consumption as we would have deducted from archeological findings.

Encephalization, or the increase in complexity and size of the human brain, coincided with an increase in cognitive ability. This increase in intelligence allowed humans to create the necessary manipulations to adapt and differentiate themselves from other species, compensating for the charactersitics that made them vulnerable to stronger and faster predators. Human intelligence allowed for the builing of weapons, traps, and tracked prey. This phenomenon is explained by the 'cognitive niche' theory, proposed by Tooby and DeVore.[5] This theory attempts to explain this achieved superiority through intelligence and technology. Whiten and Erdal consider this explanation insufficient and instead propose a 'socio-cognitive niche' by which not only cooperation, theory of mind, language and cultural transmission, but also egalitarianism would have made a difference for these hominid primates.[4] Together, bands of seemingly inferior primates would have been competitive and unique in their environment, just like hives and colonies allow bees and ants to thrive, respectively.

What the traditional societies of today tell us about earlier societies

About 10,000–12,000 years ago, hunting and gathering opened a way for domestication of animals and crops in the Middle East. Yet, some societies living in a mostly hunter-gathering style have remained. Erdal and Whiten surveyed two dozens of these ethnic societies from across four continents.[2] They consisted of groups of about 30 people, clearly different from current large societies, but not that different from the nuclear and extended families of modern society. In these societies, cooperation was glaring, with a clear division of labor that was mostly gendered, with men focused on hunting and women focused on gathering. Akin to a 'group predator,' members of these groups moved several times a year in a nomadic style. Both hunting and gathering required communication among the group members as they searched for and approached the prey, or as they decided which paths to take for gathering. Furthermore, hunters and gatherers shared information around campfires, and cooperated to care for the youngest in the band who were supervised by any adult while the parents looked for food. Food, especially meat, was distributed according to need. Members of the band did not obtain more food because of their status or relationships but because of the collective need. Humans were stronger by functioning as a group.

Another way in which these societies differed from other great apes was in that they were mostly monogamous, and the reproductive success was more egalitarian across the group, and not limited to the alpha or beta male and females of the band, so the genes of weaker members of the group could also survive.

Hunter-gatherers also had a theory of mind, which is one of the key features of the social brain. Thought to be present in some social animals but most developed in humans, theory of mind has been described as a characteristic deficit in autistic individuals by Sir Simon Baron-Cohen, a psychologist who extensively studied children and found that by age four, most were able to 'read the minds of others' or guess where the adult conducting the experiment had hidden a toy when the child was not watching. As a side note, Dr. Baron-Cohen's cousin is Sasha Baron-Cohen, a hilarious actor, director, and comedian who became known for his movie 'Borat,' a character that he also plays, and who has no mindreading abilities, which makes him an outrageous person in a foreign land, and also as endearing as a child. Observations of present hunter-gatherer societies by Avis and Harris showed that five-year-olds in those groups had the same mentalization capabilities as children from urbanized and modern societies.[6]

Language facilitated communication, planning, coordination among group members, and cumulative culture, which is the accumulation of knowledge beyond one's lifetime regarding tools to sustain the group. In addition, a long childhood, and an ability to imitate and also teach and tell stories facilitated this knowledge transmission, and contributed to the progress and differentiation of humans from chimpanzees. Despite these differences, humans have retained important similarities with other primates, one of them being the quest for status.

Evolution of equality in societies

The social evolution of equality is often described as a U-shaped curve in a graph with two axes, an x-axis for time and a y-axis that progresses from very egalitarian to very hierarchical societies.[7] Ape societies would have comprised a prolonged period in human evolution. These ape societies were largely hierarchical. Humans then evolved into hunter-gatherer societies, which were largely egalitarian (bringing the curve downwards) and maintained for several million years, shaping today's humans' brains and bodies. With the advent of agriculture in 2000 AD, humans began living in hierarchical societies again, and these have continued into modern society.

There has been extensive discussion about how egalitarian were these hunter-gatherer societies. Some argue that it makes sense to assume that humans tended to share meat, as the return of hunting is unpredictable. While one single individual may have been unsuccessful in their hunt one day, the act of sharing ensures that this same individual will still get to eat meat from others. Additionally, once hunted, the animal is too much for one person to eat before it rots, so sharing feeds everyone without cost to the individual. However, sharing was observed even when full returns were not expected, at least in the short term. Those able to hunt more meat did not always receive equal amounts in return. It was not all smooth. Sharing came with tensions, and ethnographers observed depictions of loud and long arguments, as well as cheating and stealing. However, the final outcome, sharing, overall prevailed. In addition to this research on foraging societies across continents, Marlowe and Hamilton surveyed hundreds of hunter-gatherer societies, which altogether allowed for the description of some common characteristics. These common features included: cooperation, egalitarianism, mindreading (or a theory of mind), language facilities, and cumulative culture.[8]

It appears that these societies did not have designated leaders and decisions were made through group-level negotiations and decision-making. Most of the ethnographic studies show that leaders were created when coming in contact with new agricultural and colonial societies, and were either appointed by external governments or originated due to external pressures. Those attempting to stand out from the group risked being ostracized and attacked. This rejection would help level the power in the group. This is often seen today in Western society, especially in more egalitarian and less individualistic societies like European societies, where standing out is not necessarily always respected. In contrast to the U.S., where it is expected that people will freely pursue their individual goals and identities without interference from the state, in European countries, people are more likely to prefer a more active role from the state so as to ensure a beneficial outcome for all.[9] Today, in industrial and post-industrial societies, sharing and working for the group continues to be part of our lives. However, it is not as palpable as it used to be. We now go about our days without being conscious of the work that happens behind the goods we consume, or without ever meeting the people who manufacture or collect those goods.

Status in egalitarian societies

Even in the absence of formal leaders, members of these societies would listen to and agree more often with the most skilled hunters, or informal leaders. They did not 'obey' them. Yet, other members did 'listen to' those more skilled and respected members, at least temporarily, in certain situations and at certain times. Overt attempts to achieve status and dominance were quickly stopped, through ridicule and hostility. Incipient leaders would soon learn the lesson that the highest level of dominance to be achieved was to be a 'respected equal.'

Whiter and Erdal posit that this inclination to resist dominance, just like the proneness to share, is not a learned cultural process, but an innate predisposition that has evolved and allowed the survival of those who possess it. Sharing and resisting dominance would be our natural inclination.[4] Reactions like being angry when dominated and feeling satisfaction when there is consensus would also be examples of this innate predisposition. Non-human primates also show this inclination to exert counter-dominance, but to a much lesser degree. Being caught within dominance-submission relationships, especially if you are the one driven into submission, is costlier in terms of energy expended than building the social skills to share. Eventually, those who continued to engage in the dynamic of dominance and submission would comparably be draining time and energy. In chimpanzees, behaviors like alliances between two weak individuals against a stronger one are more logical than one weak individual aligning with the stronger one, given that the alliance between a strong and a weak individual would still give less chances for food to the weaker individual aligned with the stronger one. The resulting individual psychology in these evolved egalitarian societies is one in which there is still a need to look out for the dominant members. To do this exercise, individuals need to compare themselves to others around them, to be recognizant of whether there is fairness in the division of goods, or meat carcass, in this case. One also needs to be watching developing leaders who give ideas on how to make such division, even when the intention is not to dominate but simply to get the right amount of food.

However, others disagree with the idea that egalitarianism is innate and that it evolved overtime for survival. The alternative hypothesis is that the primate legacies of dominance are the truly innate tendencies in humans and that culture and institutions are the ones balancing the most powerful by creating alliances among the weaker.[10] From this point of view, a quest for status is our nature and our behavioral dispositions include a drive to maintain territory and possessions, the creation of bonds that are reciprocal, and of groups that maintain equilibrium, as well as the avoidance of incest. For Weissner, observations in foraging societies where sanctions were placed on the most successful hunters to prevent them from becoming higher-ranking members supported this thesis.[11] More recently, other authors have developed a model supporting this idea of egalitarianism being an outcome of the development of networks of alliances.[12]

Research showing that humans have a tendency to prefer paying attention to individuals of higher status supports the idea that our brains are wired as having evolved in environments of inequality.[13] Hiearchies may have continued to exist because there are also potential benefits of being a non-dominant member of the group. Non-dominant individuals will have more predictability in their relationships, avoid conflict, and obtain protection, all of which favor reproductive success, in which case natural selection would not explain a process that creates more inherently egalitarian humans. Furthermore, it has been argued that humans may have two sets of social preferences, an older one consisting of ancient instincts that involves a quest for status, and a newer one of tribal instincts that evolved later and involved cooperation and reciprocity in larger groups.[14] Finally, Bowles and colleagues[15] discuss reciprocity in which humans adhere to social norms and in exchange, they punish those who violate them. It is well-accepted that humans gain status not uniquely by accumulation of wealth, but also by being respected and through nurturing and prosocial behavior, whereas the domination of competitors that relies more on aggression is more common among non-human primates. For status seeking, humans require recognition from others and attention directed to them.[13] When we think about political systems and waves towards progressivism and conservatism in more than a few countries of today's world, we can see these dynamics playing at the population level, with voters attempting to balance extremes. All in all, and despite differences of opinion about the innate, learned, or imposed qualities of egalitarianism, there is a general agreement among anthropologists about a human innate tension between a desire for prestige and dominance that varies with personality, skills and abilities, and an inclination towards egalitarianism that keeps humans living in groups, which ultimately benefits them as individuals. Even today's societies like the U.S., where the culture and even the institutions are extremely accepting of inequality, there is a counter pull to provide services for those in need, as shown by the many governmental programs created overtime and a culture of litigation to balance abuses of power.

The exchange among ethnographers

During the second half of the past century, ethnographers engaged in a series of arguments for and against the idea that egalitarianism was innate to humans versus imposed by external forces. One may wonder, if egalitarian behavior had been so advantageous for humans as a species over millions of years, why were individuals with a tendency to seek dominance not selected out through natural selection? And, why do we still have such strong innate tendencies for inequality, attention, and status? One explanation is that high social status gives individuals many health benefits, greater reproductive success, and more access to resources. Even in the most egalitarian societies there are signs of subtle differences in health and skills that can impact status. This argument sustains that the default organization of human societies is hierarchical and that there is a tendency to compete for prestige and dominance comparable to that of non-human primate societies. Over time, there was increased mobility and an expansion of social networks.[16] Intimate networks of a few individuals and effective networks of a few dozen did not require signaling of status as there was regular face-to-face interaction. However, extended and global networks of hundreds and thousands of individuals do require signaling of status as members of the group are not all familiar. The regular and more intimate interaction to maintain the structures of early societies has changed considerably during the last century. There is an evident display of status signs in big and busy urban areas, and in the large schools children navigate. This status signaling was fueled by traditional media such as newspapers, magazines, and television first, and has more recently reached new levels of complexity with social media.

But what was status like in early societies? Around 100,000–600,000 years ago, there was an escape from physical proximity to increased mobility and expansion of social networks. This is shown in the signaling that is often manifest in findings of ink and beads, among others.[11] The ethnographer Ames argued for a human default organization based on rank and competition for status driven by innate primate tendencies, proposing three different origins of egalitarianism.[10] One way for the rise of egalitarianism would have been through the physical dispersal of humans as the range of the landscape expanded and competition between non-dominant and dominant individuals increased. According to Erdal and Whiten, this dispersion would have made the maintaining of rank orders more difficult than when humans were more contained. A second option could have been the intense competition as networks of alliances broadened. This could also have been the preferred arrangement in a context of group extinction with environmental shifts and intense intergroup competition and violence. And finally, a third option could have been the conferred advantage to small human groups that frequently move, as those had a better chance of survival if they repressed individuals' status-seeking competition regardless of the environmental context. Most likely, this progressive tendency to egalitarianism did not happen at the same time or in the same space, and a combination of these three factors led to it.

As we saw earlier, some anthropologists like Boehm[17] rejected the idea that humans were innately egalitarian, while others like Erdal and colleagues supported it.[2] Erdal argued that data supporting non-egalitarian tendencies corresponded to post-hunter-gatherer societies, and the conclusions mixed behaviors of hunter-gathering and these other later societies. However, there is general agreement on the innate human inclination to behave in ways that create counter dominance in the group. Erdal argues that the drive for sharing comes from a sense of fairness. This thrust for sharing would create economically efficient systems, where everyone in the group could be fed, and in which a few could be better fed with the surplus. As dominant and dominated individuals created more complex hierarchial dynamics, encephalization continued (or caused this increased complexity).[17] Individuals would have overall evolved to resist domination, and would have presented motivations of dominance and non-dominance depending on the circumstances. In this context, humans would find themselves, the way we do now, assessing situations and holding multiple options in their mind to deliver the best behavior that would lead to the best outcome in every situation. To be able to do this, humans require executive functioning, or the ability to plan and deliver options, organize potential outcomes, and decide on the best steps ahead. This process, without a doubt, would have had an intricate relationship with encephalization. With new economies, the incentives changed, but the hierarchies remained.

Christopher Boehm,[18] on the other hand, diverges from this idea defending that these egalitarian societies are maintained by a conscious decision to restrict domination through sanctions of certain members in the group. This group domination is the main cause for this type of societal structure, and common in all of these societies. The change to societies ruled by a leader or chief was the cultural acceptance and legitimization of their authority and the forces of balancing power remained. Leaders are aware of their vulnerable positions. However, if they are overthrown, they are substituted by another leader, as opposed to being neutralized by a tribe of non-dominant humans.

Bruce Knauft agreed on the strong tendency to egalitarianism over the course of human evolution, constrained by non-dominant peers, with a non-extinguished primate tendency to socially dominate; the relative rising of social hierarchies among Homo sapiens sapiens (or modern humans) with increased sedentism, farming and agriculture, the surplus of foods, and the creation of more complex societies being relatively recent. Knauft also noted the existence of differences in human and ape hierarchies. For example, counter-dominance is rare among apes, while it is the norm among simple human societies. Apes also openly demonstrate subordination while humans in these societies engage in giving messages to dominant humans using 'informal status leveling through humor, inuendo, and public social support' (Knauft, p. 181).[7]

Finally, other researchers such as Richer Lee argue that perfect equality does not exist, and attempting to set a referent of perfect equality will fail and lead scholars to argue that there is no existing equality.[19] Individual differences in strength, skills, intelligence, and looks are abundant. Yet, some societies are able to minimize these differences while others, especially class societies, magnify them. In egalitarian societies, some were stronger and more skilled hunters, but these different qualities did not lead to differences in outcomes, such as more power or more wives, as societal structures ensured all members of the group had food, regardless of their ability to hunt meat.

Overall, while all these experts in the evolution of human egalitarian behaviors and societies disagree on the causes for counter-dominance in human evolution, they all agree on its existence. They also agree that the status quest was innate to humans and inherited from our ape ancestors, and that it evolved with a change from smaller, simpler societies, based on hunter-gathering economies to bigger, sedentary societies that included farming and agriculture leading to surplus and new structures of power. While we do not have the same structures, the history of evolution tells us that it is safe to assume that the behaviors observed in apes are those we have evolved from and still display in our day-to-day activities. Understanding how these behaviors affect our health, our psyche and our decisions, and how they can be observed in our children and the structures they encounter is the purpose of the upcoming chapters.

How did humans move away from egalitarian societies?

With sedentism came population growth, which led to population density, and a decrease in per capita resource availability, more production to meet the new demands, and greater social tensions. In typical foraging societies, villagers in communities of about 50 people had worked a few hours a day to sustain the community's needs for food and shelter. As societies grew, the needs under a certain type of technology increased, along with the need for space. This space overlapped with the space needed by neighboring societies, leading to turf battles, and a higher need for working adults to sustain the population.[20] Today's societies also have to balance a dwindling population that would bring current economic systems to a brink, with overcrowding that could lead to instability.

While the needs for the larger populations in these earlier societies were maintained through sharing of labor and goods, eventually these systems would break as there were too many people with different interests. The new figure of the 'manager,' comes into place to oversee people with different interests, ensuring a fair and equitable distribution of resources. The initial managers were known for their fairness and leadership skills, able to convince people by persuasion and by example and not by strength. They tended to live in humble ways, and their homes were usually identified as being the poorest huts. They were the José Mujicas of the time. The president of Uruguay from 2010 to 2015, Mujica has been considered the humblest head of state in the world, as he donated almost all his salary to poor people and lived a simple life.

At some point, through power accumulation, change from persuasion to the imposition of force, or the building of coalitions to ensure domination, leaders of earlier societies switched to self-aggrandizement and unrestricted power. This change is seen in the ornaments and regalia worn to celebrations by chiefs in some North American Native American societies, especially in the Northwest coast. The role, restrictions, and demeanor of the chief, of course, varied by society and across continents. While there is an association between larger communities and inequality, this is not a straight line of correlation and some societies remained relatively egalitarian in spite of increased population. With the coming of agriculture, property ownership either public or private becomes necessary to work the land, marking the beginning of a less egalitarian period of human history.

Were hunter-gatherer societies that egalitarian?

Anthropologist James Woodburn had introduced the term 'egalitarian' to describe hunter-gatherer societies as a way to communicate that it was intentional political equality, and not just the absence of hierarchy what lead to equality. Egalitarian systems in these societies existed not in opposition to hierarchies or the experience of these hierarchies. Actually, many hunter-gatherer societies do have systems of marked inequality, even more evident than in agricultural societies. Woodburn's argument is that only the hunter-gathering system allows for the prominence of equality.[20]

It is important to note that relationships between men and women in these hunter-gatherer societies were not always egalitarian. Two types of hunter-gathering societies have been described. One type is an immediate returns society, in which the people obtain immediate goods from their work, eat food that is not processed or stored on the same days or soon after they hunt or gather it, and use simple tools and weapons. The second type is a delayed-return systems, in which more sophisticated tools are used to obtain food, there is processing and storing of food, the products are improved by human labor, and men hold rights over women who are exchanged for goods in marriage to other men, similar to agricultural societies.

Immediate-return societies are nomadic and live in territories with one or more camps. Individuals can move freely from one camp to another without penalties and some do so temporarily or permanently. Movement is seen as desirable and not burdensome. It is likely beneficial as it gathers people around existing resources in a specific area at a given time, allowing individuals in conflict to be separate from each other, and making it difficult for an authory to impose constraint. Everyone has equal access to means of coercion. The same weapons that are used for hunting can be turned to others in the case of grievance. The ability to protect oneself from attacks during sleep or from ambush is limited if one enters in conflict and decides to stay as oppose to move to another camp. This is thought to be another leveling mechanism, as inequalities can cause resentment and make those with more possessions vulnerable to attack. Social control, therefore, is direct and not mediated by institutions or political relationships with others. Access to food and other resources is equally direct. People with ties to an area have equal access to wild resources, including newcomers. There is flexibility in who belongs to the community and who has access to resources. This flexibility extends outside the territory. In these societies, boundaries are inexistent. This helps provide a cushion in periods of shortage of resources and allows communities to adapt to changing resource availability from year to year. This lack of dependence is different from agricultural societies. Even when hunting, individuals are not expected to participate nor limited from participation in the hunt in anyway, and they are free to participate in it one day and abstain from participating on another day.

In these societies, sharing is necessary. The biggest opportunity for inequality and differential status ensues with the hunt of big animals, and in that situation, several rules are set in place. The meat is shared within the camp and never eaten by the hunter alone. The hunter is separated from the meat by different mechanisms. The hunter borrows someone else's arrow to hunt, and the arrow's owner is responsible for distributing the meat. The responsibility of distributing the meat brings status, but also potential conflict if the individual distributing it is perceived to be unfair in the distribution. Successful hunters are scorned when they boast about their hunt and little comment is made about it. According to Woodburn, this does not seem to be a process in which there is reciprocity. The hunter does not share expecting to receive in the future. In reality that often does not happen. The sharing is rather an imposition by the community. The accumulation of personal goods such as clothing and ornaments, tools or weapons is sanctioned. In the Hadza communities Woodburn studied, there is a considerable amount of time spent gambling with others in the group to transmit the own goods onto others. These goods are not basic ones such as the arrow or leather bag, but unnecessary and made of materials that are not easily accessible. However, the games played are games of chance and not skill, and the distribution of goods is fairly equal at the end of the day. The game is not a transaction that requires a contract, but a depersonalized way of transmitting goods.

There is also a lack of formal leadership. Some camps are named after older individuals with bigger families who are allowed to speak for longer periods and whose opinions may have more influence, but who are not formal leaders as known today. Those members of the group with personality characteristics that would make them distinguished and not perceived as proximal to the rest of the group are disqualified from the job. Those leaders need to be modest and generous, not arrogant or driven to accumulate goods.

In summary, traditional anthropology from the 1970s until more recently, has emphasized an egalitarian approach of hunter-gatherer societies, in opposition to the more hierarchical agricultural societies. There is no question that hierarchies are innate to humans and that status achievement is the natural impulse that drives us. These early societies were not free of inequalities as there is no perfect equality, but they offer an abundance of examples of controls that maintained these differences of status under check for the benefit of all the members of the community.

Social wealth

In spite of the well-documented observations of traditional hunter-gatherer societies and existing archeological evidence that have led to conclusions about egalitarism in hunter-gatherer societies, recent quantitative studies have demonstrated transmission of wealth and inequality within these same societies. This intergenerational wealth transmission was low, but influenced an individual's opportunities.[21] These societies are so diverse that some have questioned the utility of the classification of hunter-gatherer. Instead, framing the discussion based on the society's size or mobility has been proposed as more informative.[22]

The real effect on wellbeing may need not be measured by wealth as in accumulation of goods, which is the focus of much of the anthropological literature on egalitarianism in hunter-gatherer societies, but by other forms of wealth, such as social connections and health. Free mobility makes difficult the investment in fixed land and facilities, the accumulation of material goods, and the emergence of powerful figures who hold access to resources because people can move to other well-resourced areas avoiding control by certain individuals and institutionalized inequality. However, poor health may limit this ability to survive, and health success may become dependent on one's 'relational wealth.'[23]

Among the Ache, a hunter-gatherer society from Eastern Paraguay until its contact with outsiders in the 1970s, wealth was measured by non-material dimensions: the ability to produce resources, higher-quality relationships, and body and mind abilities such as health, body size, and cognitive abilities. These characteristics are all potentially heritable and interrelated, and can be transmitted to other generations and contribute to fertility. However, the Ache significantly changed their lifestyle after they established contact with outsiders.

Among the Hadza, in northern Tanzania, there is no property transmission or accumulation across generations. They live in very small groups of about 30 people who move from place to place every month and a half. Men hunt alone and they share the meat with everyone. The proportion of hunt retained by the hunter's household is larger than that given to other households.[24] The best hunters have higher status and their offspring have a higher chance of survival. The measures of wealth considered are weight, grip strength (necessary for the jobs done by the Hadza), and foraging success.[21]

The Ju/'hoansi from the Kalahari Desert in Botswana and Namibia are thought to be among the most egalitarian societies. Yet, those who are better hunters, or have more social skills or healing abilities, are recognized by a term equivalent to 'leader' or 'one who has things.' The measure of wealth in this community is the number of Hxaro partners. Hxara refers to a type of commitment to supporting one another in times of need. These partners can be of any age or sex. The Ju/'hoansi receive extended visits from their Hxaro that can last months. Group members with more Hxaro partners tend to own more goods, have a higher number of alternative places in which to reside, more hunting success if they are men, and more social and healing abilities than those with less partners.[12]

The Lamalera are a society in Southeast Indonesia that centered their economy in maritime foraging and trading with interior agricultural villages. Newer clans had less status and authority than those that had arrived earlier, and individuals' social status was tied to their clan's or to their own hunting abilities. Their material success was tied to social ties. Wealth was measured by household wealth, which is important as a home is a requisite for marriage; sharing network ties, which help buffer changes in harvest by having other people who share food; boat shares, which depend on kinship but can be shared with those who contribute to the boat's maintenance; and finally, reproductive success, which was defined as number of offspring living beyond one year, given the high infant mortality.[25]

Finally, among the Meriam in the island of Torres Strait, between Australia and Papua New Guinea, who acquire most of their nutrition from sea turtles, the wealth measure is reproductive success as measured by the number of children. Infant mortality was low at the time the researchers were collecting data, given the existence of a staffed medical clinic, which brings up the question of how much this is currently a measure of wealth. The researchers scored the wealth measures based on their own judgment and observation and agreed that the most important type of wealth was relational wealth. Wealth varied depending on the population's mobility. For those who were more mobile, embodied wealth was most important and material wealth was least important.[21]

Transmission of wealth across generations

Societies like the Ache and the Hadza are structured in ways in which the hunting skills of the parents are not transmitted to their sons. The sons learn from all men in the community, and not from the parent, making the transmission of this type of wealth unexpectedly low. One would envision strength and intelligence to be transmitted from father to son causing parents with superior hunting abilities to have sons with superior hunting abilities. Yet, the practice of sharing skills does not allow for the intergenerational family transmission of these skills. The Lamalerans from Indonesia also have a lack of transmission of 'wealth' related to reproductive success, likely due to the food-sharing and cooperative hunting that level the access to resources for all households.[25] There is also no advantage in the Meriam's children of parents with high reproductive success.

The only measures of intergenerational transmission of material household wealth were in the Lamalera. The investment in household construction is in itself telling of the differences between this society and the traditional hunter-gatherer societies that often moved several times a year. The other source of wealth is having a share in the boat, but those have little parental influence. Among the Ju/'hoansi, the Hxaros or partnerships were a measure of relational wealth that was also transmitted from parents to children. Overall, the coefficients of intergenerational wealth transmission are relatively low in these societies. Yet, even small coefficients have important consequences for survival, and even in those hunter-gatherer societies with leveling approaches, parents who are better off tend to have children who will also be better off.[21]

Altogether, while there is some intergenerational wealth transmission and these societies did not have perfect egalitarianism or what some have described as 'primitive communism,' wealth inequality was low comparably to any other society past and contemporary. The Gini coefficient, a measure of inequality, was found to be in the moderate range in most of these societies, equivalent to today's Scandinavian countries, and lower than in any other society in today's world, as well as lower than in agricultural and pastoral societies.[21] Again, these societies did not experience perfect egalitarianism, but they were less unequal than many of our societies today.[26]

Inequality in modern society

There is not much pre-industrial data on income inequality, but a handful of Western countries have kept records. Trends of income inequality show that farming and population density led to an increase in wealth accumulation and inequality that varied by continent depending on the ability of different societies to expand farming and their territory. The structure of hunter-gatherer societies helps us understand the hierarchies in which humans have lived for the most part of their existence before the emergence of agriculture and modern society.

As mentioned, the Gini coefficient is a measure of income inequality, or the difference between those who have the most and those who have the least amount of wealth. While it is difficult to calculate Gini coefficients in pre-industrial societies, attempts to do so suggest a progressive increase of inequality with wealth accumulation over time. Additionally, inequality increased as societies transitioned from hunter-gathering to horticulture to agricultural societies, which created the most unequal societies. As societies grew bigger, so did their socio-political scales. In essence, societies progressed from family-based structures with the lowest levels of inequality, to local, regional, and state political scales that we more unequal.[27]

It is difficult to study income inequality in pre-industrial societies given the scarcity of historical sources to make estimations. However, as a result of efforts to expand a data base on inequality estimators, economists have now been able to estimate income inequality for European countries from the Middle Ages to modern history, and for the U.S. since its creation. These data show that over the past seven centuries, there has been a continuous growth in both income and wealth inequality.[28]

More recently, there was a steep decline in income inequality in Europe from the beginning of the 1900s until the 1980s, at which point inequality started increasing again at a very fast pace. Part of this increase in inequality may have been caused by the changes in taxation that had been more progressive after the World Wars and during the creation of the 'Welfare state' policies, and that changed during the 1980s' administrations of American President Ronald Reagan in the U.S., and British Prime Minister Margaret Thatcher in the U.K. These tax changes kept the gross domestic product of these countries the same. In other words, they did not increase economic growth as promised, but instead, they increased income inequality within the population. World Wars I and II, and pandemics like the Black Death Pandemic had a way to level these societal inequalities by affecting everyone equally and making the rich less rich and closer in income and wealth to the rest of the population. These insults do not seem to be leveling the wealth these days, as inequality has continued to grow even with the COVID-19 pandemic, the war in Ukraine, and the economic recessions of 2008 and 2012. In a way, the rich are more protected than ever, and now they are also more 'seen' than ever. The expansion of traditional media and now social media has made the way of living of the wealthy accessible to watch to everyone, even children. In some wealthy countries like the U.S., the inequalities are abhorrent. The richest hold most of the wealth, which has just increased in the last two decades. Specifically, the top 10% richest in the U.S. accumulated 67.9% of the wealth in 2000 and 70.7% in 2021.[29] It takes a lot from humans to contain the drive for dominance and allow cooperation to abound, and we often only use the drive when it is in our own interest, that is, when cooperation is more beneficial for us than domination. As a species, we have had to use cooperation to survive and many societies have found a way to develop towards more cooperation. However, in some societies like the U.S., where some residents have a power of acquisition of services that is much higher than that of their fellow residents, one can create a supportive community by paying people. This is one of the hazards of affluence. One needs less of others if services needed can be paid. Many can live without needing to tolerate others, and can even isolate from others. All trends have benefits and drawbacks. It is less comfortable to share a busy bus than drive a car, go to the store than order online, and garner support from your family members than pay someone to clean your home. Money and technology allow humans to be comfortable, but this comfort and choice can also diminish opportunities to engage and cooperate with others and exchange ideas. It can also lead to isolation and even depression and substance use, as one seeks to reward the brain in other non-social ways.

In sum, traditional anthropologists discussing egalitarianism in hunter-gatherer societies did not question individual status differences among members of the group. Instead, they debated the societal structures that maintained relatively egalitarian ways of life in spite of individual differences. There is no question about the drive for status in humans, even among those living in hunter-gatherer societies. Yet, there is evidence that these societies tried to minimize the effects of this individual impulse for the common good. This is a key concept. Without a doubt, humans, from birth to death are shaped by innate qualities that put them at more or less advantage when compared to others around them. Over time, humans may also develop, through social and learning processes, other qualities that may put them at even more advantage or disadvantage in relationship to their peers. There is no question that differences in status exist and that as primates, we are naturally drawn to dominate others or become submissive for survival. It is also not a question that there is a natural tendency in humans to create social hierarchies. The questions and answers these anthropologists pose and give us are about the societal structures that minimize these differences for the survival of the group. This book is not an endorsement of any political structure. We will discuss later that the idea that communism would be a solution is misleading. Not only because it has proven unsuccessful as a strategy to improve the wellbeing of populations, but because it assumes it is possible to get rid of hierarchies and imposes an unnatural way of living. However, there is a need for a path in which we can be aware of our instinctual desire for status, and at the same time create environments that like hunter-gatherer societies, can supply needed resources to members of our society for a dignified life, especially when it comes to children. Extremes in one direction or another: either we are all different and everyone should individually succeed or fail, or we are all the same and no one should succeed more than anyone else, will miss this point.

3 What is known about social status and health

Marmot's health gradient

The clinical world of mental health spends much of its time focused on genetics, or the characteristics and risks that we inherit from our ancestors, and behaviors that we can engage in or discontinue to be healthy, such as nutrition and exercise. We also discuss healthcare access and the need for patients to follow health recommendations such as getting cancer and other screenings. Those are all factors influencing our health. However, there is more to health than these genetic, behavioral, and access issues.

In his 1984s, *The Status Syndrome*, Marmot makes a case for why relative deprivation, or how much a person has in comparison to others around them, matters more to one's health than absolute deprivation. He explains that health works in a gradient that affects not only the poor, but also those whose basic needs are covered.[1] Marmot's argument is that genetic, lifestyle, and healthcare access factors are not as important and do not have as much weight on our health as the ability to feel in control of our lives, have autonomy, and be socially connected to others. These three factors are related to our standing in the social hierarchy and define when we get sick and how long we live.

It would be difficult to rid any society of all inequalities because, as we have seen, dominance and submission interactions are inherent to human nature. We can always try to aim to work towards reducing inequalities to reduce the effects on health, or so that everyone can have a chance to live at the fullest of their potential in societies where the health of their members is not disrupted by massive inequalities.

A focus on the health gradient matters because we had always understood health and income relationships in binary terms: If you are poor, you are more likely to get sick; if you are not poor, you are more likely to be healthy. The health gradient shows that even if you are not poor or under a certain fixed income level or experiencing hardship, you are still less likely to be healthy than someone around you who is higher in the social hierarchy. This view has policy implications, because it means that reducing inequalities and not just poverty could improve the health of all.

DOI: 10.4324/9781003535942-3

The Whitehall studies

Looking at census data from 1971 in the U.K., John Fox and his colleagues followed Whitehall workers through 1980 and showed that those who became unemployed had a 20% increase in mortality rates compared to those who continued to be employed in the same social class level. Those who become unemployed may also have had difficult lives before becoming unemployed, so it would be difficult to untangle if someone presented health problems due to their challenging life experiences before becoming unemployed or because of being unemployed. Yet, these researchers found a way to prove that it was not only the lack of money related to unemployment that caused people to be less healthy, but that it was the lack of participation in society.

Whitehall is an area of London that concentrates government departments and workers in civil service jobs. The health and behaviors of around 18,000 government employees were followed over time. This was a relatively financially homogeneous group, as their government salaries and benefits were limited to a certain range. They all had access to public health services, stable jobs, and low risk of unemployment. Their jobs were similar in nature, as they were all office based. However, even within this relatively homogeneous population, there was a health gradient. These employees were not working in factories, nor they were at different risk of exposure to chemicals, other physical environmental stressors, nor were they asked to perform extreme physical labor, but they still had mild differences in their role as an office worker. Some of them were administrators, or the decision-makers who set the polices, others were executives or professionals, such as statisticians, others had clerical jobs, and finally there were those who worked as office support staff. The ones belonging to professional groups with more control and autonomy in their jobs had less disease. All workers had access to healthcare, and those who needed it more were actually accessing it more frequently. Because workers in the lower ranks of the work hierarchy had more disease, they accessed care more frequently. So, while everyone has the right to access healthcare and it is easy to argue for a right to access free healthcare, in this population healthcare access did not determine most of the workers' health.

Twenty years since Marmot's book, and after many health reports, we continue to be hyper-focused on getting people to healthcare services often ignoring the reasons why we need to access care in the first place. An obvious example is the herculean efforts of U.S. professional medical organizations to increase the workforce in their respective subspecialties. In case the reader did not know, all subspecialties in the U.S. have a shortage of providers. Currently in the U.S., nurses, physician assistants, and psychologists are all trying to gain rights to prescribe in order to cover the gap between the need for prescriptions and the availability of prescribers (which had traditionally only been doctors) for youth with mental health problems during the current youth mental health crisis. One reason for the high demand of prescriptions is the preference for faster fixes among Americans, and a predilection for medications when it comes to treating mental health disorders, instead of the longer and more tedious work done in therapy sessions over months and years. But another reason is that even if someone wanted to treat mild depression with just therapy, there would not be enough qualified therapists to treat everyone. Even when people choose therapy over medications, it is often easier to find prescribers than trained therapists. And even if we had more qualified therapists, or used telehealth or mobile applications, all laudable and helpful to attempt to cover the demand and bridge the gap, we would not be able to treat everyone. Major changes in the way we structure our society may have more of an impact in this mental health crisis and these are rarely advocated for by professional organizations. One may be tempted to think that maybe, it all comes down to adopting good behaviors. Maybe if we exercised and ate healthy enough, we could live longer and better lives. Whitehall workers who had healthier behaviors, did indeed have better health. Obviously, tobacco still causes cancer and processed foods cause obesity. But when we look at how much these behaviors determined health, we see that they still determined only a portion and did not explain the whole story. The health gradient still had a role.

One argument against this social gradient is that illness may put people at risk for social decline, but again, the social gradient of health is not explained by health-related social mobility. The challenge is that even if income was the same for everyone, the health gradient would remain, because as we have seen, it is not only about how much we have, it is also about how much we have compared to others, where we stand in the social status ladder. Money itself is not the only marker of success, and humans will find other ways to seek that superiority or to keep up with the success of others whether doing it involves money, fame, or respect. For example, when looking at health differences by sex, men's health was more associated to their standing at work, but for women, their health was more strongly associated to their social standing. This means that the health of different people and groups of people will be associated with different dimensions in the social hierarchy. As we will see, children and adolescents spend much of their time growing, figuring out their spot in these different social rank dimensions.

Income inequality

Money, of course, is key to provide individuals and communities with the basic needs to be healthy, but once those basic needs are covered, more money does not improve health, if we still we have a lot less than others. A person surrounded by people with higher incomes will not have as many opportunities to fully participate in society as those wealthier neighbors. In the Whitehall studies, workers' income and lack of control were not the only factors that contributed to health. Those who had a feeling of reciprocity did better than those who did not. As a social species that has evolved through cooperation, we are wired to feel as part of a community. When people were not rewarded appropriately, not just with money, but also with esteem and career opportunities, they were more emotionally distressed. Those who engaged in high effort and had low rewards presented more cardiovascular disorders. The opportunity to participate in society and have a sense of purpose was vital for their health. Sense of purpose and social support are two of the basic tenants of communities with large numbers of people who grow to be very old. Furthermore, individual income is very intertwined with what a society offers. In societies with weak public services, individual income will make a big difference, because money will allow people to cover those costs that society does not secure, but that are still vital for a good life.

Wilkinson compared different countries' level of income inequality[2] showing that the more unequal a country is the shorter the life expectancy and the worse the health outcomes. It is easy to think that this effect of inequality on life expectancy is due to more people falling under the poverty level, but inequality in itself, regardless of poverty, seems to be bad for health. Deaton studied differences between U.S. states showing that the states with higher mortality rates were also the ones with higher percentage of Black people.[3] Race and income are strongly intertwined in the U.S., but other factors like racial or class discrimination may contribute to stress and poor health.

Power and health

Marmot argues that the lack of ability to socially engage, rather than the material deprivation itself, is the issue affecting health. He concludes that there are three levels of social stratification and health: the absolute or objective level of resources, status, or the subjective rank and power. Objective resources are beyond this text and have been described extensively. In essence, being poor predicts all sorts of poor health outcomes, including all-cause mortality.[4] Subjective rank will be discussed throughout the text. Let's focus on power for now.

Power is related to stress levels. Having less power leaves people with no control over their lives. A good example is the health of women under the Taliban government. Given the variety of circumstances and evolution of Islamic societies, it is not possible to generalize, and it would be an inaccurate exaggeration to say that all women in Islamic-majority countries are oppressed.[5] However, the example of the Afghanistan gives us a pre- and post-comparison of women's health while living under an oppressive extremist religious government, and accounting for the same circumstances of culture, genes, and geography. During the 1990s and early 2000s, Afghan women were forced to wear coverings, and were denied access to healthcare, jobs, education, or autonomy, having to be accompanied by a man. In the post-Taliban period, starting in 2004, women recovered their rights, had access to healthcare, and there was an increased enrollment of girls in primary schools from less than 10% in 2003 to 33% in 2017. Secondary schools saw a rise in enrollment from 6% to 39%. In only two decades, life expectancy increased from 56 to 66 years of age. While these changes were mostly seen in urban areas, they are an example of what it is like to live without having control of your own life and how it affects your health and lifespan. A sign of this lack of control is their inability to leave marriages that may be traumatic, as 80% of Afghan women are thought to experience domestic violence, which in itself leads to poor health as we know from the extensive literature on traumatic experiences and health.[6] Unfortunately, Afghan women have now had to surrender to yet another Taliban regime era.

What makes stress toxic?

Not all stress is bad. A certain degree of stress is not only benign, but necessary. The Yerkes-Dodson Law,[7] which was based on an initial study with mice in 1908, later replicated in humans, proposes that very little stress will generate an insufficient level of arousal for the animal or person to perform well, but if the stress is too high, performance will also be poor. This U-shaped curve applies to complex tasks, while with simple tasks that don't require as much cognitive involvement, more stress leads to better performance. Too much stress may not matter when you have to run a 400-meter race, and it can help when you are trying to run away from a hungry predator, but it probably will block your ability to plan and think when you are trying to do more complex tasks such as taking a test or finding a new hunting path.

Stress helps organisms perform to the best of their abilities. The amygdala is the part of the brain that will become more active in situations of extreme stress. It will prepare the body to fight or flight. But its overstimulation will overwhelm the prefrontal lobes, which allow humans to plan and strategize. Imagine trying to concentrate enough to respond to complex math questions in a test. You don't want to be completely relaxed or distracted and not respond to all the questions on time, but you also don't want to be so stressed that you can't think clearly and get the questions wrong or that you freeze and cannot proceed with completing the task.[8]

The question is, what happens when stress is constant and chronic, without escape or any control? Several aspects of stress make it not-so-good. The control an individual has over the stress is one of the key elements that determine its effects. Whether one can leave the situation, hide, or retreat when faced with a threat are key factors. Will you have to stay in that situation regardless of your efforts to control your environment? Adults will often tell children who are being bullied by their peers to 'just ignore' the bullies, or avoid them, and some times that is possible; but what happens when you are in a school that you need to attend every day and where you will encounter not only one bully but many? Often, especially in big schools with hundreds of children, the administrators and teachers are not able to keep track of the subtle interactions that take place among middle schoolers navigating these years of social skills development with limited experience and perspective. Those children may feel trapped in environments they can't change or control, and in which they may be victimized.

Another aspect involved in stress is predictability. As a physician, I have experienced a narrow range of unpredictable events, and for that I feel fortunate. My choice of career was largely motivated by my wish to avoid stress and uncertainty, and the reason why I did not follow my first choice of being a war correspondent. But even within my profession, we experience the differences in medical rotations during training, transitioning from the emergency room or hospital services, to the life of more stability in outpatient clinic settings. These differences are well-known to medical professionals, and can determine the type of jobs they choose as other demands, like family, enter the picture, because one can only handle so much. For many children and adolescents, even in developed countries, there are few choices when feeling trapped. Not knowing when food will run out, if their families will have enough to pay for their school uniform, or whether the walk to school will be safe that day are unpredictable threats over which they have little control.

Social support is another key aspect related to stress. Even having only one trusted adult can make a difference in a child's life who has experienced trauma or deprivation. Social support can make life smoother. It allows individuals to keep afloat when they feel like they are sinking. The threat to status is another aspect of stress. This one is not only relevant to teen girls of the likes of the movie 'Mean Girls.' Number one seed tennis players can be extremely stressed over others ranked below them trying to take their spot, CEOs falling during an economic crash, more and less democratic presidents fearing loss of popularity and votes, and egos hurt due to office politics are all examples of stress related to threats to status. This stress is different if you are coming up than if you are going down the social rank, because trying to meet a demand that will put you higher in the ladder is not as stressful as fearing going down and losing your position in the ladder.

That leads us to the last characteristic that affects the impact of stress in our psyche: the availability of outlets. This is the reason why afterschool activities and sports in children are so essential in underserved communities. Stress is inevitable. We live with it every day, in our personal life, at work, and in our social relationships. For children, the lack of control (as they depend on adults for almost everything in their lives), unpredictable environments (which they have little capacity to escape), lack of social support (as they may be part of struggling families without the ability to care for them), a threat to their status (which can be constant in poorly supervised settings or in middle school) can feel like a threat to their life. For those in communities that are deprived of basic resources in an environment with multiple stressors and high inequality, respect is the last thing to hold on to, and a lack of respect can feel like a stab in a wound, worthy of risking one's life. For some, a threat to status can actually mean a threat to their life, as losing status is perceived as being weak and can be the deadly recipe that may lead to being bullied, attacked, and potentially killed. In those cases, there is a psychological threat to status and a potential real threat to life.

The stress on our bodies

Stress also has direct effects on hormonal systems, and hierarchies affect the level of stress, leading to changes in cortisol, as mentioned earlier. Cortisol is a stress hormone that in excess and when constantly elevated can cause a multitude of problems, including metabolic syndrome, leading to increased risk for cardiovascular disorders and cancer. Obviously, a perfect diet with a good amount of exercise will make it more difficult for a person to develop atherosclerosis, or the clogging of arteries, and will lower their risk of cardiovascular disease. However, given the same diet, someone in a higher position in the hierarchy, will have better health than someone experiencing more stress in a lower position.

Higher stress also weakens one's immune system. Immunotherapy for cancer treatment is now showing that a strong immune system may be the key to rid one's body of cancerous cells, as opposed to using the chemotherapy, which rids the body of all cells, cancerous or not.[9] Just as with infections, there is a dance between the microbe and the host's defense system leading to more or less severity of disease. A recent example is the infection by the SARS-COVID-19 coronavirus. Some hosts were more vulnerable due to older age, which comes with a weaker immune system or obesity, which generated an overreactive inflammation. For those who were more vulnerable, the virus could be deadly, while for others, it consisted of a temporary headache or a cough. The same process happens every year with the flu, every year a virus that finds vulnerability at extreme ages. With non-infectious diseases, our body may react to internal inflammation. In the case of cancer, for example, an insult (agent) to one's body, like tobacco, may lead to cancer often, but the response of the body will vary depending on the person's immune system, which will also vary depending on their stress levels and standing in the social hierarchy.

Social support as a human basic need

One of the things that makes people more resistant to insults, either internal or external, is social support and the quality of their social relationships. These social relationships and the level of cohesiveness are driven by individuals, but can be influenced by societal structures, cultures, religion, and even historical events. For example, suicide, tightly linked to social support, decreases in periods of war or during catastrophes, as people find purpose and band together to fight common enemies. Additionally, income inequality is associated with less trust, social capital, and social engagement. This burdens those in highly unequal societies twice, by exposing them to more stressors and depriving them of social support buffers.[10]

Sociologists and mental health professionals have recently engaged with intensity on a debate regarding the role of social media on the increase in suicide rates among adolescents. Many identify social media as the cause for these increased rates in youth suicide. However, one could also explain the rise in social media use as caused by more isolation and a need for young people to find communities when other aspects of society prevent them from experiencing a sense of community and social integration. I believe most healthy children and teenagers with the opportunity to interact with peers in safe spaces will likely have a preference for that option over social media unless the child or teenager has social skills deficits or social anxiety. However, without those opportunities an alternative can be found online. Due to fear for their safety and curtailed autonomy, or because of over-structured schedules, and inexistent free time, the time to socialize in person may be threatened. There is no question that for many children social media-based relationships are easier, less risky, and more comfortable, but for many they are just a substitute. There is rarely one single cause for changes in patterns of relationship and mental health disorders among youth, which is why it is important to look beyond the introduction of social media to fully understand the current youth mental health crisis.

The essence of status lies in people's ability to be active participants in social life. Whether it is by having basic items that make life less hard, socially-oriented items that allow one to keep in touch with the world, or luxury items, these are related to health as they signal a certain status to others and a sense of continuity and stability. These issues are universal. Even within communist societies in Central and Eastern Europe during the second half of the 20th century, and with very narrow differences in individual incomes, cardiovascular disorder and violent deaths affected more those who did not have autonomy, social support, or control. Additionally, these societies had low social capital and social cohesion. They were structured as two entities: the people in power (the state) and the rest of the population, without the organic communities that grow out of trust, social support, and reciprocity. Naturally, trust-based relationships of parents with the local school board of education or the family business meeting with the local chamber of commerce were the essence of early political structures in a big democracy like the U.S. Big government is often in the conservative psyche of the 21st century. Libertarian Americans still remember the monster of Europe's failed communist societies prior to 1989s end of the separation and destruction of the Berlin Wall. While neoliberalism in the U.S. and Communism in Europe are completely opposite economies, they have something in common: the big government of big societies, which many resist. It is not difficult to imagine more civil, naturally constrained and collaborative local governments with more opportunities for informal relationships. In fact, Marmot surveyed Russians and asked them if they relied more on informal or formal institutions. Those who relied on informal networks had better health. Truly, big bureaucracies can lead people to experience some of the most stressful moments.

Finally, an aspect to highlight is the imbalance in effort and reward, in other words, stress.[11] Very hard work that is poorly rewarded, either monetarily or with a pat on the back, is stressful. Other factors, such as insults to one's body, substance use, unhealthy behaviors have an obvious role in our health, and are also associated with lower social rank.

Health gradient and children

Sir Marmot points out that differences in schools' scores, which are known in the U.K. as 'the league tables,' have little to do with how well one is taught in the school and a lot to do with the level of deprivation of the children in that school and the location of the school.

Parents' level of education has a linear association with children's literacy levels, meaning that the higher the parent's level of education the higher the children's literacy. This effect is stronger in certain countries like the U.S. when compared to countries like Sweden. In other words, if you are a child whose parents have a low level of education, your literacy scores will be lower than if your parents have a higher level of education, but if you are born in the U.S. you will feel the difference much more than if you are born in Sweden. Or put in yet another way, your parents' education level matters less if you are a child born in Sweden than if you are born in the U.S. Most of what makes the difference is the social capital, the environment outside of the school, and parental participation. Marmot recognizes that increasing funding to existing systems will likely continue to keep inequities with those children who may benefit more from schools advancing even more, while the children who don't benefit continue to remain behind. It is also not plausible, or at least not well-accepted, to take away funding from children who are doing well to fund the children who are not. After all, they are all children. There are no 'bad' children for being born to families with a higher level of education. So, what would the answer be to be fair to all children? Obviously, one step would be to ensure the same access to quality teachers or facilities for all children. Some states in the U.S. may have brought it up a nudge by removing quality teachers from wealthier schools to place them in low performing schools. I am not sure that is the right answer. It is not like public schools in wealthy neighborhoods don't also have struggling students. Another much more productive way to deal with inequities in education would be to try to address the family and social circumstances that place kids at disadvantage. While there has been much talk about the equalizing power of schools, Marmot essentially says, schools cannot be the answer to all the societal ills, as those remain even within the best schools.

Like in the U.K., these school rankings exist in the U.S. The *U.S. News & World Report* rankings of grade schools or websites like *Great Schools* and *Niche* are an easy find for any concerned student or parent. These rankings are somewhat of a self-fulfilling prophecy in the U.S. where the parents with more financial means and more mobility choose neighborhoods with schools with good ratings, which will then become even better ranked as the children will come from well-resourced families. Schools are largely funded by property taxes, so those neighborhoods with little value in their housing are understandably taxed less, and there is less funding for their schools. Parents in neighborhoods that are starting to be gentrified make herculean efforts to diversify and support lower performing schools. By diversifying, I don't mean adding more minorities, but the opposite, adding more White children to largely minority schools. Race and social status are closely intertwined in certain urban areas in the U.S., and Whites tend to be wealthier. This diversification, which works to improve outcomes, is also a socio-economic status level diversification. This is not an easy task and involves resisting decades of economic and racial segregation driven by poorly regulated housing markets.

Interestingly, this is a hot issue related to education in the U.S. right now. After the very public death of a Black man during an arrest that went viral on social media during the COVID-19 pandemic lockdowns, an event that unfortunately had happened before, Americans recognized that their problem with racism was not entirely resolved. All sort of institutions (educational, news, professional organizations, and others) made changes to be more racially inclusive. One of the institutions that began to recon with their practices was the educational system. A new wave of teaching antiracism and creating 'equity' committees was inflated to the point that some middle-income families or those of children who were more academically advanced began to question whether the interests of their own children were being served by the public education system. An example of practice change that took place and upset many parents was the erasing opportunities for advanced placement courses, as these tended to be occupied by higher-income White students.

Many families left public schools for private schools, which at the end of the day, only contributes to even more increased inequities at the societal level.

Modern societies are constantly changing, and even in the apparently most stable times, from the Western world's perspective, massive changing demographics have created changes in societal dynamics in which the powers are switched. It seems like hierarchies and the will to dominate and get ahead will always be a part of human history. The question is, what are we striving for? If it is to improve the health of all people, we then need to consider improving the social circumstances that make life very hard for some and an easy walk in the park for others.

Low control in one's life is not only associated to physical health, but also to depression. It is possible to be in a lower hierarchy at work or at home and feel more in control. Compare a woman working at home whose husband works outside of the home but assigns a salary and monetary control over home expenses versus a woman whose husband unpredictably decides if he is going to allocate money to home activities. Imagine the women from Tehuantepec, Mexico. This is a matriarchal society in which women make decisions in and outside of the home and take a lead in the commercial activities, even though the men do the fishing and farming. These women will all experience very different levels of control over their lives. Among the Zapotecs, the founders of Tehuantepec, some identify with a third gender or "Muxe." Muxes are men who adopt female dressing and characteristics. While these societies are pretty equalitarian and men still hold most of the political positions, one has to wonder if the higher status of women sparks a desire to emulate them among young men. The Whitehall studies found that low control also predicted coronary health disease independently of the effort and rewards balance. This means that if you had low control in your job, you had worse health, and if you had low rewards for your efforts, you also had worse health and that these two associations happened on their own, whether or not the other one took place.

Equitable societies

What would be our health like if we lived in the most equitable societies, with minimal rank differences, and no one taking away other people's autonomy or control? An attempt to answer this question was made through the study of a very equal society in the Bolivian Amazon, the Tsimane.[12] This group of foragers and horticulturalists are thought to have the 'healthiest hearts on earth' as they have lower risk factors for heart disease than any other population known to this day. Accumulation of coronary artery calcium (CAC) in our arteries, a sign of clogged blood vessels that increases risk of heart attack, affects 25% of Americans by the age of 45, but almost no Tsimane has it at that age. By age 75 years, one out of three Tsimane have any CAC versus 80% of Americans. At the time the study was conducted, obesity, hypertension, elevated blood sugar, and cigarette smoking were rare in this population.

The Tsiamane lead very healthy lives. They get their steps in, with men walking an average of 17,000 steps daily, and women and adults older than 60 walking just slightly less. Their diet consists of mainly calories from carbohydrates, followed by fat, protein, fruit, and nuts. The observations of this group tell us that coronary atherosclerosis can be avoided in most people by leading healthy lives and maintaining very low LDL (bad cholesterol'), low blood pressure, low glucose, normal body-mass index, no smoking, and engaging in plenty of physical activity. This lifestyle would take care of the conventional risk factors for coronary artery disease, which contribute to 90% of the risk for heart disease. However, while the Tsimane are relatively free of cardiovascular risk factors, they have a high infectious inflammatory burden, and many become ill due to respiratory infections. Even in this very equalitarian and healthy society, there were differences by rank and stress hormones, and in who became ill from infection.

Social rank and health can also be measured by the influence a person has on the people who surround that person. Those with more influence will have more cooperative partners, and social support is associated with less stress. This effect of social influence happens regardless of age, body size, or one's health-related behaviors or lifestyle. This social influence is associated with cortisol levels, showing that social influence affects stress hormones.

Those with more informal political influence had lower cortisol levels and lower chances of having a respiratory infection, which was a frequent cause of disease. The differences in social influence had no effect on cardiovascular health.

This phenomenon was studied in an egalitarian small-scale society where greater informal political influence among men was associated with lower cortisol. The differences in cortisol levels depending on social influence were equivalent to differences between leaders and non-leaders in U.S. samples.

Status has clear health benefits in both non-human societies where dominance is physically imposed, and in institutionally-granted authority in large scale human societies, but in a society like the Tsimane's no one has control over others and wealth accumulation is limited. And yet, the social benefits of having social influence mitigate health risks over time. Those of lower status do not have that 'social insurance.' Sometimes money can buy this social insurance, but it is costly.

Social health

Social genomics is the science of studying how social factors such as stress, conflict, isolation, or attachment affect our gene expression. While we are glued to the genes we inherit, genes are only a map for the development of proteins, which are transcribed from our DNA. This transcription can be affected by the external environment. Social factors, as part of the external environment, can also affect the expression of individual genes, or clusters of genes.

Loneliness can be an environmental factor affecting our biology. John Cacioppo, a professor of psychology and behavioral neuroscience at the University of Chicago, and Steve Cole, a professor of medicine at the University of California, Los Angeles, among others, have identified a link between feeling lonely and genetic expression. In a small study, which has been since repeated in larger trials, Cacioppo and Cole[13] compared blood samples from six people who felt socially isolated or lonely with samples from eight people who did not feel isolated. Among the lonely participants in the study, the function of the genome had changed in such a way that the risk of inflammatory diseases increased and the antiviral response diminished. It appeared that the brains of these subjects were wired to equate loneliness with danger, and to switch the body into a defensive state. In historical and evolutionary terms, Cacioppo suggested, this reaction could be a good thing, since it helps immune cells reach infections and encourages wounds to heal. But it is no way to live. Chronic inflammation promotes cancer cell growth and the development of plaque in the arteries. It also leads to the disabling of brain cells, which raises susceptibility to neurodegenerative disease. One thing to note, though, is that social genomics research consistently shows that the *perception* of social stressors is a much better predictor of social stress than the objective presence of a social stressor. For example, subjective perception of isolation more strongly predicts proinflammatory gene expression than the objective size of one's social network. This is why therapy can be good. Because it can change the perception one has of a social situation and reduce stress. Essentially, this is what one does in cognitive-behavioral therapy. One learns techniques to make situations be something we can handle as opposed to something overwhelming.

At the population level, social factors such as social isolation can have large effects on various diseases and all-cause mortality. For example, individuals with chronic social isolation have different profiles of genes transcription related to the immune system. People with chronic social isolation will have higher expression of cytokine genes, which are proinflammatory, and a lower expression of antiviral genes. These individuals are also more likely to develop diseases of inflammation, have more morbidity and higher mortality.

Acute and chronic social stressors such as social rejection, isolation, stress, or social rank are also associated with variations in gene expression of breast tissue, lymph nodes, brain cells, and cancers such as ovarian, prostate, and breast cancers.

Perceived social status

The research on social rank had traditionally been focused on socio-economic status. With the turn of the century and through work on inequalities, Wilkinson and others[2] had claimed that inequality and relative standing actually mattered more than socio-economic status. Nancy Adler began exploring the health correlates of subjective social standing examining not just the person's social position based on objective measures such as income, employment, or education, but also how they perceived themselves to be placed in the social hierarchy.[14] To measure subjective social status, she introduced a tool consisting on a 10-point self-anchoring scale with two items, *The MacArthur Scale of Social Status*. Participants in her study were presented with a ladder. They were asked to

think of this ladder as representing where people stand in our society. At the top of the ladder are the people who are the best off, those who have the most money, most education, and best jobs. At the bottom are the people who are the worst off, those who have me least money, least education, and worst jobs or no job and place an X on the rung that best represented where they thought they stood on the ladder. She found that this subjective measure was highly correlated with psychological functioning like stress, affectivity, and coping, and to a lesser degree with physiological measures, like Body Mass Index, waist-to-hip ratio (associated with worse cardiovascular health and higher cortisol levels), sleep and blood pressure, even when controlling for negative affect. Later research studied subjective social status and its associations with other health disorders and found that even when controlling for objective measures of status, subjective social status was predictive of health outcomes.[15] Additionally, this ladder later included two items, one in which adults were asked to compare themselves with their society and another one in which they compared themselves to their community.

While this original study was focused on adult White women, Elizabeth Goodman later studied other racial populations and designed an adapted tool for adolescents (the *MacArthur Scale of Subjective Social Status – Youth Version*),[16] asking the same question, but with two items, one in which the adolescents were asked to compare their family's status to the rest of society and another one in which they were asked to compare their own status to the people in their school. She found the ranking was associated with obesity and depression.[17]

With time, subjective and not objective social status has been settled as the measure of social rank most predictive of mental health disorders in adolescence.[18] What is most interesting, and relevant to current times, is that in children of families of lower education, subjective status is not as a powerful predictor of mental health disorders.

More recently, our work has shown a relationship of lower subjective social status with depression, suicidal ideation, and prior suicide attempts, even when taking into consideration (or controlling for) parental education and employment, and household income. The fact that these findings were from a clinical sample brings up the question of whether it would be worth using this tool with adolescents coming to health services. Using these two simple questions and asking them to pick a rung in the ladder may be a low-burden screen in general pediatric settings as the score is related to many health outcomes, and the tool is less onerous to administer compared to the many screening tools and now multiple social determinants of health we inquire about.[19]

Effects on children

As mentioned before, the social position of the parents has effects on children's health and social success. While our focus here is on hierarchies, it is important to briefly note the consequential effects of objective measures of status. A child's socio-economic status also has effects on their health when they become adults. Of course, this could be the result of the child of lower socio-economic status growing up to be an adult of lower socio-economic status. But studies that look at childhood socio-economic status controlling for the adult's, meaning that they study socio-economic status in childhood regardless of whether the child ends up being an adult of lower or higher socio-economic status, also show higher morbidity and mortality in those children who grow up in families of low socio-economic status. That is, if you grow up in poverty as a child, you will be more likely to die younger and be sicker when you are an adult, regardless of how much wealth you accumulate as an adult. Obviously, everyone's circumstances are different, and not every single child growing in poverty will be sicker as an adult than other children growing up wealthy, but when looking at populations as a whole, poverty in childhood, just like adverse childhood experiences, is a risk factor for poor health outcomes as an adult. This is one of the many reasons for which children should be protected from hardship, and this is especially true for cardiovascular disease.[20, 21]

The physical and social environments in which children grow can affect their development in multiple ways, including directly exposing them to toxins, injuries, or weakening their immune systems, and increasing their levels of stress. Changes in stress hormones and hyperactivation of areas of the brain like the amygdala also cause the frontal cortex to not function at its maximum potential.[22] Finally, epigenetic changes, or those that happen without alternation of the basic DNA sequence but that change the activity of genes nonetheless, also play a role.

Different models explain when does this exposure to low socio-economic status matter most in childhood. The timing model hypothesizes that experiencing factors related to low socio-economic status would have the highest effect on adult health when experienced during specific developmental periods or sensitive periods at which children would be most vulnerable. The effects would also vary depending on the outcome. For example, being exposed to smoke may affect younger children most, and this same environmental condition may not affect adolescents with more fully developed respiratory systems; but adolescents may be more susceptible to exposure to peers who engage in risky behaviors or to poor modeling related to use of substances, poor sleep or nutrition habits. Though overall, the earlier the exposure in time, the more of an impact it will have on health. Another model is the accumulation model that suggests that the addition of adverse events and not when they happen is what matters. And finally, the change model posits that it is the direction in which socio-economic status changes that matters for adult health outcomes, such that going down on the hierarchy ladder would be more detrimental than going up. However, we still don't know what the proximal factors for these relationships are. Is it the substance use for cancer? Is it the exposure to pollution?

In essence, this chapter reminds us that where we stand in the socio-economic ladder, the jobs, the education, and the income, we have, and even how easily we can access health services tell us just a part of the story of how social factors and inequalities 'get under our skin.' That looking at an entire group of people in the same socio-economic stratum will give us different ranks of their subjective experience and stress within that position, and that these processes influence many aspects of children's lives. That health is affected by the stress suffered and accumulated in life due to one's social rank. Our task is to strive for societies that ensure that these health differences are minimal, especially while children grow. One way to do is by ensuring that all people have autonomy and control as those are related to health.

4 Social status in adolescents, from the playground to social media

Social status identity in adolescence

Erikson described different stages of psychosocial development over the course of human life. In each stage, a key developmental task needs to be realized before the individual is ready to move on to the next stage. The key task in adolescence is identity formation. This process involves testing different roles until the adolescent finds his or her own identity. Those who succeed will develop a stable sense of identity. Those who do not will remain in a state of confusion.[1] During late adolescence, there is also a process of maturation of one's ability for abstract thinking from the more concrete and less flexible ways of viewing the social world in early adolescence. These changes in cognitive style enable the formation of status-based identity as the adolescent evolves to a view that is also more adaptable to changes in perspective.[2] This ability to think differently leads to more awareness of how one is perceived by others, and of phenomena such as one's standing in the social hierarchy.

The concept of 'self' was coined in 1922 by Cooley who envisioned the 'self' as a product of society and introduced the idea that individuals construct it based on what they learn from how others see them. He labeled this phenomenon as the "looking glass self."[3] This experience of seeing ourselves based on how we perceive others see us has relevance in many dimensions of life. It plays a part on the roles we take in our families, on the dynamics between a therapist and the client, and on how our bosses make us feel validated at work. During adolescence, the perceptions of peers become especially relevant. Being accepted or rejected by them can impact how we feel.[4] Social status, often ignored in the popular discussions about identity, matters just as gender and ethnicity identities matter.[5] The concept *status-based identity* is used to describe the meaning that people attach to their social status.[6] There are social expectations of individuals of different races and these expectations can condition their social interactions, academic anxiety, and motivation as early as in elementary school.[7] It is likely that these social expectations of the self are not only exclusive to race identity and also apply to social status.

In contemporary society, another aspect of adolescence is that there is an expansion of the number of possible social reference groups with whom adolescents can

DOI: 10.4324/9781003535942-4

compare to help build their self-identity. This expansion of reference groups is much broader now than ever before, as adolescents have access to reference groups from all over the world and to the lives of individuals of all social ranks through social media.

In 1978, Rosenberg and Pearlin explored differences in self-esteem by look-ing at social status as individuals developed.[8] Self-esteem is a symptom consid-ered in the diagnosis of depression, and those with depression tend to have low self-esteem. In their sample, social status and self-esteem among pre-adolescents were not associated, but as adolescents grew, self-esteem and social status were modestly associated, and the relationship was solid when individuals became adults. As we grow older, we become more aware of inequalities. Therefore, how we assess social rank will depend on our age, with a growing importance of social rank for one's self-identity and self-esteem in adolescence as compared to ear-lier stages of development. More recent research confirms that the points of refer-ence for comparing social status differ in adolescents and adults.[9] Furthermore, the dimensions in which we compare to others may vary in adolescence. For exam-ple, Scottish adolescents socially identified with different groups and considered themselves to be of higher status in some of those groups. For example, some adolescents perceived themselves to be of higher status in a status-peer group that included those who identified as being popular, respected, attractive, or trouble-makers; and others ranked higher in scholastic activities, which meant doing well in school and not being a troublemaker, or as being sporty. Furthermore, these self-classifications were associated with health-risk behaviors in that those who ranked themselves higher in the 'peer' dimension tended to use more tobacco and alcohol, whereas those who ranked themselves higher in the dimensions of scho-lastic and sports tended to engage less in these risky behaviors.

How early do hierarchies play a role?

Hierarchies, especially socio-economic hierarchies, play a role as early as in-utero, and arguably even before through epigenetics. But, how do human self-perceptions of hierarchy evolve during development? The perception of social hierarchies evolves in humans from a very early age.

Children perceive differences in social status or dominance from infancy. By the end of infancy, children associate size with dominance. They expect larger-sized individuals, and bigger rather than smaller groups to win in winner-loser situa-tions. For example, around one year of age, children tend to focus their attention on bigger blocks rather than smaller blocks when the blocks bump into each other as they understand that the direction of the blocks will follow that of the stronger and bigger block.[10] Sooner, they will understand the consistency of this outcome across conflicts.[11] As they grow older, they will develop a more nuanced perception of who is in power. To decide who holds higher status, they will observe posture and facial expressions, the quantity and quality of resources individuals hold, like toys, whether they control these resources, and their own influence over others (e.g., whether they can get those toys from others).

Toddlers expect those who won in the past to win in future conflicts and in different contexts, and expect that those who win will accumulate resources. During toddlerhood, dominance is signified not only by body size like in infancy, but also by age and resources, and the understanding of dominance will grow in complexity in the middle and high school years.[12] By four and five, as children play with peers and group formation continues to increase, dominance and preferences to interact with group members of higher status are evident, and in elementary school these hierarchies are formed very quickly.[13] While historically, the accepted thinking was that there was a preference and favoritism for one's own gender group; that is that boys preferred playing with boys and girls with girls, status also seems to have a role in this preference. As early as in elementary school, both boys and girls view boys as more powerful or of higher social status than girls.[14]

Anyone spending any time observing an understaffed daycare center will see these dynamics come to play. Boys of bigger size will likely dominate, and smaller size children will either retrieve or bite in self-defense. Obviously, an alternative is to have better staffed centers that understand the realities and human behavior. The newer *laisse faire* approach to childrearing by not interfering with the development of their 'true self,' that assumes that adults are toxic to children's true personas, might not always work, and is contrary to centuries of childrearing approaches in which adults had an active role in socializing children. Do-nothing approaches may actually create bad experiences for all, the children who are receivers of aggression, the children who are told they are misbehaving, the parents who cannot do much about the environment in the school or center, the teachers who stress about the climate in the classroom, and the administrators who are constantly putting away fires. In these situations, adults ignore the reality that the true nature of all humans, starting with the most adorable two-years-olds, is to dominate when allowed to do so, and that dominance, in the absence of more sophisticated ways to communicate, manipulate, or impose oneself, usually shows in the form of aggression and counter-aggression.

These hierarchies continue as children grow, and in adolescence there is more differentiation by status. However, there are some differences in social rank differentiation by sex, with females having more unstable and fluctuating hierarchies. The visual preferences for members of higher status continue, meaning that they will tend to stare longer at those individuals of higher status.[15]

One's position in the hierarchy as an adolescent may impact health and behaviors as an adult. A longitudinal Swedish study of women born in 1955 followed them from ages ten until they were in their forties. The study found differences between the cluster of girls who were rejected by peers and those clusters of popular and average girls. The rejected girls tended to drink more and present more legal problems in young adulthood than those who were not rejected, likely because the rejected girls may have steered towards outliers and have been more likely to be involved in alcohol use and illegal activities. The popular girls went further in their professional careers, whereas the rejected and average girls did similarly in mid-adulthood. The good news for the not-so-popular is that the differences in health-related behaviors disappeared by mid-adulthood. It would be interesting to see if the same applies to women born in later generations and in other countries.[16]

Being popular

Popularity seems to be a good measure of social status in children and adolescents, more than social preference or acceptance. If you want to be popular these days, you can do it within the walls of your home. Social media offers plenty of opportunities for children to be very popular, and you can measure that popularity with the number of 'like,' 'loves,' and 'shares' you have on one or more social media platforms.

Children tend to be seen as of higher status by their peers when they are popular. But not all popular people are well-liked. Popularity tends to be linked to dominance, but is not necessarily linked to being liked. Being liked in a peer group has also been labeled as 'preference' whereas popularity is a measure of a person's level of prestige or impact in the peer group. Accordingly, individuals in a group may have 'preference' for a certain individual while considering others to be more popular. As children grow, and especially from late elementary school to the end of high school, the correlation or association between being liked and having prestige decreases, meaning that younger children like the most popular peers, while older children or adolescents like peers who are not necessarily popular.[17]

Status and dominance dynamics continue through life after childhood and adolescence. However, the dimensions of interest vary as individuals mature. For example, children may be more focused around the developmental tasks of establishing friendships and excelling academically or in sports, while emerging adults will be more centered around romantic relationships and work, and adults' focus will be on workplace relationships. Status is so important that some research has shown that adolescents and young adults prioritize popularity over romantic relationships.[18] Any fan of Netflix shows depicting college students will see the repeating story of the college boy disappointing his girlfriend when trying to impress his male peers to gain status. It is a captivating narrative because it is so common in real life.

Peer nominations are a way to assess status even in emerging adults, and the differences between likeability (or preference) and popularity persist in young adults.[19] There are also different types of popularity. For example, in a popularity study, those who fell on a factor labelled *prosocial leadership* and included people considered attractive, leaders, respected, and successful were found to be both popular and liked. The group of peers who engaged in *relational aggression*, or who tended to exclude and/or ignore, intimidate, and gossip were popular because they had influence over and status within the group, but they were less liked. Finally, those who had *dominant leadership*, and received attention and had power, were also popular, but not necessarily more liked or disliked. The fourth group was the *social exclusion group*, which included those who were neither liked nor powerful. One interesting finding of this study was the gender difference. Men tended to fall more frequently in the dominant leadership or in the social exclusion group.

In other words, they were more frequently perceived as of high status (central and powerful), or as not fitting in, than the other two groups. Women were less frequently in the dominant leadership or the social excluded groups. Interestingly, men in the prosocial leadership group were more liked than women in this group. The authors' explanation for this difference is that social stereotypes expect for men to be dominant and for women to be cooperative, well-connected, and taking a selfless interest in other people. Instead, being popular in women would give the impression of having an underlying personal and self-interested agenda and not a genuine interest in others. These assumptions would not be made of men.[15] This is still true today. To this date, women in many cultures receive messages that communicate to them that being ambitious is unattractive, while it is considered a positive attribute in men. Overall, this study's findings showed similar dynamics in peer status among adolescents and young adults. While these factors may seem inconsequential to humans' health, they are not. Social status gives you connections and social influence, and as we have seen, this social influence has effects on health outcomes. These differences in popularity can also be key when considering interventions, if we want those who are more popular to set a positive example. Furthermore, this finding is especially relevant in today's society and the discussions about men feeling marginalized and at loss in their identity within society, given the changing economics and roles in the job market.

Adolescence and young adulthood are risky periods in human's life. It is a time when individuals begin experimenting with drugs and alcohol, having sexual relationships, driving independently, and when the rates of violent victimization and perpetration are at their highest. For those who survive these tumultuous times, the behaviors in which they engage may have consequences in the short and also the long term. While as we have seen, popularity in childhood does not always equate to worse outcomes in adulthood, much of the existing research in behaviors adopted at this age shows that the earlier one engages with a behavior, the hardest it is to disengage from it, and the worse the health and social outcomes are later in life. One clear example, supported by extensive research, is substance use. Those who start using alcohol and drugs earlier in life will be more likely to end up suffering from a related disorder of addiction. One of the major limitations for the generalization of this particular study on popularity is that it was conducted in college students in a small classroom environment. These results may be different in young adults engaged in the workspace, or adolescents navigating much larger classroom environments.

Dominance in bullying dynamics

A study with adolescents[20] categorized individuals as populistic popular and prosocial popular, in a similar way to the 'popular' categorizations of prosocial and dominant leadership respectively in the study discussed previously conducted with emergent adults.[19] In the adolescent groups, the populistic group was not well-liked and considered antisocial and arrogant, but was still considered as 'attractive and hip' as the prosocial popular group that was also considered cooperative and engaged in academics. The dynamics of bullies and victims parallel those of dominance and submission in non-human primates, and show similarities with these popularity categories. While bullies are often disliked, they also tend to be popular.

We know less about how social status affects the way children process social information than what we know about it in adults, but it is likely that what happens in adults may be amplified in adolescents given that this developmental period is one of extreme sensitivity to social status cues that signal rejection or acceptance. Overall, in adolescence, brain areas involved in affect are overactive and more sensitive to social information, and the areas involved in inhibition are more immature, as the prefrontal cortex continues to develop through the mid-twenties. More than children and adults, adolescents are very sensitive to peer rejection.[4] All these lend adolescents very sensitive to status cues as peer rejection and low social status are associated.

Aggression and popularity

In younger groups as well, children tend to like peers who present prosocial and not aggressive behaviors, but consider those who have both antisocial (including aggressive) and prosocial behaviors as popular.[17]

One way to establish dominance is through aggression, which tends to be more common with more unstable hierarchies. This is seen not only in monkeys, but also in preschool classrooms when at the beginning of the year aggression is relatively high, decreasing as the year advances. Girls tend to engage in more relational aggression, and boys use physical aggression to impose dominance. With age, aggression declines in part as children weight the costs and benefits of being aggressive.[21] Yet, there is still a fair amount of both physical and relational aggression well into the middle and high school years.[17] In order to socialize children to not be aggressive, having natural consequences that are appropriate for the age for aggressive behavior can extinguish the behavior. Overtime, aggression may be replaced by assertive behaviors.[22]

Why are adolescents more biologically vulnerable?

Adolescents have developing frontal cortices involved in emotional regulation and executive functioning. As certain areas of the brain mature with age, such as the connectivity between the ventro-lateral prefrontal cortex and the ventral antero-cingulate cortex, the sensitivity to rejection decreases.[23] Interestingly, without going into excessive detail, the activation of certain brain regions parallels what is observed in behaviors. It shows that those adolescents that are more able to refocus their attention from negative to positive social information, and those with more positive social environments, are less sensitive to rejection. Imaging studies to assess how individuals process social status have been conducted in adults but not in children or adolescents. However, data on social acceptance and rejection can be an approximation to adolescents' social status, even if not directly studying it.[24]

How do children form perceptions about group-based hierarchies?

Group-based social hierarchies involve social stratifications of power and status by social group, and these are linked to social categories like race and gender. While there are objective social hierarchies, like differences in household income, there is also a perception of group social hierarchies that exists in the individual's view of the world. Being aware of the existence of these hierarchies can motivate people to strive for social justice, driving them to minimize these hierarchies or their effects, and to avoid acting on pre-formed biases.[14]

Researchers have used vignettes depicting interactions between individuals to understand group-based hierarchies. For example, in one vignette a faceless figure 'tells' another figure what type of activity (i.e., game) they will undertake. Then the observing child is asked if the person giving the order about the activity was a boy or a girl. Another vignette consists on matching resources or roles such as matching a beautiful wealthy home to a darker or a lighter-skin picture of a girl. Some researchers have used abstract depictions using a preschool version of the subjective social status ladder. This version, designed for three to six-year-olds, involves a rope ladder in which the top of the ladder corresponds to those people with more clothes and toys and with more influence over others. Children across multiple countries in Europe, the Middle East, and the U.S. tend to place boys higher up in the ladder. This placement of boys above girls is stronger among boys. However, girls of all ages also placed boys higher up than girls, and over time their placement of other girls in the ladder declined. These experiments suggest that these little girls were internalizing boys or males as more powerful as they grew older. As mentioned before, there are different dimensions of status in children and adolescents, and these dimensions may parallel what is valued in society. Children may see a group as more powerful and resourceful because it is more valued in society, while they may see the less valued group as 'kinder.' Again, the more powerful and resourceful group may not always be the most respected.[14]

In addition to gender, another important and common group-based category is race. Cues regarding people's race are thought to develop over time and less quickly than those involved in gender categories. Children prefer the group race that is most valued in society. Those belonging to groups of higher status or wealth tend to prefer their own race group, while those of lower status tend to prefer other groups of higher status, or have no racial preferences at all.

With the advent of social media and all its flaws and dangers, there has been a certainly positive coming out of the dark and into the light of many minoritized groups, both in the gender spectrum and racial minorities. This acceptance or rise in status may or not change the social status of these groups in certain age groups or culture circles, but it can give a space in which people feel more included and accepted. Time and research will provide a bird's eye view of these changes. What is clear now is that, the social environments in which children live condition what they learn about group-based hierarchies. These social conditions vary by country and culture. For example, in the Dominican Republic most people are of mixed race and there is less of a categorical division by race. Race is seen as a continuum (darker or lighter skin) rather than binary (White or Black). Pre-pubertal children from the Dominican Republic are less likely to use race to cue social status or wealth. Based on this example, and the growing and changing landscape of racial categories across countries, one has to wonder how people in countries like the U.S., with rapidly growing racial minorities, will view race in the near future and how will children (and adults) in these countries link race to status, if they even do.

There are other group-based categories used by children to assess the status of a perceived group. Some examples include nationality (U.S. versus Iran) or region (northern versus southern accent in the U.S. or British versus Indian English speakers in India). There are likely many other areas of group-based categorization that are understudied but may be just as important.

Children learn about these hierarchies and status rankings from society. They learn through direct observations, and when these aren't possible, they do so from the media. They can also learn from other people around them, such as adults at home and in school, and their peers. They learn through other people's non-verbal behaviors (e.g., watching how other people treat and interact with people from other groups). These observations take place as early as in preschool age and based on these, children will perceive others as more or less competent. Perhaps, more obvious to children than the non-verbal statements are the verbal statements made about other groups, even when these happen only once, and even when they are not directed at the child, like when they are overheard. It is not always easy for parents and other caregivers as well as teachers to get it right. Even comments that are intended to erase hierarchies, such as saying that one group (girls) is as good as another (boys) in an activity, can make the child perceive that the reference group is the boy and that the boy group is more competent to begin with, when the adult's intention was to equalize both groups. Likewise, one may perceive as more beneficial to not mention to children anything related to group differences or the structural causes of these differences, but this may lead children to believe that there is something inherently disadvantageous about the group, or that the current situation is how it is supposed to be.

Overall, a general good practice is to avoid group generalizations when talking to or around children. This is an exercise that would benefit everyone and seems to be an exercise in the literal sense of the word, as it requires consistent practice. But beyond the need to understand people as their own unique entities and not just part of a group, children may also need to understand that external factors can affect one's status in society. Children who understand that are more sympathetic to members of lower-status groups and more likely to befriend them than those children who believe the disparity is explained by the inherent characteristics of the individual belonging to that particular group. The tendency or default position is for children to explain these differences through inherent causes.

Humans' natural tendency is to make assumptions about groups of people. Doing so takes less mental effort when we navigate our very complex social worlds. It is harder to get to know people as individuals with their own characteristics than to make judgements based on external features. As adults, we are tasked with teaching our children to avoid these default assumptions and take it a step further to get to know others without preconceptions. Maturation helps in this process. The child will evolve from a view of the world based on group hierarchies to a more structural-level perspective, one in which they understand that the context in which people live affects their state. This change starts being noticeable in the late elementary years when children also start trying to rectify social inequities. Interestingly, even though adults are more able to explain the world from a structural perspective, the default is also to explain inequalities from an inherent or individual-level perspective as it also takes more mental energy and a more complex cognitive process for adults to think in structural terms. Additionally, it is easier to go with the tide than challenge already established social structures. Finally, how an individual is oriented towards social dominance, or whether they view social hierarchies as more or less desirable, will also affect how much they will be willing to work to rectify social inequalities, and their tendency to favor out-group members over members of their own group. This individual orientation appears to happen early in life and not just in adults as previously assumed.

One important factor conditioning group-based hierarchies is how the child views him or herself within the social hierarchy. Children who perceive themselves to be higher up (e.g., wealthier, of the dominant class) are more tolerant of inequalities or even interracial exclusion in both observational and experimental studies. These children with more advantages have more difficulties appreciating their privilege or understanding other's experiences. There is an evolution in how children place themselves in the social status ladder. As we saw earlier, the younger the person, the more likely they are to place themselves higher in the social rank. As they grow older, they start placing themselves lower as they gather more information from their context, and are able to also place themselves in a rank that correlates with their families' education and income levels. In a way, developing humans go through a process of progressive social rank humility.

These cognitive processes in children's thinking about group-based hierarchies bring to question the recent support of antiracism programs in American schools. These programs are well-intended and attempt to correct decades of systemic inequalities linked to race. However, some questions remain about their effectiveness, and their application in educational settings. As we have seen, children have a natural tendency to make group-based hierarchies. Teaching them about differences by race group may just reinforce this natural tendency. In other words, if children struggle more than adults to understand structural barriers and tend to blame the individual for their shortcomings, teaching them that Black people have been oppressed may temporarily switch the order of hierarchies, but it does not change the division of people by race that they have already internalized, and it may not make them understand the systemic causes either as the emphasis continues to be placed on the individual. An alternative would be to help children understand three basic and compatible ideas: (1) that those who are disadvantaged are likely to have suffered from situations that are not under their control and that may have contributed to their disadvantage. These situations may be historical, familial, peer, or school-based events and circumstances, among others; (2) that individuals are complex and have many layers; that their race, gender, and class are just a few of the many aspects of their persona; (3) that those who are more advantaged may also be so because of their circumstances. This last point is important. Advantage can be acquired through historical privilege, or through skills or abilities. Assuming that those with privilege are all oppressors has the danger to alienate groups from one another as it assumes malintent on the side of the privileged. A better approach would be to expect those more privileged to contribute to society in ways that would make individuals in disadvantaged situations live in more dignified ways.

Status in school-age children

Another Swedish study interviewed 57 teenagers between 7th and 12th grade to explore their subjective social status in school. The study essentially showed that social status in schools was complex and multifaceted. It was perceived as a complex game that the adolescents could choose to participate in or ignore. The adolescent's position in the social status ladder was determined by factors that were relatively fixed, like ethnicity or age, or more malleable and controllable by the participants, such as how they chose to interact with others or how they looked. Using social comparisons was a strategy that allowed them to understand their social rank position if they wished to participate. Some participants, while aware of the social status game and stratifications, chose to not participate actively in order to 'play it safe.'[25] Younger participants seemed to want to engage more in this status game, while more of the older participants would feel they could disengage from it. These findings are interesting when we compare them to the very similar dynamics of non-human primates trying to avoid positions of risk at the top of the hierarchy.

Girls, again, ranked themselves lower, and tended to compare themselves with other girls more than boys did, suggesting higher social awareness among girls. Girls also mentioned that dating popular boys would help them gain popularity. White Swedes who spoke Swedish well were more popular and less bullied. Older age gave status. This effect of age or grade is known across the Atlantic as well, where just mentioning the word freshman (versus senior) evokes a certain degree of stress in students. There were also status markers, such as having a driver's license that were more easily achieved or purchased by those students from wealthier families. There were also demands for social desirability that were heavier on girls than boys, at least when it came to their outfits.

Clearly, in this study conducted in 2020, gender norms were very strong. Boys gained status by being strong, athletic, self-confident, and promiscuous. Girls gained status by dressing well, and being good-looking and nice. Girls also had to navigate a very fine line and needed to strive for moderation in everything, as they could easily lose status. This finding concerned the authors as Sweden scores high on the Gender Development Index (GDI). The GDI is a measure of gender equality and ranges from 0 (more inequality between men and women) and 1 (higher gender equality). The GDI measures standard of living, opportunities for education, and health. If children in Sweden, a country that almost approaches equality between men and women, experience such strong gender norms in which girls are expected to sit and be judged or liked, whereas boys can actively better themselves, one could guess pressure to acquiesce to these social norms would be even higher in other countries. On the other hand, stronger gender roles may not translate into worse health for women, except of course, in situations when there is forced subordination and gender violence. However, having to navigate constant self-evaluation to maintain one's status in a world that values girls for their looks, something they cannot completely control, while also trying to succeed professionally and academically, may become a stressful balance for girls growing into women. The increase in depression that has been more pronounced in girls since the introduction of smartphones and applications, 'apps' like social media, has often been explained by their more intense engagement with these apps, where they can constantly compare with others. While the relationship is not clear, it is true that girls are now exposed not only to their immediate environment, but at the expense of the likes of many other people, some of which are people they don't personally know. The expectations about their appearance are higher as well, as filters and time spent curating one's photos have raised the accepted threshold for beauty among ordinary people. The points of reference when it comes to looks often seem unattainable. Finally, the exposure to these images without context increases the pressures and expectations on girls.

In this study, friend groups also helped gain or lose status, and having more friends made one more popular. The type of school program also mattered. In Sweden, academic gave more status when compared to vocational programs. Interestingly, among members of minorities and groups regarded as of lower status, there was a strong sense of unity that protected against the threats of being considered of lower status. While some students forced their social position, many others did not respect them. Overall, the participants were aware of narrow norms and rules to gain and keep status, and the potential of these norms to change at different times, environments, and situations. The truth is that reading the quotes collected from Swedish students in this study brings one back to American movies from the 1970s and 1980s. The essence of status dynamics has not really changed much in schools in half a century, not only in the U.S., but it looks like neither in some parts of Europe.

In spite of the societal differences in racial, cultural, and income inequality, this Swedish study's results are strikingly similar to those of interviews conducted in Baltimore, the essence of which is explained in an upcoming chapter. They suggest the existence of some universal (at least in Western culture) mechanisms underlying the perception of social status in adolescents across countries. In broad terms, our sample also talked about the complexities of status in schools. While our study was more focused on exploring mechanisms of association between subjective social status and mental health and well-being, our participants also mentioned clothes, possessions, and access to activities as markers of status, in addition to the social comparisons made to gage the environment. Some differences existed, such as the levels of exposure to community violence. While exposure to violence may be explained by higher income inequality and firearm ownership in the U.S. in comparison to Sweden, the status dynamics being so similar in adolescents from two countries with very different levels of income inequality show the innate quest for status in adolescents regardless of their environment.[25]

Another level of complexity is added by changing norms when children switch schools and need to relearn these hierarchy dynamics. This can be especially difficult for children with poorer social skills who may have found a stable group in a school, but have a hard time navigating complex hierarchical systems of newer and/or bigger school systems. I was an exchange student in a public American high school after having spent most of my life in the same all-girls school. For much of that year, I was completely unaware of the social hierarchies in that school. As a senior, the rules of status did not seem to matter as much as everyone had already found their place in the pecking order. However, at the end of the year, during a conversation with a peer, I asked where he was planning to go to college, and he responded that he had no plans to go to college. He actually had never thought of it. Meanwhile, others in the classroom had never questioned their future in a university.

Unlike Europe, American adolescents do not always secure a spot in a college just by working hard. College level education is expensive. Many students just cannot afford to go to college, even if they are hardworking. Newer programs like those providing the opportunity to attend community college without a cost are changing the game. However, this is a slow change. While there are differences in income inequality within Europe, with the U.K. having larger income inequality than Sweden, for example, the levels of income inequality are far greater in the U.S. than in other developed countries. For example, in 2024, according to the World Bank, the Gini coefficient of Iceland, the Netherlands, and Norway was among the lowest in the world. Meanwhile, the U.S. ranked among the countries with highest income inequality in the world, and at the top of all developed countries. This means that differences in status for students in the U.S. will be more determinative than for students living in Europe. If your family is at the top of the income bracket, you will likely attend college. For those without a financially strong family environment, the process is much more delicate and a minor setback can be decisive. Being higher up in the status at school may land you opportunities for academic or sports scholarships, distinguish you from your peers, or motivate a counselor to help you navigate the paperwork for a scholarship, and that could determine whether you attend college or not.

Perspective-taking

Anyone immersed in a highly hierarchical environment at work and who happens to be in the lower rungs of the social rank ladder will have experienced this ability to take perspective. In my opinion, that is what makes those who have lived in more deprived environments great leaders, and leaves those who have grown in privilege more lacking in their ability to empathize with some parts of society and their experiences. Contrary to what the imaging studies in animals would suggest, power and higher status do not necessarily help you with your ability to take perspective. It could also be that those in power are savvy about those over them, and not so much about those below them in the social ladder. Those in power tend to control resources and they depend less on others to reach their goals, so they do not need to understand others who are less powerful. Additionally, those with power also have more demands for their attention, and in a way, less time to worry or pay attention to the struggles of the less powerful. Additionally, the less powerful tend to adapt more and their identities are less rigid than the more powerful individuals. When you are powerful, you distance yourself from others. When you are not powerful, you understand other's perspectives and feel more similarities between yourself and others.

More powerful people tend to have worse mentalizing abilities. That is, they are worse at estimating other people's interests, form more simplistic impressions of others that are based on stereotypes and expectations, and take credit for positive outcomes while blaming others for negative ones when compared to others who are better at perspective-taking (and likely lower in the rungs of power). Perspective-takers also are more altruistic and tend to help others more, while those who are more powerful tend to present more antisocial behaviors.[26]

Some experiments have investigated people's sense of power and their ability to take perspective in their relationships. In one experiment, participants were asked to draw an E on their foreheads to see if they would draw it as if others would be reading it or as if *they* were reading it. This task was done after the participants were primed with a high-power or low-power task, in which they were told to think and write about a situation in which they had power over someone or someone had power over them, respectively. Those primed with the high-power task were more likely to draw the E as if they were reading it, and not as if the audience was reading it. In a subsequent experiment, the participants were given information about a speaker's intentions, and they showed more or less difficulties adjusting to the fact that other listeners did not have that information. Usually, individuals who have advantage in knowledge about the speaker's intentions adjust well to the other person's perspective. This was harder to do by those in power, causing their social judgment to be worse than in those who were better at perspective-taking. In a third experiment, participants were asked to describe the emotion expressed in images of faces. Those primed with power had more difficulties detecting the emotions accurately, and more issues experiencing empathy than a control group. In these experiments, the 'powerful' ones were not aware that the experiment gave them more power than it gave those in the control group. Therefore, this was not believed to be a conscious effort to ignore the perspectives of others, but rather an inability of those in the powerful group to see other people's perspectives. In a way, this is reassuring for those who have been belittled or ignored by the more powerful. It is easier not to take things personally when you know the other person is likely not engaging in the behavior consciously. Should the powerful be reprimanded for not seeing the harm they do to the non-powerful when they do not do it consciously? Probably not. But do we accept the behavior to continue if it harms the less powerful? Hopefully not. In essence, these experiments showed that those holding power can have a defective social judgment and ability to pay attention and understand other people's emotional states, and that their perceptions of and thoughts about the world may be reduced at least in comparison to control groups of people with less power.

It is possible that we are designed to look upwards and not downwards. In a way, those down in the social hierarchy automatically become invisible during these experiments, even with an extremely brief assignment of power. It makes sense that as primates, we are wired to capture social cues of those more powerful than us as a way to survive in the group. The more powerful have more capacity to threaten us and our status, while those below us don't necessarily pose a threat to our status. In other words, it may be that we are ladder-climbers by nature.

The authors in this study suggest that this lack of attention to other people's concerns may make the powerful more likely to act and achieve their goals efficiently; they may also tend to objectivize others and see them not as whole humans, but as the parts that make them useful in achieving their goals.[27] Additionally, there are relationships between power and stereotyping, in that power increases stereotyping, but also between perspective-taking and stereotyping, as the latter decreases with perspective-taking. Furthermore, the authors acknowledged that the powerful can gain perspective by increasing their knowledge about other's perspectives, feeling responsible for others under them, and seeing them as individuals and not as part of a stereotypical group.[26] Finally, cultural and individual beliefs have a role in how people use power. When you do have power, do you use it like Gandhi or the Dalai Lama, or do you use it like Hitler or Mussolini? Do you use it to create change and help others, or only to benefit yourself through wealth and power accumulation?

The individual differences in dominance

Hierarchies in children have been studied since the beginning of the 20th century. The research on rank processes in children was in part driven by the interest of female researchers like Helen Wooley,[28] Lois Jack,[29] and Marjorie Page,[30] who were based in community child care centers, observed children playing, and suggested that some presented more dominant or non-submissive personalities.[31]

Abraham Maslow (1936), the creator of the hierarchy of needs that posits that humans must have basic needs fulfilled before they can move towards other developmental goals like transcendence and self-realization, was also a student of social hierarchies.[32] He was mentored by Harry Harlow who studied attachment in primates. Maslow considered dominance as a universal drive and natural dynamic of any relationship and believed dominance was expressed differently depending on the context. On the other hand, his contemporary researchers saw dominance as a perduable disposition. These observations were partly due to the fact that Maslow observed primates in captivity with an environment highly determined by the researchers. When given the opportunity, the subordinates would behave as dominants. Maslow made a connection between context, self-esteem or confidence, and dominance feelings.

Meanwhile, and separately, in Europe, the study of hierarchies derived from human ethology, or the study of human behavior from a biological and evolutionary perspective, and observations of children would follow the animal behavioralists' methods. For example, they would focus on how individuals who were socially dominant received more visual attention and associated with more attractive social partners. However, little attention was paid to individual differences, psychological variables such as temperament, and relationship dynamics. More recently, adolescent ethology has had a resurgence, especially to explain bullying, and romantic and sexual relationships.[33]

Resource control theory is an evolutionary developmental theory of social dominance that provides a perspective on individual differences on social status hierarchies and dominance. Although ethologists and animal behavioralists focus on contests and aggression to describe competition suggesting that individuals maintain status by coercion, from an evolutionary perspective, prosocial behaviors and emotions would be just as important for survival.[28] The answer may be in the middle, where both coercion and prosocial behaviors are necessary to maintain status. In fact, the motivations for coercion and prosocial behaviors may be the same. People can be prosocial and completely self-serving, expecting an immediate or more delayed reward; or they can be prosocial and completely altruistic and oriented towards others concerns. Preschoolers actually tend to use prosocial strategies twice as often as they used confrontational strategies.[31]

From the time children start to socialize in preschool, through their school years until they reach university, in more or less structured groups, in person or in the virtual world of social media, or when they reach the epitome of social status ranks in Greek sororities in American universities, the learning about and search for social status is omnipresent in youth's lives and prepares them for their adult lives.

5   The context of status

Societies, culture, and the media

Societies: happiness-income paradox

Does money bring happiness, and are wealthier societies happier? These are questions related to income and happiness that economists have tried to answer. These economists are divided into two groups. One group has shown that higher income is associated with higher levels of happiness. The other group supports the concept of the 'happiness-income paradox.' The first group has shown a positive relationship between income and happiness looking at cross-sectional data, meaning that societies with higher income have happier people. If that was always the case, wealthier societies would be happier than less wealthy societies. By extension, the entire world would be getting progressively happier as the World's wealth progressively rises, and as people migrate from poorer to wealthier countries. The second group of economists has shown a paradox using time series analyses; that is, looking at relationships over time and not just at one point in time. With this method of data analysis, as countries become wealthier, happiness appears to increase, but only to a certain extent. After a certain period of time, the levels of happiness remain the same. This observation applies to developed countries, countries in eastern Europe that transitioned from socialist regimes to capitalism, and developing countries.[1]

But what is happiness? The levels of happiness in populations are often measured with subjective well-being scales. To measure well-being, people are asked about both their life and their financial satisfaction. With growth in the economy of countries worldwide, there tends to be a short-term increase in people reporting being happy. However, after some time, the relationship between economic growth and happiness is null. Worsening and expanding economies will make people unhappier or happier, but just for some time. A study examining these income and well-being associations highlighted three countries with rapid increases in per-capita-income, which have doubled in relatively short periods of time. The countries were Chile, China, and South Korea. Life satisfaction has increased very mildly in both Chile and China during this period of growth, and only mildly in South Korea. In the case of South Korea, the largest increase in life satisfaction was concentrated around the months following the assassination of President Park Chung Hee in 1979. This president had ruled under a dictatorial regime for almost 20 years. Later significant increases in per capita gross domestic product GDP

DOI: 10.4324/9781003535942-5

did not see a growth in life satisfaction. The study did not focus on the reasons behind this phenomenon, but the authors suspected that the results may have been related to an increase in material aspirations. As countries become wealthier, people's aspirations also change. Suddenly, it is not enough to have a nice weekend away on the house beach nearby, if your friends are traveling out of the country. It is also important to note that this phenomenon applied to countries where the average income was higher than $75,000 in 2010. Therefore, it would not apply to very poor countries with unmet basic needs.

Absence of happiness is not depression but social factors affect both

We need not mistake lack of happiness with depression. Population surveys ask people about happiness and life satisfaction. Sociologists and other researchers make assumptions about the general mental state of those surveyed. While surveys are a good thermometer to track symptoms and perceptions of populations overtime, we cannot ignore the fact that diagnoses were designed to be used in the clinical setting, where not only a subjective report of the patient (symptoms) was gathered, but also an objective report (signs) was taken into consideration. Two people can report problems with sleep and appetite, low mood, and trouble concentrating, and the reasons for those symptoms may stem from very different diagnoses that may not necessarily be depression, even if the surveys suggest a depressive disorder. Other times, the questions asked are not validated depression questionnaires, but only one question about mood. Furthermore, people can have those symptoms and continue to function well. In a clinical visit, a psychiatrist is able to determine if those symptoms reported also match what the clinician sees, how the patient moves, and their affect and expression. The clinician can also ask follow up questions to ensure that those symptoms are depression and not another disorder like attention deficit hyperactivity disorder, and that they indeed cause a loss of functioning. Notwithstanding, these surveys can be useful to gather data from large numbers of people, and make inferences about social factors influencing mental well-being. Symptoms of depression, even major depression, are also influenced by social factors.

Based on one of these surveys conducted with people age 15 and older across European countries, older people whose physical and social health are preserved tended to be less depressed.[2] In other words, while there is a higher percentage of people who are depressed in older age groups when compared to younger age groups, this is explained by the greater share of people with health conditions in this age group, and not attributable to growing older per se. In fact, the happiest people are the ones in their 70s. If you stay healthy, you will be happier as you age.

The survey also showed that women were more likely than men to be depressed. This is a consistent finding in both non-clinical and clinical samples. Social health or the health of our relationships protected people from depression. People in good marriages were less depressed than those who were separated or divorced, single, or widowed. This social health also applied to relationships beyond a partner, like those with friends, work colleagues, and other relatives. Those who engaged in these relationships daily had 9% lower chances of being depressed than the ones who never did. Education was also important; the more education, the less risk for depression. Interestingly, being in the far left was associated with 1% higher probability of depression than being in any other political position. Regarding income, those of higher income had a lower probability of being depressed. The people in the highest bracket of income had more positive reports of their mental health.

Despite this effect of income, health and social relationships were the most important factors contributing to depression, followed by the relationship with one's partner, and only then, income and education followed behind. There is something to spending time with friends and going to the gym to preserve one's mood. But, when these researchers asked participants how satisfied they were with their incomes, or whether it was 'possible for them to live comfortably with their present income,' those in the lower bracket who found it most difficult to live comfortably with their income had a high probability of being depressed, as high as those with poor relationships. Again, income matters to mental health, but only to a certain degree. Of note, this survey asked participants whether they had 'been depressed most of times or all time in the last week' and this is not a measure of clinical depression. It is an approximation of one's mood that week. In this context, for the responders, having been depressed could mean having had a few bad days, or having been irritated.

How do we become happy people?

An explanation for the income-happiness paradox has to do with social comparison and what we think about when we assess our happiness levels.[3] When looking at data on happiness or life satisfaction at one point in time, we are asking how people feel about their life in general, and comparing their life satisfaction currently to that of their own past. However, when looking at life satisfaction over time, we ask people about how they feel in the moment, and their response refers to how they feel today compared to how they could potentially feel in the future. Happiness has also been described as comprised of two facets.[4] One facet tracks income and involves an evaluation of one's life. The other facet is happiness as aspiration or experienced well-being, and this facet does not track income after a certain threshold has been reached.[3]

Whether you assess your happiness based on past experience or future hopes makes a difference in how you respond to questions about it. In the process of thinking or dreaming about oneself in the future, we create a gap between our current situation and the goal or dreamed situation. This thinking process generates excitement. However, it can also be dangerous and costly, as one can realize that the gap between the present and the future self is too broad to achieve, causing the opposite of excitement. Dreaming about oneself in the future is different from daydreaming. The latter is the activity of dreaming about a goal without taking the steps needed to achieve that goal. It's what you do when you want to play soccer like Messi or tennis like Rafael Nadal, but you don't put in the work, don't train frequently and intensely, don't take care of your diet and sleep, and instead choose the couch and potato chips. Or you dream of being Taylor Swift, but do not take the steps to learn how to play an instrument or sing.

Daydreaming has been compared to a form of consumerism, or the activity of focusing on acquiring objects. Like an addiction, consumerism is the opposite of mindfulness. It is an 'inactive entertainment' in which our senses are busy, but we are not engaging them fully. When we daydream, just as like when we consume goods, we obtain pleasure by imagining our future self, a self with the possession of new goods, or goals achieved, but we are shutting down full engagement with the present. In the long term, this process keeps us from achieving our goals of connection with others, of academic achievement, work well done, or care for others.[3]

Social media combines these two aspects of daydreaming by promoting an absence of full engagement in the present and easy access to consumption. First, it removes us from our present while we scroll watching others live their lives. And second, it facilitates our consumption of goods, as tempting and personalized adds pop up for us to make purchases in an effortless way. In addition, it offers plenty of opportunities for comparison, which may motivate people to improve themselves by consuming more, or it may make people daydream about their future selves while they click on links to explore the goods that will make them feel closer to their dreamed future selves.

Relative income theory is based on the idea that our well-being is relative to our social rank position, or dependent on whether we have less or more than others. One can also choose to compare one's current self to one's previous selves, and make an assessment of where they are now compared to where they were in the past. Either because the object of comparison is another person or several people, or oneself in the future, reactions of misery or exhilaration take place when we are daydreaming instead of doing. Some studies have found that passive use of social media, or the scrolling without actively posting may be more detrimental to one's mental health than using social media in active ways, by posting and sharing. As mentioned earlier, daydreaming generates a positive edge by allowing one to spend some time in an imaginary, better place, but it also opens one up to experiencing the negative feeling of seeing a growing gap between our actual and our desired reality. While the question of happiness and well-being is complicated, one thing is clear: all of these theories highlight that income alone is not the answer to happiness, and that social comparisons are involved at every level.

Daydreaming tends to happen when the external environment does not demand your full attention or the needs to process information from the external world decrease. It is harder for a mother of two young children to daydream as much as an idle adolescent during a low intensity summer break, even though mothers can get creative with their mental time. As we age, we may process information more slowly and with the same amount of information from the external world, we have less time to daydream. At the same time, we have less concerns and worries. Younger people are then, more likely to daydream, and teenage girls are the best at doing it.

Dr. Giambria, a psychologist, conducted a study with over 3,000 patients recruited from 1971 through 1996 in several U.S. cities across states, including Baltimore, to study daydreaming across ages and sexes.[5] This is an impressively long time of recruitment. Some participants were tested several times over time.

In all aspects of daydreaming, women scored higher than men, and in both men and women, people scored lower in the frequency and intensity of daydreaming as they aged. This was true even when memory capacity was considered, meaning that having less memory capacity was not causing this decrease in daydreaming. The results were also not explained by people censuring or trying to control their daydreaming as they aged. The idea that older adults were less able to pay attention to internally generated stimuli because their attentional capacity was occupied processing information from the outside due to slower information-processing was also not supported by the data from this study. Additionally, the older adults in the study were active in their communities, so the thought that maybe they were engaging in less stimulating environments that required less processing of information was also not supported. It looks like older adults were actually choosing sleep over daydreaming, or focusing their attention on external events, which both seem smart alternatives to ruminating. It can also be that there is decline in the functioning of the central nervous system that allows for less thoughts and length of the thoughts as we age. Finally, and most likely, it could be that over time, older adults learn strategies to decrease the number and intensity of their worries, as shown by cognitive development theories that explain the ability of older adults to use successful strategies for emotional regulation.[6] It may be that as we grow older, we have less concerns and can live more in the moment.

We daydream to compare ourselves with our future selves, but we also compare ourselves to others. Naturally, adolescents trying to define their identity and daydreaming more will also spend time engaging in social comparisons, many of these comparisons will be with celebrities, as they are easy to find, now more than ever.

The media and birth of celebrities

The admiration and need to look up to others higher in the social rank is not new. In a streaming show giving insight into the tribulations of the British Royal family, a constant need to keep appearances is made evident. Queen Elizabeth's (or at least, the fictional character in the show) is open in her description of the role of the monarchy: to make people (the lower people, the poor, the ones with hard lives) believe that there is something to look up, to strive for, and to get closer to God. The notion that a family would be between reality and perfection or the afterlife where no suffering or hardship will be experienced, seems delusional, but is too ingrained in our psyche to not have an effect on how we behave and how we respond to these prestigious personalities. Hollywood celebrities have the same role; to let us think they are without flaw, and superior to the rest of us who need to floss our teeth, remove sleep crust from our eyes in the morning, and struggle to keep up with dirty dishes. More recent efforts to not maintain that distance either by choice or by the lack of limits of newer media have resulted in less dreamy situations around celebrities, but adolescents are still infatuated by them.

And yet, the phenomenon of the celebrity, as we know it today, is a relatively recent one. In a survey conducted in 1898 in which adolescents were asked who would they want to emulate, they mentioned no celebrities. Instead, most wanted to mirror historical figures like presidents, roman emperors, or discoverers. Fifty years later, in 1948, another survey showed that 37% of adolescents wanted to be a professional entertainer or athlete. This proportion increased to 90% adolescents surveyed who wanted to be entertainers in 1986.[7] In 2019, 86% of adolescents wanted to become an influencer.[8] Two years later, another survey showed that becoming a Youtuber/Streamer was still less popular than being a doctor or a nurse, but entertainment professions like actress, musician, and professional athlete ranked among the five most coveted occupations.[9] This is proof that the media world has crept into our lives, and that adolescents, attuned to their social environment and perceiving what would make them worthy adults, have been looking up to the successful people in the media as role models. Our environment suddenly became much bigger when we went from our small communities with town pamphlets and newspapers to TV and now social media.

For many decades in the second half of the 20th century and the beginning of the 21st century, the Oscars Ceremony was thought of as among the gatherings of people with the highest status on Earth. People like movies more than they like G8 Summits, which congregate the truly powerful. But the Oscar ceremony only started in 1928 as a small hotel gathering of a few hundred people that paid tickets that today would be worth less than the entrance to most museums.[10] The rise of the film and television industries at the beginning of the 20th century promoted this and other public ceremonies, bringing the concept of celebrity to a new level, and creating a transition from heroes, which were the characters with which regular people would identify or create imaginary relationships with, to today's celebrities. The media not only brought actors to this celebrity level, but also musicians, athletes, and political figures who occupied the front pages of sports magazines, newspapers, radio shows, and TV news and programs. The rise of social media has also given rise to other subgroups with their own celebrities. In a way, social media has made being a celebrity more democratic. We now have 'influencer' moms being flown in first class to influencer mom gatherings, video game player influencers, traveling influencers, and political commentator influencers, among many others. Influencers are at the top of their status rank in their own newly created subgroups, and there are more opportunities for everyone to rank high or even reach the top in these multiple dimensions. Today, celebrities have thousands or millions of followers on X (twitter), YouTube, and Instagram. Whether seeking monetary rewards, votes, or simply status, the media is a tool that, when well-used, can put people at the very top of humankind because being a celebrity equates to success, especially in countries where people spend most of their time connected to one form of media or another. For children in the West, this is especially true as much of the time children spend awake they spend it on screens.

For these reasons, celebrities have a certain moral responsibility to give messages that are beneficial, especially as adolescents look up to them, turning them into role models. Their public behavior, whether they like it or not, matters. Or the celebrity can choose to continue celebrating unhealthy behaviors, with the risk that their followers will imitate them. A study interviewing Elvis impersonators found that people who consumed media saw celebrities as role models and tended to adopt the celebrities' values and behavior. Ordinary people actually developed psychological relationships with alive, but also dead celebrities.[11] Because people identify with them, celebrities can potentially promote certain values and behaviors in the general public. Whether because people gravitate to identify with celebrities who share their values, or because they adopt those values from said celebrities, celebrities' behaviors can positively influence the behaviors of their followers. An example would be an adolescent who admires a singer who idealizes drugs and suicide. Adolescents listen to the music and follow the celebrity online. The celebrity could change and model healthier behaviors and influence the followers who may want to imitate these new healthier behaviors.

One example is the Angelina Jolie effect.[12] We know, and so do marketing companies, that celebrities have power to influence others' behavior, what they buy, and their attitudes towards the products marketed. And we also know that celebrities can create interest in health issues and sometimes even influence health behaviors. For example, the announcement of cancer diagnoses of Kylie Minogue (breast) and Jade Goody (cervical) were followed by an increase in breast and cancer screenings in Australia and the U.K., respectively. However, to change behaviors, the person receiving the message needs to not only be exposed to the message, but also identify with the person giving the message. The actress, Angelina Jolie, underwent a double-mastectomy due to her genetic increased risk for breast cancer and wrote an opinion article about the reasons why she did it. Her announcement had an impact especially among women who identified with her.

Other examples of the power and positive use of messaging by celebrities are seen in the practice of Edutainment. Edutainment involves a planned campaign to influence the masses. For example, after the war in Ruanda, a radio soap opera showed the reconciliation of two members of the two different sides of the conflict.[13] An organization with programs in southern hemisphere countries has used media to help educate people around the world about health issues.[14] This type of health campaigns can be invaluable in locations where there is a shortage of health workers.

People tend to identify and compare more with those who are similar to them. That is what makes marketing on social media so extremely powerful. Models who look similar to us will be showing bathing suits on Instagram that suddenly seem attainable and proximal, and worth any reasonable amount of money at the touch of the screen. This imitation applies to all ages, from the child who imitates heroic movie characters to the teen adopting the ripped-up jeans and crop tops of this new wave of 80s and 90s clothing with minor modifications, to adults engaging in any of the many paths for self-improvement.

There is a darker side to this imitation, and it is the problem with suicide contagion.[15] This phenomenon has been especially well-studied in the case of suicide. Celebrities who have died by suicide have sometimes influenced other suicides in youth. The term suicide contagion first arose in the 1970s to describe rises in deaths by suicide following celebrities' suicides. It includes the effects of the publication of a late 18th-century book by Johann Wolfgang Goethe named 'The Sorrows of Young Werther' that features a fictional character who dies by suicide. It is known as the Werther Effect. Following this literary publication and more recent public suicides, as well as streaming shows like '13 reasons why,' there was an increase in suicide rates among youth. There are existing media recommendations on how to best report deaths by suicide. The challenge with social media is that it is difficult to track the content, and even when some posts containing certain red flag words are blocked by the platform, users can quickly come up with new ways to describe suicide. For example, after TikTok blocked the word 'suicide,' users came up with new words to discuss the topic, such as 'unalive' and 'sewereslide,' allowing for discussion of the topic of suicide in an unmonitored environment, with adolescents serving as both content creators and consumers of this delicate information. It is worth mentioning a positive side of social contagion called the Papageno effect, where someone sees a celebrity struggle and then overcome their problems in healthy ways and mimics this healthier behavior.

Social comparisons

Humans, as social beings and primates, have evolved to live in groups for their own survival. While in these groups, and especially when food and other resources are not abundant, modern humans have had to gage the environment to see if they were dominant or dominated. While our parents give us a break when we are babies, as soon as we gain some independence, we need to start learning to fend for ourselves. This process starts as early as infancy, when we take our first steps in the neighborhood playground, and a stronger toddler takes our spot in the line to come down the slide, or in our daycare, when another toddler pulls away our blanky. We are constantly required to check out who is stronger than us and who is weaker. If someone is stronger, we can retrieve or we can fight. If they are weaker than us, we take what we want without much of a fuss. If our culture encourages domination, we will be rewarded for imposing our wishes onto those of others. If we live in a culture that encourages cooperation, we will learn to share.

As a kid, my grandfather used to take us to the zoo in Barcelona, which at the time was a zoo with little concern for animal rights. The highlights of the zoo were the dolphin show and Floquet the Neu, an albino gorilla who became more and more rebellious with time, and made fun of the visitors, while engaging in some grotesque behaviors, like showing his genitals and smearing feces on the window, behaviors which were most likely reinforced by the attention and reactions of the onlookers. He sadly died of melanoma in 2003. Floquet the Neu (in Catalan) or Copito de Nieve (in Spanish), which means snowflake, was to the zoo what La Gioconda is to the Louvre. The main attraction and very busy. Another much less popular attraction was the monkey pit. It was a sad and inhumane gigantic well with dozens of monkeys. At the same time, it was the biggest open book on primate behavior. Dozens of monkeys could be watched for hours in this huge pit that grew underground so that the top could remain open and monkeys would not escape. Moving from place to place, those monkeys, deprived of everything but a few crumbs, would fight with each other, occupy themselves, avoid each other, and then fight again. The bigger ones looked calm and the smaller ones struggled. Any observation of other primates shows similar behaviors. In gorilla groups, the alpha male usually appears calm. Mothers carry their babies until they are old enough to be on their own. Then the struggle begins. Tentative approaches to get food will turn into quick escapes when a bigger animal approaches or bluff charges. The weaker gorilla will hide in a corner, or will have isolated fights that can end quickly depending on who is involved.

In middle schools, the scenario is not that different. Children are now more on their own, constantly gaging the environment, looking at who dresses better, who has newer shoes, who is wealthier, who has skills in sports, or who is good in academics. With changing hormones and brains, the quest for status is most palpable in early adolescence. Suddenly, even if not taken to the consummation, you can become a desirable mate or be a non-desirable one. And even if your intentions are not to mate, at least not consciously, knowing your status allows you to invest in certain abilities or decide to focus on others. The intensity of these years can be exhausting. As bad as middle school can be, it is good preparation for competitive workplace enviornments, where the scenario is not that different. In the workplace, you can be part of the group or be excluded. If you are isolated, chances are your life will be harder, as you won't get help from your colleagues. If you are part of the group, you risk being excluded, and that can be damaging to your ego, but you can also be protected from predators. Being isolated, you could face exploitation or public humiliation with no one running to protect you. Depending on your ability to fight back or stand your ground, you will present as stronger or weaker, and how others perceive you will allow you to get things done, or not. Once you understand the dynamics, you have a choice to play the game of office politics or not, with the advantages and disadvantages each of those decisions bring. Obviously, some office environments are not as extreme as the one described, and cooperation is the rule.

Adolescents engage in this quest for status through social comparisons. Festinger proposed that in order to continue to belong to groups, humans engage in these cognitive processes to evaluate their own opinions and abilities and as a means to continue to belong to the group.[16] We are wired to live in groups, because as we saw, humans, like ants, would not make it on their own trying to fend off other predators. Upward comparisons are those we engage in when we try to compare to others who are better off than us or higher in the social rank, while downward comparisons are those we engage in to compare to others below us in the social rank ladder of skills, possessions, or positive personality attributes, among others. We use one or the other depending on whether our goal is to compare for self-improvement or self-enhancement. If we want to improve ourselves, we will focus on those who are better off than ourselves to try to understand what we need to do to improve. If our focus is on making ourselves look better (to our own selves or to others) or feel better about ourselves, we will engage in downward comparisons. While Festinger suggested that proximal comparisons with family members and close friends were the most common, social media may be changing the types and frequency of comparisons in which adolescents, the future adults of society, engage.

Social media as a feast of social comparisons

Social media appears to contribute to negative mood as it can create patterns of addiction in which children and adolescents spend less time sleeping or engaging in traditional social activities. This time being taken away from activities that are good to prevent depression like sleep, in-person socialization, and time outdoors could theoretically have an impact on mood and possibly depression. Social media also allows for a virtual space in which victimization can take place with little supervision or awareness from adults through cyberbullying.[17]

A well-understood aspect of social media is that it drastically changes the number of opportunities one has to engage in upward social comparisons.[18] As adolescents work hard to define their identities, which are highly influenced by peers, they also seek more feedback from others and inevitably engage in social comparisons to gage where they succeed and where they fail in progressing in the rank ladder. Those with a tendency to become depressed engage in social comparisons in maladaptive ways. Alternatively, those who are engaging in making social comparisons with a certain style, may end up being more depressed. In social media, especially those sites that are highly visual or based mostly on photographs and videos, and where the text is not as important unless it comes as a means to validate the person posting, people can curate the images they share to a significant degree. When other people post, they will use these unrealistic images as a reference, and try to compete. Some will compete to become more relevant than the original poster, or simply to keep up with the level of the initial poster and remain included in the group. The same dynamic happens with information related to the activities someone does. For example, people will start posting about their trips to Portugal, and suddenly people are taking it up to the level of actually moving to the country. For those adolescents who already have emotional difficulties or low self-esteem, these comparisons can be detrimental. Social media use may help them engage in frequent upward social comparisons, which could potentially have negative effects on their mood.

One area of significant concern regarding mental health and social media is body dissatisfaction and the social comparisons made on line, with potential consequences for people with or vulnerable to suffering from eating disorders.[19] Body image dissatisfaction can be multifaceted. People may feel dissatisfied with their bodies for a variety of reasons, such as not having enough muscle, not being thin enough or being too thin, or having a body shape that is not accepted by the person. There is a gap between the body that we think is ideal and the actual body we perceive we have. For women, the general drive is to be thin, while for men, it is to have a muscular body. Research has shown that exposure to images of thinness for women and muscular images for men in the media can motivate behaviors to achieve those body types. As with other comparisons that people make on social media, comparing one's body to that of celebrities and peers becomes complicated, not only by the constant flow of information and updates from an expanded number of contacts, which is a change from times when traditional media dominated, but also by features and tools that facilitate the enhancement of images and self-portraits, in addition to one's ability to select the images that are most attractive before sharing them. Finally, the information posted online is one piece of the story of a person, just like the photo posted is only one moment in time of that person's looks or activities; the best one. That post raises the bar for the passive observer watching updates of their peers who now look much better and in very realistic ways. Adolescents who engage in more social comparisons about their weight or looks feel worse about their body image. However, there seem to be differences between women and men, as women compare more with people better off than themselves (upward comparisons) in addition to their peers (lateral comparisons), while men tend to restrict their comparisons to people like them. Even among women, comparisons with friends matter more for body dissatisfaction than comparisons with celebrities.[19]

There are good reasons for the rise in the popularity of social media influencers. They seem like regular people, but just a little better, a little wittier, slightly more beautiful, or more talented. This relative proximity makes them great to make the consumer dream that they can achieve and surpass that discrepancy, whereas more distant characters like the flawless British monarchy and the Hollywood celebrities may be less motivating, because that gap seems unsurmountable. If a hat looks good on a commoner, why not click the link that allows you to instantly buy that hat? It is extremely tempting. Just three decades ago, you had to first go to the hat store, make sure they had the hat, try it on if they did have it, watch how it did not look like you had hoped, and then, if it did look good, decide if it actually was good for you in an environment where really no one wore hats. But now, by the time you would have needed to get out of the door in the past, you may have already bought the hat if you can afford it, or have been left with the feeling that something is missing in your life because you never bought it.

Population-level studies show a rise in mental health problems among youth around the time of the introduction of the smartphones,[20] and there is no question that there are addictive features of social media platforms that can lead to people using them in excess.[21] Like other behaviors that are positively reinforcing in the short-term, and given that social media companies have a business model that requires engagement of the user, and results in more revenue with more user engagement, it is no surprise that many people feel addicted to social media platforms.

Around 95% of adolescents are now using social media.[22] Some longitudinal studies show that use of social media and depression go together, especially with excessive and problematic use. However, the research regarding the effects of social media on depression is not definitive. Other studies show no or weak longitudinal associations between social media use and depression. When looking at groups of people who use social media versus those who don't, the ones using social media in excess tend to also have more people in the group who are depressed, but whether or not this is just a sign or a red flag is unclear. It seems that more than causing depression, social media tends to be used more by those with depression. We showed that same finding in a recent longitudinal study with adults younger than 25 years, in which we also examined this relationship accounting for other behaviors.[23] Greater social media use at baseline was associated with more depression, even when accounting for other behaviors, like substance use and time spent outdoors. Depression was also associated with more use of social media at all points, even after adjusting for other behaviors. This only means that youth who use social media more frequently also tend to be more depressed, and that those who are depressed also use more social media. However, it does not explain depression as caused by social media. Depression and suicide are multifactorial. Like most mental health disorders, depression is caused by a combination of a genetic predisposition that conditions your personality, stress tolerance, and how prone you are to be depressed, your tendency to become addicted to drugs and behaviors that may make you feel depressed, your experiences in life, and many other factors. It would be hard to pinpoint only one cause for the rise of depression in adolescents. This is important to take into consideration when we advise parents and schools. However, just like isolating a monkey in a pit may make their behaviors peculiar, isolating children with a screen, may also affect their behavior. In the same study, we saw that the association of social media use and depression was strongest in females. In summary, social media use may encourage unfavorable comparisons, which may, in turn, lead to low self-esteem and depressed mood, but the picture is not clear as depressed mood can also condition the way we make comparisons. Additionally, factors such as bullying, addiction, and sleep disturbances are involved and poorly understood in the processes associating social media use and mental health outcomes in young people.[17]

Can social media be used for good?

Social media can also be used to promote health among adolescents. Social media could be used to repair negative mood by focusing on downward comparisons or favoring positive content. Certain social media sites, such as *BeReal*, encourage adolescents to post photos of themselves at any moment of the day, no matter what they are doing or how they look, avoiding the curation of images and selective posting.

But, like any type of media, social media transmits information, including health information. Most teens and young adults go online for health information. They frequently search for topics such as anxiety, depression, and stress, as those are also the main topics of concern for most adolescents. Even more, those adolescents with symptoms of depression search for mental health information at even higher rates than those without depression. They also report having both positive and negative heightened responses to social media. We know that media in general has been used and is often recommended for mood management, for example, by encouraging watching comedy to improve mood, but we still don't know enough about how to use social media for mood regulation. Some evidence, however, is starting to suggest potential for certain uses of social media to induce positive affect and improve self-esteem.

Media literacy is not new. It has had a role managing media engagement and has potential to address digital media use.[24] For decades, programs in schools have taught children how to interpret media content and commercials, how to use media in moderation, and when to use it, giving the child control over their use.[25] Social media literacy is fiercely needed now to help youth manage their social media use. Especially among youth with emotional disorders who may be at greater risk for engaging in negative social comparisons and more vulnerable to cyberbullying, literacy programs can help with avoiding negative interactions on the platforms and addressing cognitive distortions related to social comparisons. There are some social media literacy interventions focused on body image and sociocultural issues related to eating disorders. Some are very brief and consist of 15-minute-long videos providing education, and others are longer and more intense. These interventions have the purpose of empowering youth to think critically about the information disseminated on social media. Some studies consist of two media literacy training sessions in which the adolescents watch a documentary and have interactive discussions on social comparisons. They have shown to be effective with students at high risk for eating disorders.[26]

Because the associations of social media with depression are a little muddier, the interest is now growing towards understanding the psychological mechanisms involved in social media use. Social media, as a tool, can influence depression in many ways. Going to school also has an effect on mood, and so does playing on the street. But focusing on the tool has its limitations. With social media, there are issues with addiction and less time spent on healthy activities like exercise, which can contribute to weight gain and depression. However, there are also issues related to how people use social media and the things that happen to them on the platforms. It is important to consider not only if adolescents are using social media, but if they are being cyberbullied, if they are active and posting or ruminating about other people's posts, if they are receiving positive feedback or being criticized or made fun of in public, or if they are using social media in compulsive ways that affect their daily functioning, as these will matter more than how much time they are spending on the platforms.

TikTok, a platform that became highly popular during the pandemic, has also had a role in decreasing mental health stigma. Young people are creating videos about topics ranging from depression and anxiety to suicide and eating disorders. Not all of them contain accurate information, but many have hundreds of thousands of viewers. While some of the creators have good information to share, not all of them do, and no one is monitoring the content they share. What is popular becomes viral, and mental health is now popular to a certain degree. A boom in mental health tic diagnoses during the pandemic revealed that many had found a specific audience online that felt supportive of people with tic disorders who then would become influencers. Doctors started to see a rise in functional tic disorders in their clinics.[27] This phenomenon is called social contagion, and it is similar to the earlier mentioned phenomenon of suicide contagion. This social contagion of psychiatric symptoms has been observed not only with tics, but also with eating disorders, and ADHD,[28] among others. Obviously, there are well-known dangers to social media, as it moves masses at unprecedented levels, and sometimes the masses are misinformed.

This is the first time in the history of humanity in which a person can have endless points of comparison with others because of social media. Moreover, the platforms contain features that allow for an objective measure of one's popularity or success that is visible to the user and others through 'likes,' and that allow for quantitative comparisons of this success or social status. You can now see how many people liked a picture of yourself and compare it to how many people liked other people's pictures. These other people could be anyone else, people who are distant from your life experience or very different from you, but they could also be similar to you or people you know. These comparisons may seem unimportant to adults with life experience and perspective, and stronger self-esteem built from achievements in other parts of their lives, but they occupy a big portion of adolescents' worries.

Certain platforms, like Instagram, which are largely based on images and short videos, bring the focus onto how people look. This makes the online environment of social media one in which the comparisons rise to an unprecedented level. Because many young people spend much of their time on social media and increasingly less time seeing others in person, it is easy for the observers to fall into a trap of not distinguishing what is real and what is not, or at least, it becomes hard for their brains to make that distinction. Additionally, those with a tendency to be depressed may turn to social media for emotional regulation and social contact in a relatively effortless way, avoiding in-person interactions.[29] The problem is that those who are depressed tend to also have low self-esteem and when comparing themselves to others, they may focus on negative aspects of themselves, or what they see themselves as lacking. Envy arises when one feels inferior to others; the person feels she/he does not have as much or is not worth as much as others, or does not do things as well as others do, and at the same time compares to others who are perceived to be better off.

Studies that have explored the relationship between depression, social comparisons, and the feeling of envy one experiences when using social media have mostly found that people who are more depressed also tend to compare themselves more with others.[29] The studies looking at causal relationships, meaning that they have examined whether one thing causes another to happen, have found that if you are depressed, you will be more likely to compare yourself with others, but that comparing yourself to others does not necessarily cause you to be depressed. More and more, research is showing that if you are depressed, you will tend to engage with social media in ways that are harmful, but that social media use may not necessarily by itself cause you to be depressed. For that reason, people with a tendency to become depressed or who are depressed, and vulnerable groups of people, like children and adolescents, especially girls, will need to be careful with their use of social media.

But what if we took media out of the equation? Would we rid ourselves of rank concerns? In the following chapter we discuss how our larger environments determine how children develop, and how much their lives are affected by social rank differences as they grow.

6 Social status and mental health and the larger environment

Poverty and violence

After families, the closest environments youth traditionally encounter in their lives are schools and neighborhoods. I say traditionally, because with interactive media, like social media, the landscape has changed and social spaces have become very prevalent in the online world. However, traditional spaces still matter in young people's health. As an example, in the U.S., socially and racially segregated neighborhoods often lack the transportation, tax base to sustain public services, and access to employment for a dignified life. Children in these neighborhoods also have poor access to healthy foods, high-performing schools, and health providers, and are often deprived of basic human rights such as security.[1] Other countries around the world encounter similar problems. Children living in deprived neighborhoods suffer from direct insults to their health. For example, lead exposure in water causes neurological and cardiovascular problems, and affects people's kidneys and intellectual coefficient, leading to lifelong negative consequences. And yet, in cities like Chicago, Illinois, an estimated two-thirds of children under six years of age are exposed to water contaminated with lead. Minorities and lower-income children have higher rates of lead exposure and lower rates of lead testing.[2] Neighborhood poverty impacts cognitive function and the volume of brain areas such as the prefrontal cortex and right hippocampus, even after accounting for household income.[3] In other words, while household income is an important determinant of cognitive function, neighborhood income matters on its own.

Additionally, segregated and deprived environments are isolated from opportunity and will push young people to engage in illegal activities such as drug dealing.[4] For clarity, drug dealing is not always motivated by poverty. A U.S. national study showed differences between White and Black youth. White youth tended to engage in drug dealing if they were personally using drugs themselves and not necessarily when their parents were receiving public assistance, suggesting it was their drug use and not a deprived background what motivated their engagement in underground economies. Whereas in the case of Black youth, there was no relationship between using drugs and selling drugs, other than with marijuana. Black youth either used only marijuana or only engaged in other drug use later on, suggesting that their selling of drugs was motivated by other reasons, such as social

DOI: 10.4324/9781003535942-6

and economic factors, and more availability of drugs in their neighborhoods. It is possible that, in this study, the families who received public assistance had children with less of a need to supplement family income by selling drugs.[5]

Violence is a feature of many deprived neighborhoods and more prevalent in lower-income brackets. But economic recessions or poverty at the societal level are not associated with increases in crime rates. We actually see declining trends in crime rates even with economic recessions. Intuitively, one would expect violence to increase and by extension, crime rates to go up during periods of scarcity and during recessions, if we think that people under more economic strain will engage in more criminal behaviors. And yet, there was no increase in crime in the U.S. during the recession of 2008. Instead, the recessions experienced during the last quarter of a century do not seem to have affected crime rates negatively, which shows that crime may not be related to economic factors alone, or at least, not to poverty alone. For example, in periods of economic expansion, like in the 1960s, crime actually increased, while it continued to decrease between 2007 and 2010 around the recession, following the crime declining trend experienced since the early 1990s. It could be that during economic expansions, people are outside doing more things and more exposed to being a victim of crime.[6] Additionally, the wealth of a country as a whole does not equate to low-crime rates, as we see in the case of the U.S. In Canada, where government assistance is focused on poor provinces that are also less unequal, inequality, and not poverty, is associated with violence and homicide. However, it is likely that prolonged recessions will have an impact on systems that support those who are more vulnerable.[7] For example, a sustained recession may impact budgets on crime prevention or other public services like education that would otherwise support children and adolescents.

Income inequality

While it is not the case for poverty, the association between income inequality and crime rates is evident. The differences between some low- and high-income neighborhoods can be abysmal.[8] In the U.S., these differences are particularly obvious as the U.S. has the highest index of income inequality of all developed countries, meaning that the differences in income between the wealthy and the poor are very large. The U.S. also has had one of the highest increases in income inequality in the last few decades. However, this country is not alone. There has been a trend of increased income inequality in most Organisation for Economic Co-operation and Development's (OECD) countries since the 1980s.[9]

Income inequality is associated not only with higher levels of property crime, but also with lower-social trust. Low social trust can have effects on how people treat each other, even at the institutional level. The U.S. has five to seven times higher rates of incarceration than other democratic countries and the highest total number of incarcerated residents per 100,000 in the world. It jails as many as the population of the entire state of Massachusetts. These high rates of incarceration do not seem to do much to prevent crime. The U.S.'s rates of incarceration have increased since the early 1970s, and yet, crime rates continue to be higher when compared to the crime rates of other democratic countries. While there has recently been a slight decrease in incarceration, largely due to placing more people on probation, the rates continue to be high compared to decades before they began to rise. Minorities and those with a lower-educational level continue to be the groups most affected by incarceration. It is likely that this has been due to the criminalization of problems such as homelessness, and mental or behavioral problems. The problem with putting and keeping people in prison for issues that would require social assistance or treatment is that this practice does not make societies safer.[10] It perpetuates the transmission of poverty across generations and maintains inequalities.

One may think that if you are rich in a country with high-income inequality, you will be better off than if you are a regular person in a less unequal society, but that is not the case. Income inequality affects everyone, not just the poor. It is associated with poorer mental health and overall health outcomes, and with greater rates of violence. The cost of income inequality falls on everyone. The Rockefeller Institute compared the most populated U.S. metropolitan areas between 1970 and 2004 and their levels of 'Intercity Hardship,' which is an index that includes data on unemployment, educational attainment, poverty, and crowded housing. The good news is that there has been a relative improvement in the majority of the country's metropolitan areas over time. However, those areas with higher disparity between the central city and the suburban area presented less improvement in Intercity Hardship.[11] The problem with inequality is that those who can will build their own comfortable spaces, and the public space and services will be neglected. The reality, however, is that everyone, eventually both rich and poor, will be needing to use some public services or spaces. You may choose to live an isolated life between the country club and your mansion in some areas of the U.S., but if you decide to travel a little bit outside of your bubble with your Lamborghini, you will encounter potholes on the roads, delayed services, and even violence. You will have less trust in the people around you, and they will trust you less. Additionally, children, with no earning power, will be less protected, which is why in wealthy countries many of them still suffer from lead exposure, just one example of the many health-risk factors that will cost society for years to come.

Why is inequality associated with violence?

De Courson and Nettle talk about a 'desperation threshold' at which one would choose the risk of getting caught committing a crime over continuing in the same position that could lead to starvation if we were foraging, or to other desperate situations in our current societies.[8] Under that threshold, agents can take different actions. They can choose to forage alone, in which case there is less risk for exploitation but not much revenue, as they only get back what they put in. They can cooperatively forage, in which case both agents benefit from the relationship and they get more than what they put in individually. And finally, they can become an exploitative agent, join in a cooperative group, and selfishly take the resources produced by the group. If they are successful and not punished by some authority, they obtain a reward. The peers do not do the punishment. When you have little to lose, it may be worth for you to take the risk of being punished for exploiting others, if there is any chance that you will succeed.

If this seems too abstract, imagine a deprived neighborhood in a wealthy city, where some families will fall under this 'despair threshold,' and the child or teen, already a risk-taker, given their stage of development and/or because of their personality, will make the decision to try a robbery at a time of desperation. The peers (other neighbors) will have little to do with it. If the consequences (i.e., incarceration or death) are not as scary as the prospects of not having a future (or a dignified present, in some cases), the individual will engage in the criminal behavior. Alternatively, the child could decide to isolate, and get small rewards for his efforts, or to cooperate. However, cooperation could be difficult if the level of trust is low, as it is in unequal societies. If a deprived neighborhood is far from your reality or imagination, think about your workplace. And of the people there, who depending on the environment, will decide to isolate, cooperate, or exploit. Some very competitive environments may have a high rate of people who exploit and go unpunished. In those environments, one may need to isolate and avoid cooperation to protect themselves from exploitation.

High inequality can affect how much exploitation takes place. In highly unequal environments, those with a wealth of resources will also engage in deviant behaviors as they will be able to pay off the fines or punishments that come along with the deviant behavior. The expectation will be that in highly unequal societies, those with less resources will be concentrating the perpetration of crime, which is exactly what happens. However, this concentration of crime within poverty-stricken communities applies only to claims of property crime, and not violent crime. Violent crime is associated with inequality and not necessarily mediated by poverty rates. The strain theory of deviance posits that the goal of individuals is to remain above a threshold that allows them to participate in society, and that when they do not have the legal resources to achieve that goal, they engage in deviant behaviors. A good example of these deviant behaviors manifested in property crimes are car thefts. Since 2020 there has been a spike in car thefts, with an increase of 105% from 2019 to 2023.[12] The National Insurance Crime Bureau attributes it to the pandemic and the economic downturn, but also to cuts in public budgets that would support youth and other public programs.[13] Some have attributed this phenomenon to social media delivered instructions on how to steal certain electric cars.

Not only inequality of resources, but also lack of social mobility can affect the level of trust and the prevalence of exploitation. Countries and neighborhoods with less social mobility make people think that their only way out of misery is by engaging in crime. One would expect that if a society had enough wealth in average, there would be less crime regardless of the levels of inequality because with more wealth, those at the bottom would also have higher wealth. But that would assume that the threshold of desperation remained static and fix. The reality is different. There is not an absolute number of dollars that defines this threshold. You can live in a wealthy country with an average mean that is high, but if you are on the lower bottom, you will still compare with those higher in the ladder, so wealth is redefined by what those who are higher up can afford.

Finally, places with more social mobility also have lower crime rates as they provide legal opportunities to leave poverty for those who want to climb up the ladder without having to engage in deviant behaviors. More unequal societies do allow smaller groups of cooperation and trust, which are needed, given that more people will be out to exploit. At the same time, segregated spaces will be more common, as with low-trust levels, people will rely on these smaller social networks that are more homogenous and use measures to stay separated from others who are different or not seen as part of the group. In some American urban areas, private schools are often perceived as the way to create that smaller, more trusted atmosphere for children, but there are many other settings in which both children and adults find their tribes.

While for some, it may seem counter-productive, and it has definitely become a political issue across countries and regions, lifting the ones in the lower brackets of wealth or decreasing exorbitant levels of inequality, would probably solve a few problems in crime-ridden societies. For example, the rates of minor offenses among youth decreased sharply in a natural experiment that distributed royalties from the casino to Eastern Cherokee Native Americans. This process took place without changes in judicial cases, showing that a monetary intervention had positive effects with no increase in punishment.

From societies to individuals

What happens with inequality at the individual level is less well understood. It could be that in more unequal societies, the poor feel or may be poorer and fall under a threshold of desperation that leads them to exploit others and commit crimes. Alternatively, it could be that people in unequal societies become more competitive, stressed, and self-oriented as they see the massive differences between them and those around them. The lack of or inadequate services to maintain a dignified life or even one that approximates that of those living in the higher strata of society, less social mobility, and a sense of hopelessness may lead to more risk-taking. Having nothing to lose and having to compete for scarce resources may lead to killings when inequality and poverty go hand in hand.

As we have seen, the effects of income inequality on people go beyond the objective economic needs and include a lack of trust. One of the most obvious consequences of this lack of trust is the creation of neighborhood gangs. Gangs are usually formed in very deprived environments, but their purpose is not only to secure resources; they also help provide protection. In dangerous neighborhoods, going solo can be dangerous and protection from the group is important. The same happens with college fraternities or sororities. Big colleges are massive places where for the first time, youth who had never been fully independent need to find their space and their tribe. They can be confusing. What better way to find another family than to join a brotherhood? As with gangs, the process of entrance is brutal, although to a different degree given that college groups now have more insitutional restraints. If you are able to go through it and put yourself at risk in order to be a member of the group, you are considered trustworthy. Once in, you belong to the group, with its advantages and disadvantages. More generally, young people make a realistic appraisal of their environment, meaning that they assess whether they have any chances to make it successfully. They look at their schools, at their neighborhoods, and at their futures, and decide if engaging in deviant behaviors for a reward is worth the risk.

Aggression and social status

Given certain contextual factors, psychological factors related to social rank, such as one's perceived sense of control can have an impact on an individual's levels of aggression. There is nascent research on the associations of social status such as low sense of control, and aggression in adolescents.[14] Theories of social rank propose that when an individual is confronted with a threat or when they perceive they are being threatened, they tend to escalate their behavior towards those who are subordinates, and de-escalate behaviors towards those individuals that are higher up than them in the social ladder. This behavior has been observed in humans in the workplace.[15]

Lower socio-economic class as measured by low income and lower levels of education has been associated with increased levels of aggression, but so has *perceived* lower-social status.[16] The mechanisms by which low sense of control increases aggression may involve the perception of threat, such as in facial expressions,[17] or an increase in perceived threats in the person's life.[18] The perceived threat does not necessarily have to be a threat to one's physical integrity. Social status loss is also perceived as a threat and individuals who have few alternative resources may use aggression with the purpose of increasing or maintaining their social status.

Suicide and its contributors

Harm towards oneself is another behavioral concern in today's society. In 2023, the U.S. experienced the highest rates of suicide since 1941 when 15 individuals per 100,000 in the U.S. would die by suicide. The rates of suicide have been increasing since its lowest rates of ten in 100,000 people in the year 2000 to rates of 14.3 per 100,000 people in 2022. The highest rates of suicide were during the Great Depression in 1931 when almost 22 individuals per 100,000 died by suicide.[19]

While the strongest risk factor for suicide is depression, the social factors that trigger and contribute to suicide are many, and include access to firearms and other lethal means, traumatic experiences, the effects of the COVID-19 pandemic, technological changes, and loneliness. Clinicians do not have the ability to change these big societal factors from their office. They have very little capacity to impact economic or technological changes. They do have the tools to address related symptoms such as trauma or depression. Often, underlying many of the social contributors or directly related to suicide are economic changes. However, it is important to remain humble, as bigger forces in society are likely driving the upward trends in suicide, and the healthcare system can realistically do so much with a medical model of healthcare delivery. Below are some of the factors that unlike depression and the consequences of traumatic experiences, clinicians often feel powerless to address, when attempting to prevent suicide-related deaths.

Firearms

Deaths by suicide are closely related to the access a person has to the tools or means to die. One of the most obvious and deadly means Americans have access to are firearms. In the U.S., lack of state firearm access regulation correlates with higher suicide rates. Of the methods people use to complete suicide, guns are certainly the most effective, with nine out of people who attempt suicide with a firearm dying. Survivors do not go on to attempt suicide in large numbers, so one would expect that people who survive a first suicide attempt would not necessarily end up dying by suicide.[20] The problem is that when someone attempts suicide with a gun, it is very unlikely the person will survive the attempt. Other people attempt suicide by other means, such as by drug overdose, which is more common in females than males, and less lethal. The chances of someone dying by overdose are a little over 10%, meaning that one person out of ten would die of an attempted overdose, in comparison to 90% if they had attempted suicide with a firearm. Laws like the Extreme Risk Protection Laws (or ERPO) have been enacted in more than 20 U.S. states to prevent people in crisis from accessing guns. The guns are removed temporarily and returned to the person when the crisis is over. About 3% of those who had their guns removed and then returned ended up dying by suicide.

The U.S. ranks first in percentage of firearms per person, and is the only country in the world with more firearms than people, with 120 firearms per 100 people. The vast majority of these firearms are not registered. The number of firearms per capita has continued to increase.[21] And yet, while the U.S. has higher rates of suicide than most European countries, firearms do not explain all suicides. The U.S. does not rank first in suicide rates, and is behind many other countries with stronger regulation of firearms. Arguably, those other countries may have easy access to other means of suicide. For example, until public health campaigns and regulations were established, Chinese rural young people were using pesticides to attempt suicide.[22] However, the likelihood of dying by suicide in the U.S. is lower than in some other OECD countries.[23] If it is not the access to means only, what other social factors may be contributing to the rise in deaths by suicide?

Deaths of despair

Deaths of Despair is a concept born out of a study conducted by Case and Deaton in 2015.[24] These authors noted an increase in deaths related to drug overdose, liver disease due to alcohol use, and deaths by suicide between 1999 and 2015, and a reversal in mortality after a years-long trend of decreased mortality rates. During that period of time, all-cause mortality rose by 134%. These deaths of despair were thought to be associated to specific social conditions and social inequalities, both objective and perceived. Objective social inequalities include low socio-economic status and educational levels, jobs with insecurity or unemployment, and living in rural areas.[25]

Youth have also experienced an increased trend in suicides, for which blame has been placed on the advent and popularization of social media. However, it is more of a logical leap to also blame social media for the sharp increase in adolescent deaths by opioids, the group most impacted by the fentanyl crisis. It would be more plausible to assign this increase to a spill into the adolescent population of a general trend already taking place in the adult population. The same could be argued for the social inequities driving deaths of despair. Put differently, it could be that what we are seeing in youth today is an extension of the effects of economic and social crises that adults are also experiencing.

Over the past two decades, changes in economic trends have taken place in part due to larger level policies. The North American Free Trade Agreement (NAFTA) in the 1990s opened American economic markets causing a movement of jobs and workers across countries.[26] Some have blamed NAFTA for the decrease in the middle class and stagnation of wages in the U.S., as well as the distribution of income to the elites, after decades of growth of the middle class since World War II. The argument is that the purpose of the deal to expand trade only benefited corporations that were freed from U.S. laws that provided protection for workers and the environment, while U.S. workers' standard of living was cut. These effects have been felt strongly in cities that held manufacturing jobs such as Baltimore and Detroit, which despite tremendous efforts by local governments, have suffered depopulation, growth of underground economies produced for the survival of those left behind, and community violence among city dwellers who continue to reap the consequences. In reality, this deal had a negative effect in Mexico's small business sectors and agriculture, driving workers to the U.S., which ended up putting more pressure on less skilled labor. While a democrat, Bill Clinton, closed the deal, it was a a bipartisan process, as Republican presidents Reagan and George H.W. Bush had proposed and negotiated the agreement with Mexico and Canada. In July of 2020, NAFTA was replaced by the USMCA (U.S.-Mexico-Canada agreement) with the promise of balancing trade, supporting workers with higher paying jobs, and growing the American economy.

Others argue that NAFTA may have had more benefits than disadvantages, and that the real problem lies in the increased presence of China in the global economy. An eight-time higher increase in U.S. spending on Chinese goods between 1991 and 2007 has changed the landscape for American workers, especially in the absence of a bilateral free-trade treaty. This would not surprise any consumer growing up seeing goods largely 'Made in the U.S.' and living in the now ever-present 'Made in China' world.[27]

Regardless of the culprit, the analysis of which is beyond this text, over the past two decades, economic crises and recessions have impacted the quality of the life of average American workers. Unsurprisingly, many voters among the U.S. working class have been disillusioned with the political class and have been switching parties from Democrats to Republicans to more Libertarian or anti-system politicians.

Deaths of despair are largely caused by underlying distress related to the conditions in which people live, or the social determinants of health.[24] For example, while the lack of regulation in the supply of opioids was a significant contributor to deaths by opioid overdose, social pressures like the changes in the labor market also put people in a process of 'cumulative disadvantage,' especially those with less than a college degree.[28] A comprehensive review of studies pointed to economic conditions, employment, education, geographical setting, race/ethnicity, and gender as the factors associated to deaths of despair.[25] Contrary to expectation, one study showed higher-than-average income to be associated to the risk of a death of despair.[29] This was thought to be related to the fact that in areas of higher income, a person's income had less utility compared to in lower-income areas, which can lead to more despair. While this study was conducted in adults, this comparative income reality is also perceived by adolescents. For example, an adolescent of a middle-class family with an average absolute household income living in a wealthy neighborhood will attend a school with wealthier students who may travel abroad, sometimes several times a year, spend vacations skiing, and afford expensive outings with parents, in addition to buying expensive clothes and other goods. In comparison, said student will perceive himself or herself to be, even if they are not, poorer than the average student. The student, of course, may not end up engaging in behaviors that would lead to death, or even feel despair, but this is an example of how the income relative to those around you matters, even when your absolute income is above the general population's average.

The above mentioned review showed that factors such as economic insecurity or loss of income or assets may affect mortality related to despair.[25] About 20% of U.S. counties experienced economic insecurity between 2000 and 2010. Loss of income influences deaths of despair especially among those with lower-education levels. Conversely, mortality is reduced when one's home increases in value. Finally, those with public health insurance have a higher risk of deaths of despair than those with private insurance, which is likely a reflection of their employment status. Minimum wage and earned income tax credits are two policies to consider that benefit low-income workers and have been shown to reduce deaths by suicide.

Professions with more economic insecurity, such as fisherman, construction workers, or home aids, have a higher risk of deaths of despair. However, having a job seems to be better than having no job, or having never been employed, with a difference in risk of death of despair ranging between 2.88 deaths in 100,000 for those in professional groups and 19.32 deaths per 100,000 among those who were never in the labor force. As expected, U.S. counties that lost manufacturing jobs also had more deaths by suicide, alcohol, and drugs. Clearly, having purpose and feeling part of society by contributing through labor keeps people alive. For those with a job, having lost it recently was strongly associated with suicide deaths. Those with lower education attainment were also more likely to die by a death of despair, and this was especially true for opioid-related deaths. The association of low education attainment and higher risk for suicide and drug use was explained by financial losses in one out of five cases. White people and those living in rural areas of America were also more likely to have increased death rates. This pattern varied depending on the area of the country, and it did not apply to Mountain, Pacific, and Mid-Atlantic areas, where White Americans living in rural areas did not experience higher mortality rates. Deaths by drug poisoning were higher in metropolitan areas.

The type of economy driving rural counties also matters; for example, mining counties had higher deaths of despair than farming counties, and these deaths were higher in southern states compared to northern states. It is still not clear if deaths of despair are different by ethnicity. Initially, these deaths were attributed to non-Hispanic Whites, with studies pointing to both directions; some showing deaths of despair being a phenomenon in White groups, while others showed it to be present across races and ethnicities. Regardless, these deaths may be increasing in other ethnicities, such as Hispanics and Blacks, which is a phenomenon also reflected in changes among children and adolescents of minority groups. In addition to the continued high levels of suicide in Native American adolescents, minority groups like Blacks and Hispanics have also seen a rise in suicide rates in recent years.

If anything, these data tell us that suicide rates are linked to societal stressors and that we should not ignore the power of stable economies on people's health and mortality. There have been three recessions this century starting with the early 2000s recession, and after a period of economic growth and stability in the 1990s. The second one was the Great Recession after the subprime mortgage crisis in 2007–2009. Just a decade later, the COVID pandemic caused another recession, thought to be the worst recession since the Great Depression, which has been followed by a period of severe inflation. There have been many economic cycles with recessions in U.S history. Fortunately, bank regulations and technology have led to more stability and moderate recessions overall in the last few decades. Surveys that examine mental health in children find that economic recessions significantly affect their mental health and that this effect cannot only be explained by parental unemployment.[30] However, the mental health surveillance of children and adolescents is relatively new, making comparisons with past periods of higher economic instability difficult.

Finally, inflation may have a similar effect on individuals as being poor.[31] After the COVID-19 pandemic, Americans were hit with this new economic blow. If you were a healthy, middle- or upper-class house-owning American, the effects of inflation may have been more insidious and you may have been able to adjust. If you were not one of the lucky ones, you were likely affected badly as the price of basic goods such as rent, food, and gas to get to work increased by 8–10%. The House Pulse Survey showed, as expected, that people of higher income were the ones least stressed about inflation. According to the United Nations, in 2021, worldwide, the price of food increased by 22%.[32] In lower-income countries with less on the budget for luxuries, these prices directly impacted the food supply. It is not a surprise to see more political instability around the globe coinciding with economic changes, especially considering the strong interconnectivity of the current human, jobs, and goods markets. At the same time, more conflict creates more inflation. Among our most vulnerable are children, who suffer the effects of inflation and poverty. Protections for children are most needed during these times.

Economic downturns and effects on children

There is solid evidence that economic downturns are associated with poorer mental health outcomes in adults. Studies of the impact of the 'Great Recession' have shown effects on eating habits, demand for emergency visits, hospitalizations and psychotropic medications, as well as suicide. But economic downturns do not affect adults in isolation. Administrative data between 2005 and 2009, during the foreclosure crisis, show a relationship between home foreclosures and emergency room visits for mental health problems among children.[33] State-level job losses have also been associated with suicidality in adolescents.[34] However, overall, there is very little known about economic conditions and mental health in young children, even though mental health problems dominate the health issues affecting children and can have consequences in many areas of their lives such as their academic, employment, and substance use outcomes, even into adulthood.[30]

There are multiple ways by which children may be affected during economic recessions. Children may experience more stress and family conflict at home; they may live in neighborhoods with decreased social cohesion and supporting structures; and they could lose their health insurance, which would limit their access to services. A study examined Data from the U.S. National Health Interview Survey from 2001 through 2013. The data contained questions regarding psychopathology across the domains of emotional symptoms, conduct problems, hyperactivity, peer problems, and prosocial behavior gathered with the Child Strengths and Difficulties Questionnaire from children 4–17 years of age. The study showed that increased state unemployment rates and housing prices were associated with more psychological problems in children, while periods of decreased unemployment showed better mental health outcomes, especially among children with several mental health symptoms. The effects of this relationship were not that different when family measures of social-economic status, family structure, and parental age were considered.[30] In general, the effects of economic stress are expected to be greater in adolescents who are more aware of the household dynamics, have stronger psychological responses to stress, and are more likely to be directly affected by labor market changes.

Economic changes seem to have an effect across ages and sexes. A study looked at parental educational level, race and ethnicity to assess if parental employment affected children's mental health during economic changes. Race and educational level are good proxies of parental unemployment because minorities and those of lower-educational levels are more likely to be the first to lose their jobs during economic recessions.[35,36] Interestingly, the authors found that parental unemployment had a certain influence in children having poorer mental health outcomes during an economic recession, but that this was not the only factor explaining their poorer mental health in these conditions. Other factors during economic downturns would have also had an impact on children's mental health. Essentially, the effects of the economy on mental health seen in adults were also seen in children. These effects are not insignificant: a 5%-point increase in unemployment rates at the state level was associated with a 35–50% chance increase in mental health problems in children. Additionally, there was an increase in need for special education services, which can have effects in the stress placed in school systems, with its estimated cost to local and state governments of hundreds of millions of dollars yearly. However, in some families, unemployment was linked to worse child mental health outcomes while in other families it was not, showing that unemployment was not the only driver of these mental health states. This study could not tell whether these effects were short- or long-term, but because of the developmental process children undergo, even short periods of poor mental health could have long-term consequences. For these reasons, systems that provide more cushioning to prevent poor mental health outcomes in children are important. This prevention can be done at multiple levels, from providing more direct family support through extended unemployment benefits, to supporting schools to ensure special education services are well-funded in times of crisis, to funding mental health services for children. Futhermore, ensuring a more stable economy could be a preventive intervention that would avoid expenses in other domains.

Instability and threat of loss

Threat of loss tends to be more motivating than the prospects of gain and it may affect more those living in high-income countries. In lower- and middle-income countries, economic instability does not seem to affect suicide rates. In a way, loss of status or feeling deprived may be more significant for one's feelings of despair than actually being deprived. Social inequalities are more obvious in countries with wealth disparities than in countries where there is generalized poverty across groups. This is not an excuse to keep all people or countries in poverty, which is also associated with poor health outcomes. Yet, it reflects the association between suicide rates and income inequality in men.[37]

Relatedly, economic uncertainty seems to have an impact on suicide. A study looking at economic uncertainty across 141 countries by income level found that the more economic uncertainty between the years 2000 and 2019 the higher the suicide rates, but only in high-income countries, and not in middle- and low-income countries.[38] The study controlled for income, mental health diagnoses, unemployment rate, and population size on a logarithmic scale. The authors controlled for population increases because rapid population increases cause an acceleration of change and unexpected events, which may cause disruption in the integration of society. Depression rates, unemployment, and lower gross domestic product (GDP) per capita were associated with higher-suicide rates, whereas population size was not. There were also differences between higher and lower and middle-income countries. In higher-income countries, one of the main determinants of suicide rates was economic uncertainty, whereas there was no significant association between depression and suicide rates. In lower- and middle-income countries, depression and unemployment rates were associated with suicide, whereas economic uncertainty was not. The authors explain these results through the 'vulnerability paradox.' This paradox explains that while wealthier countries may be less vulnerable in many aspects as a whole, the culture of individualism and lack of restrain in personal pursuits actually puts individuals at risk of being more sensitive to social failure.[39,40] In an environment with more economic instability, when it may be harder for individuals to achieve their goals, despair may ensue at the prospect of losing status. However, there needs to be caution in interpreting results of studies that include data from low-income countries as suicide rates may be underestimated due to lower-suicide reporting. It is also key to note that mental illness, specifically, a diagnosis of depression, continues to be the strongest predictor of suicide at the individual level. Technological changes such as the introduction of the internet, smartphones and apps, and Artificial Intelligence more recently, signify progress for humanity, but may threaten jobs and create instability. It will be important to consider ways to prevent more deaths of despair in this context of economic and job uncertainty.

Social rank and suicide

In addition to these objective aspects of social status, there are the subjective aspects of a perceived decline in status for new generations. To clarify, when talking about declining quality of life, one has to consider not only the nation's GDP, which in the U.S., it is the healthiest in the world as it has been for years, or even the stock market, but the ways in which this translates into the lives of people. In 2024, the U.S. had the highest GDP in the world, with 28,783 billion U.S. Dollars (USD) and 85.37 thousand USD per capita according to Forbes. The U.S. is way ahead of the second (China) and third (Germany) largest economies, and has ranked first since 1960.[41] And yet, the U.S. has the highest poverty rates, and the highest rates of income inequality of all industrialized countries, and these correlate with poor mental health. The wealthiest country in the World has the highest poverty rates among children, adults, single-parent homes, or any other measure of poverty examined. Since Americans also tend to work more hours than people living in other developed countries, the only logical explanation is that Americans have made the choice to live in this risky way by making decisions about our collective wealth that do not prioritize the reduction of social inequalities, and that do not prevent families from falling into poverty.[42] Alternatively, it could be that Americans (or at least the ones who vote) desire stability, but do not think they will be the ones falling into hardship.

Generally, there is evidence to suggest that economic conditions in the U.S. have been significant drivers of deaths of despair and that these have affected different groups in different ways. One aspect that has changed has been the perceived social status decline in White American blue-collar workers, while other groups may not perceive themselves to be in the same downward trend, especially when compared to other generations before them. White American workers working in manufacturing jobs with a high-school degree in a Midwest rural area could afford housing and possibly college tuition for their families at the end of the 20th century. Today, providing a good education and appropriate housing to their children may prove more difficult, and not as different from the difficulties a Black family may experience today, when decades ago they had to overcome unsurmountable obstacles to send their children to college. Therefore, while Black Americans have worse absolute mortality outcomes, the prospects of White American blue-collar workers may have put them at risk for deaths of despair.

Another sign that loss of status may be key to explain deaths of despair is that among people with mental health disorders, low social position is not as important in predicting suicide as it is in the general population. For example, when a group of researchers studied people who had died by suicide over a decade in the 1980s and 1990s, they found that those with higher income and mental illness were actually at higher risk for suicide than those of lower income with mental illness.[43] They explained that those of higher income with mental illness may have suffered more stigma or shame related to their mental illness.[44] In a way, these people fell from higher up in the ladder than those already struggling with psychosocial stressors, or living among people who were all struggling. Although it is important to acknowledge that in this study, people who were wealthier and ended up in the public hospital may have been more ill and at higher risk for suicide than the average person. They may have ended up in a public hospital as a last resource after exhausting many other community resources that had failed to stabilize them due to the severity of their illness.[43]

Suicide is not just related to one's absolute income. A risk factor for suicide is also how much others have in relationship to the individual, or the individual's relative income. Economists have explored suicide deaths related to relative socio-economic status.[45] Higher county median income, or the income that we would find to be in the middle if we looked at an entire population in a county, has been associated with more suicides if the individual's income stays the same. This finding applies to both higher- and lower-income individuals, but with larger effects for those of lower income. The question of suicide, however, is complicated. Suicide is not always associated with economic recessions,[46] as we saw at the beginning of the COVID-19 pandemic, when suicides initially decreased in certain groups, or with subjective well-being.[47]

Well-being and income

From the 18th century to this day, it has been clear that people are affected not only by their own socio-economic status, but also by that of others.[48] This turns into an easy experiment for many of us. We wake up on a Sunday morning in the best of moods, excited about our upcoming trip to Mexico in the summer, just to scroll down our Facebook News Feed while we drink our morning coffee and see that our close friends are spending their Spring Break in Patagonia, something we will not be able to afford any time soon. The level of happiness suddenly drops. A confusing feeling of unease emerges. You were happy before opening that page and you will be happier soon, if you are able to understand what just happened, but you may not if you have that Patagonia trip nagging in the back of your head for the rest of the day.

However, the relationship between income and well-being is not always a straight and smooth line. Economists have studied how income relates to happiness and found that it varies within income strata. More specifically, it seems like all strata of income appear to have the same rates of happy people, but those who are richer have less misery than those who are poorer. In other words, money does not make you happy, but it keeps you from being very unhappy. This has been named the Anna Karenina principle, which is a concept that applies to a multitude of disciplines and is based on the opening statement of Leo Tolstoy's novel 'All happy families are alike; each unhappy family is unhappy in its own way'.[49] The principle implies that many things can go wrong to make someone unhappy. People without money could be unhappier for a multitude of reasons, reasons to which people with more money would be less exposed. In U.S. samples, for example, bad health and unemployment affect poor people more than they affect wealthier people. Notably, these samples may not represent other countries with more cushion during periods of unemployment and with universal health care. This may also be why rich people tend to look calmer than those of lower-income levels. Research looking at the same people after gaining income shows that indeed, the wealthier you become, the more emotional stability you display, and this has also been shown in samples outside of the U.S., like in the U.K.[50,51]

The differences in wellbeing apply to education as well, and not just income. Those with a higher level of education consistently have higher well-being scores. However, a study examining changes in well-being by income bracket showed that while social status explained some reduction in wellbeing differences when income increased, lifting financial constraints was a bigger concern than status.[49]

The U.S. spends more in healthcare per capita than other countries, but has the highest levels of suicide among developed countries.[52] Most of the excess in spending is driven by private and out-of-pocket spending. In addition to a better managed healthcare system, public investment in stabilizing economies and communities may be an important and efficient way of saving lives.

7 Common clinical presentations related to social status

Why study depression in the context of social status?

Suicide is a symptom of depression and one of the leading causes of death among adolescents in the U.S. and around the world.[1] Over the past two decades, both adolescent depression and suicide have increased in industrialized countries at an alarming rate.[2,3] The focus to understand these increased rates of suicide is often on the many physical, psychological, and environmental factors such as one's family and community, but the stress caused by social hierarchies is generally ignored. The increase in suicide rates has been associated with a parallel rise in adolescent depression. Understanding depression in the context of social rank is important in an environment of growing income inequality and opportunities for social comparisons with the expansion of social media use.[4] Some common reasons for presenting to mental health services in youth, like anxiety, depressive symptoms, suicide-related thoughts and behaviors, and disruptive behaviors, are all related to status to some extent. In this context, the topic of social rank and its associations with mental health may need a closer look.

Much of the research discussed on social rank and mental health focuses on general populations. However, little research has been done in clinical populations, as this is not a topic that is consciously or purposefully included in mental health practice. Instead, in studies conducted in the mental health field, we tend to control for socio-economic status and focus on other variables. For example, we will study parental attachment, but control for socio-economic status. That means that we will try to understand how parents' attachment to their children affects children's mental health regardless of their income or their perceived social rank, when the reality is that perceived social rank and socio-economic status influence attachment styles between parents and children. We try to make up for the differences of rank by focusing on other factors, but what if social rank and socio-economic status were the main factors to focus on to understand mental health better?

Theories of depression and social rank

While psychiatrists and psychologists do not usually focus on rank in their day-to-day practice, several evolutionary psychological theories have tried to

DOI: 10.4324/9781003535942-7

explain depression through the lens of social rank. Some of these theories have been briefly mentioned earlier. The social competition or *social rank theory of depression*[5] explains depression as a strategy individuals use when they accept defeat and retreat in competitive situations. The goal of the behavior would be to inhibit aggressive reactions from the more dominant peers. The subordinate individual submits signals to dominant individuals that communicate that said individual is not a social threat. In contemporary human society, dominance would be determined by prestige. Less prestigious individuals would behave in ways that would not alter the hierarchy, by maybe being very respectful, or bowing when someone more prestigious interacts with them, or for the common people, letting the more prestigious person speak more in a meeting, or frequently nod or smile to the comments they make. According to this theory, affiliation and rank are core processes underlying many psychological disorders. In psychopathology, individuals who perceive themselves to be of lower rank would be less assertive in their relationships and isolate when there is conflict. Similarly, the *social risk hypothesis of depression*[6] suggests that depression would be an adaptive response to a threat situation. The individual feels threatened when navigating an environment in which others are of higher status. In order to overcome this perceived threat, the person (or animal) will reduce expectations of success and send signals that show that he/she is of relative low value to others. Showing low value can also be done by not imposing on others, speaking softly, socially retrieving and isolating, and surrendering to others. In both of these theories, under a stressful threat to status loss the individual would take a stance of avoidance and retreat from the stressor, the extreme presentation of which would be depression. An alternative to responding to a threat to one's status could be confronting the threat (or confronting the individual threating one's status). Although depression as a response may be adaptive in certain situations, it is highly non-adaptive in other situations or as a long-term strategy.

There are also theories that apply to suicide. Some of the best-known theories of suicide are the *interpersonal theory of suicide*[7] and the three-step theory.[8] These theories consider suicide thoughts or ideation as only one aspect of suicide, and the progression from suicide ideation to action that culminates in a suicide attempt as a separate process. A model called the *integrated motivational-volitional model of suicidal behavior* combines the ideation-to-action framework and the diathesis-stress framework in which one's predispositions and stressors would cause the individual to reach the moment of crisis. This combination is a model that includes a pre-motivational, a motivational, and a volitional phase.[9] Within this framework, background factors such as life events, genetics, and deprivation would constitute the *pre-motivational phase*, certain moderating factors would facilitate the transition from defeat to entrapment in the *motivational phase*, and factors that influence the likelihood that someone will engage in action (e.g., impulsivity, exposure to other people's suicides, and capability for suicide or access to lethal means) would constitute the *volitional phase*. Stress, social status, and belongingness fit into these theories. Social comparisons have been proposed as an element of social rank that would represent a pre-motivational factor that makes the individual more likely to interpret life circumstances in a way that makes them feel defeated or entrapped.[10] Loss of status as in loss of employment and acute financial stress could possibly be one of the moderating factors that would lead someone to enter the volitional phase. Another model is the *Schematic Appraisals Model of Suicide*.[11] This framework includes self-appraisals as an influence on suicidal thoughts and behaviors and proposes that these, especially when appraising a situation as defeating and entrapping, modify suicide risk. Suicide is often the endpoint of the concurrence of multiple factors ranging from biological and psychological to sociocultural. Essentially, all these theories include social status as a key component to attempt to explain depression and suicide. And yet, social status is rarely considered in clinical settings, or at least, it is not directly and openly addressed.

The strongest risk factor for an individual to die by suicide is having depression. However, psychosocial adversity also has a large role in suicide. Genetic changes alone cannot explain the rapid recent rise in the prevalence of depression, and depression alone does not completely explain suicide.[12] A study conducted in China compared the characteristics of people who had completed suicide with living controls by interviewing family members.[13] The authors found that relative deprivation, or how much less the individuals who died by suicide had in comparison to others, along with individual characteristics such as lack of coping skills and unrealized aspirations, were associated with suicide even after controlling for mental illness, showing that social status along with one's ability to cope with social rank-related stress, were more important suicide risk factors than mental illness.

Social rank, depression, and suicide in clinical settings

By now, the reader may know, or may have guessed, that socio-economic status and perceived social status are different concepts, but it is important to clarify these concepts in more detail here. Socio-economic status refers to one individual's social standing or class but also the social standing of a specific group. We usually measure socio-economic status by combining education level, income, and occupation.[14] Perceived or subjective social status, on the other hand, is the person's subjective experience or beliefs about where they fall in the social ladder, their social status, or how they see themselves compared to other people around them who they may or may not know. This perception of one's social rank appears to be more strongly and consistently associated with health outcomes than objective measures of social standing like socio-economic status. The reason behind this concept as a better predictor of health is that one's perception of social standing may capture nuanced aspects of social status that more objective measures cannot capture.[15] For example, an individual may have a certain household income that may objectively seem adequate or even high, but may live in an environment where, to keep up with the lifestyle of surrounding people, that income may be inadequate. Perceived social status would be able to capture that subtlety, whereas socio-economic status alone would not. Likewise, a teenage girl may belong to a wealthy family and live in a big home, have access to a good education, and have parents with good jobs, but she may rank low in her school as she may not be popular, may be, or feel, bullied or rejected, or she may struggle with her grades or have little ability to play sports well. Socio-economic status would not capture the stress she would be exposed to by ranking low in social status at her school.

This ability of subjective social status to capture stress better than socio-economic status measures is especially true in adolescents. When the relationship between social rank and mental health has been studied in adolescents, the associations between social status and mental health have been found to be more directly the result of subjective social status than absolute socio-economic status.[16] Again, those who perceive themselves to be lower in the social hierarchy compared to the group of reference are more likely to suffer from poorer mental health. The subjective experience of being higher or lower in the social status hierarchy has been extensively studied with the MacArthur SSS ladder mentioned earlier.[15] The youth version of this scale has been validated in adolescents and its use has shown that low perceived or subjective social status is associated with poorer health outcomes in adolescents compared to higher subjective social status. These health outcomes included depression and risk behaviors such as substance abuse.[17]

In data collected in clinical settings, we examined the perceptions of adolescents when they compared the status of their families to the larger society and when they compared their own personal status to that of other students in the school they attended. Among these adolescents, their social rank assessment in these two dimensions was associated with depression scores and suicidal thoughts and behaviors. In both cases, adolescents's lower perceived social status was associated with higher depression scores and more suicidal thoughts and behaviors. This is not a big surprise, especially because this was a cross-sectional sample, meaning that it was a one point-in-time assessment of their symptoms and thoughts. It could be that perceiving your family and yourself as being of lower status causes you to be depressed and that because you are more depressed you also may have more wishes to die. On the other hand, it could also be that those who are already depressed (and sometimes feeling like they would be better off dead) are also feeling bad about themselves to start out and are comparing themselves more negatively with others around them. When we looked at whether objective socio-economic status played a role in this association, we found that it did not. The association remained the same if you were wealthier or poorer in this sample. These findings validate previous research in adults and adolescent clinical and non-clinical populations. What they tell us is that using this two-item scale may give us the information we need in order to understand how social rank affects our health. This is relevant in busy clinician's offices in which capturing all the aspects of a person's social environment can prove challenging. It is a bit surprising to see that two decades after the research of doctors Nancy Adler in adults and Elizabeth Goodman in adolescents validating this scale and demonstrating that its results were associated with health outcomes, the scale has not become part of the regular set of questionnaires that children are given in outpatient clinical centers. Clinicians may not understand the purpose or know what to do with the results. In my opinion, this is a brief and good measure of social stress and rank. Given its association with mental health outcomes, it could be used to prompt the administration of assessments and screening tools related to mental health, such as depression or anxiety scales, that are already starting to be provided in primary care settings.

Another finding in our study was that older adolescents tended to have a lower perceived social status than younger adolescents, both when they compared themselves to others in their school and when they compared their families to the larger society. This age difference can be due to two things: on the one hand, depression increases with age, so it could be that the older adolescents had higher scores in depression, which may have led them to see themselves in a more negative light when they were comparing themselves to others. On the other hand, it could be that as individuals age and their social environment expands, they have more opportunities for comparison, which brings their assessment of their social status closer to the average. This is in part what has been previously shown in studies on self-esteem.[18] The process of growing up involves migrating from the rewarding environment of one's parental home, to school and work or college, where progressively, we encounter more competition and less rewarding feedback, or at least, not as consistently positive rewards as those one may receive from loving parents and extended family.

Finally, the comparison of one's family within the larger society and the adolescent's own status within their school were not strongly correlated, meaning that just because you feel your family is positioned lower in the social rank when compared to the rest of society does not mean that you also feel you are of lower status than the rest of the peers in your school. This finding suggests that these two measures are assessing different aspects of social rank. It is also a hopeful finding in that even if you are an adolescent who comes from a background or a family of lower socio-economic status, you may find ways to see your position as higher in the school setting, and vice versa.[19] This finding is also predictable if we think about some schools being more or less homogeneous in their population. For example, it may be that all the students in one school are of lower socio-economic background. A student of little financial resources may not feel of as low social status in that school environment as when he or she compares to the Kardashians. It could also be that one individual's school gives more opportunities for comparisons in other dimensions of social status beyond socio-economic status. For example, you may not be the one with the best grades, but you may be someone who is really good at sports. In that case, you may find a way to focus on sports and not feel bad about yourself for having low grades.

In another study, sense of control and perceived social rank both in the school and in society were explored together as risk factors for depression and suicidality. Other factors explored included family and childhood health factors such as early life adversity including in-utero and perinatal complications, and a family history of mental illness, as well as environmental factors that measured how much adversity the adolescents were exposed to at school, in their neighborhood, and personally. The goal was to elucidate what was a stronger cause of stress among adolescents from an urban setting in the U.S. The obvious answer is that it was most likely a combination of individual and environmental factors. But what had more weight? Was it the early insults or predispositions, stressors in the environment, or the current interpretation of one's social status as measured by perceived social status and a sense of control?

We confirmed two factors: a perceived control and status factor, and an environmental risk related factor. The results showed that measures of social rank like sense of control and perceived social status could be used together as a measure of social rank to predict depression and suicidal thoughts and behaviors in adolescents from an urban area. The findings also showed that a higher subjective social rank measurement (a greater sense of control and perceived social status) was associated with lower symptoms of depression and suicidal thoughts and behaviors. Finally, a history of traumatic experiences was highly associated with suicidal thoughts and behaviors but not with depression. Suicidal thoughts and behaviors are consistently and strongly associated with traumatic experiences. Children who are physically or sexually abused are known to be at high risk for suicide. Not being able to escape humiliating and damaging situations affects a child in many ways. It not only threatens their lives, but also their psyches. Therefore, this finding was not surprising. Most importantly, though, when entering all these individual-centered and environment-centered variables in the model, environmental stress variables, including traumatic stressors, had less of a role in the association with depression and suicide than subjective social rank variables.[20] This finding is also a hopeful one. It tells us that even though things may happen to us and we may experience traumatic events that put us at risk for depression and suicide, how we perceive ourselves and how much control we feel we have, is more strongly associated with mental health outcomes such as depression and suicidality. This part of the contributors to mental health is malleable. While we cannot change what happens to us, we can change how we feel about our self-worth and social status with good therapy and good relationships. All of these factors explored (early life stress, interpretation of one's social rank, and environmental stress) are proxy measures of stress. Again, screening for those subjective stress or rank measures may at the end be a good thermometer of someone's risk for mental health problems.

Other research has also found an association between lower perceived social status and a higher risk of suicide attempts and behaviors among adolescents.[19,21] Children and adolescents have little control over their lives as they depend on immediate and more distal environments such as their families and communities. Giving adolescents choices within their families and schools by using more collaborative problem-solving and authoritative parenting approaches, as opposed to authoritarian parenting styles, can have the benefit of helping adolescents gain developmentally appropriate autonomy. Parents who use authoritative parenting have high warmth and high discipline, meaning that they are loving but they also set strict limits and have high expectations for their children. Authoritarian parents will be strict as well, but will show less warmth. Children of parents who are authoritative have better outcomes than those who are authoritarian. Parents who are very warm and do not set any limits and parents who are cold and do not set limits have children with poor psychosocial outcomes. Limits are important. They socialize children and guide them. They also allow them to understand who they are, as one can only do that when they know what they cannot be. Understanding that limits are necessary to ensure safety and education, and that giving controlled choice can also be beneficial are compatible approaches that help children become responsible and independent adults.

Mechanisms involved in the associations between adolescent social rank and well-being

What is behind how adolescents define their social identities? To answer that, we asked adolescents how they understood relative deprivation and social status and the ways in which they constructed their social rank and coped with their assessments of social rank. The adolescents explained that they appraised their *environment* by observing its physical aspects, such as the state of their neighborhoods. The physical aspects were considered first. However, social aspects of this environment such as the ability of their peers to participate in activities, or the way they behaved were also taken into account. They frequently used *social comparisons* to gauge their status. They made these comparisons by using various dimensions of comparisons. These dimensions were not the traditional dimensions that adults use to compare their status to that of others, namely income, occupation, and education. They used dimensions that had to do with personal values, perceived popularity, and physical appearance, as well as skills in certain areas, including academic achievement. Very often, they protected their self-esteem by focusing on those dimensions in which they were most successful. For example, for those without opportunities to excel in a particular field such as sports or academics, being nice was a measure of pride. Yet, financial status was still a relevant point of comparison in this group of adolescents. They were well-aware of the differences in power of acquisition of different families, although this only became a problem when their lack of resources impeded full participation in society or an ability to keep up with their peers. Many adolescents also explained feeling a lack of control over their situation, and feeling anxious and discouraged about the future. These observations are relevant in clinical practice, as some adolescents found the discussion about socio-economic status, in particular, validating. They explained that after discussing the topic, they took a perspective of not internalizing their lower socio-economic status and seeing it as a result of societal forces over which they did not have much control. Finally, they used negative and positive *coping* strategies to either avoid or deny social comparisons, focus on positive aspects of their lives or personalities, or rationalize their situation. A few adolescents were able to create a plan with steps to change their situation, and many discussed environmental or societal changes that could take place to ease the experience of inequality.

Schools, neighborhoods, and status

Neighborhoods, but especially school environments and their culture had an important role in how adolescents perceived and handled their social status position. As the primary gathering places of adolescents of diverse backgrounds and as a second home, schools have a role in mitigating the effects of stress related to social hierarchies. Schools can educate on social issues related to socio-economic status and also social rank more generally, poverty, citizenship, and social comparisons. This education may help collective groups of adolescents understand and address the effects of inequality on health. Additionally, schools can create more inclusive and less segregated environments, with not only less racial and socio-economic segregation, but also with less separation by academic ability, without compromising the pursuit of academic excellence. Schools can also create environments that promote and value a wide variety of strengths and skills so that every adolescent can find a space to which they can feel they belong. These steps could create school climates that are better equipped to buffer social inequities. To that end, investment in public educational systems needs to follow. However, educational systems are funded differently by country and region. As an example, the U.S. funds its schools with property taxes. In areas of poverty and devalued homes, property taxes will be low as they are a percentage of the value of the home. This mechanism will allocate less money to those schools in poorer neighborhoods, which is exactly the opposite of what should be happening to reduce inequalities. Families of children from less resourced homes will have less opportunities to pay for activities and other stress outlets, or to supplement their children's education. This system keeps educational inequalities alive, which translates into other inequities over that child's life course. Taxing wealthy people to help those in need is seen with distrust in the U.S., but it does not have to be a zero-sum game. The people who would be taxed most in a fair taxing system are those who can afford it. The very wealthy may have earned their wealth, but can still be responsible citizens who ensure the well-being of all children in society.

But before the world is fixed and made fair for all children, smaller, easier-to-implement actions can have an impact in buffering the effects of rank on children. Practices like free lunches can continue to be a role of public schools. These efforts help to not stigmatize those who need free lunches and are not able to bring a packed meal from home. The use of uniforms or aid for clothing without stigmatization of those who needed it could also help equalize school environments. Finally, while separating classes into different academic degrees can have educational benefits, those should be carefully balanced with the emotional consequences. Offering more challenging curriculums for those who are ready for them, without creating academic hierarchies is a problem to be solved. A solution to this problem would prevent these divisions from contributing to definitions of identity as more academically or less academically capable students, given that this labeling can potentially be internalized during adolescence, a key time of identity formation. Many children are told they are not among the smart ones, and that is the identity they adopt, sometimes for years to come, and even for the rest of their lifetimes. Thinking that you are not smart enough not only limits what you can do, but also how hard you will try at things, making it a self-fulfilling prophecy: 'If I am not smart enough, why even try?' And if one does not even try, one certainly cannot achieve. A more detailed explanation of what adolescents said follows in the next chapter.

Because adolescents engage in social comparisons using multiple dimensions, expanded options for adolescents to be successful or of higher status in at least one area of their life may help with their self-esteem. Some urban areas in America have a dearth of activities for children who are also unable to pay for private sports clubs or music programs, among others. This is also the case, to different degrees, for children in other countries. Expanding resources in schools serving lower-income students is important and should be an effort focused not only on providing high-quality education comparable to wealthier schools, but also offering broad opportunities to engage in activities outside of academics.

Some school systems in the U.S. have the practice of punishing students who perform poorly in academics by not allowing them to be part of a sports team. Exercise has many benefits for mental health, including preventing mood problems, channeling aggression, helping with focus and concentration, giving a sense of belonging to a team you cannot let down, and relevant to this topic, providing an additional opportunity to experience a higher perceived social status for adolescents who may not be successful in other areas of their lives, but excel in sports. Needless to say, this practice is probably not a great idea. An alternative would be to give those children more support when they are struggling with academics, or keep them as part of the team with less play time, if they lack the motivation to study, but without excluding them from sports altogether. Given the scarcity of resources in certain urban areas, affordable extracurricular programs for children and adolescents programs are often cut. Opportunities for adolescents of lower socio-economic status to engage in diverse activities outside of academics can offer them alternative environments to test their abilities and gain self-esteem.

Social media, status, and mental health

Additionally, due to the rise in social media use among youth and the complexity of the virtual social environment, it has become essential for schools to educate adolescents and younger children on safe and healthy approaches to social media use. This education needs to involve not only teaching students about how social media affects their behaviors. It is also important to advise families and students to limit social media use until they are able to consume it more critically.

Nearly all adolescents are now connected to the internet, and they spend an average of seven hours daily on digital media.[22] Social media expands opportunities for adolescents to explore other social environments beyond their neighborhoods and schools, or the fictional character on a TV show or a magazine. With this expansion of points of reference also come more opportunities for comparing one's social status to that of others. Social comparisons on social media are associated with depressive symptoms, regardless of how often social media is used and whether there was depression prior to using it or not.[23] In fact, how you use social media may be more important than how much of it you use. The association between social comparisons on social media and depressive symptoms is especially true among females and less popular adolescents[24] and among individuals with low self-esteem. Highly visual social media sites such as Instagram, in which the content is mostly videos and photographs with little text, can also predict internalizing symptoms and body image concerns. The widespread use of social media, the risks of neglecting healthy and more wholesome ways to maintain relationships, the tendency of individuals to share more positive depictions of themselves on social media, as well as the ways in which social media provide objective opportunities for comparisons through 'likes,' 'comments,' and 'shares' may lend young people more prone to making these comparisons, which if not managed well, could contribute to depression.[25] However, this is also an opportunity for intervention through social media literacy. While schools are largely powerless to change the content of social media to a more positive one, or the features of social media sites to less addictive ones for younger users, they can catch up and prepare children for this new world of intense interactive media presence, by limiting the exposure in the school, and preparing students for a responsible use of digital media.

To summarize, social comparisons have a critical role in the construction of adolescents' perceived social rank. Adolescents will give more weight or focus more on those dimensions valued in their environment but also on those in which they perceive to be lacking. These social comparisons, if done wrong, can potentially contribute to adolescent depression. While longitudinal research is needed to understand causality, there is indication that the perception of one's rank is associated with depressive symptoms, suicidal thoughts, and potentially with other behaviors such as aggression.

Aggression and status

While girls tend to present more internalizing behaviors, such as depression or anxiety, externalizing behaviors are more common in boys. Externalizing disorders are difficult to ignore as they are more easily seen by the people living around the child or adolescent than are symptoms of anxiety and depression. Externalizing disorders impact the environment, whereas internalizing behaviors mostly affect the person who suffers from them. Externalizing behaviors include disruptive behavior disorders like ADHD, oppositional defiant disorder (ODD) and conduct disorder (CD). In the latest diagnostic manual of mental health disorders of the American Psychiatric Association (DSM-V), ADHD was classified as a neurodevelopmental disorder, and not a disruptive behavior disorder. ODD and CD are common presentations to clinical services across the world, with between 1–2 out of ten children presenting these behaviors.[26] One potential symptom of disruptive behaviors is aggression. Both ODD and CD, as well as aggression, are strongly linked to dynamics of dominance and rank.

Aggression manifests as a combination of predisposing factors such as the person's schemas or the ways in which the individual perceives the world, their learned social behavior, and circumstances that may precipitate the episode of aggression. Most animal species present aggressive behaviors as these have a role in survival, sexual selection, and group cohesion.[27] Both genetic and environmental factors contribute equally to people's aggression.[28] Aggressive behaviors in humans peak in preschool and start declining after, as children and adolescents progressively gain the skills to regulate their emotions.[29] Some children will continue to present aggressive behaviors and these can lead to problems in adulthood, such as unemployment, criminal behaviors, and social isolation.[30] Both low socio-economic status as measured by income and education and lower perceived social status are associated with higher levels of aggression.[31] Low perceived sense of control, a proxy measure of stress, has also been associated with aggression in Asian adolescents.[32]

As seen in the Whitehall studies, low sense of control explained part of why people in lower social status positions presented poorer health outcomes. People's low sense of control in domains such as the workplace, their finances, and their contributions to society have been associated with higher stress in other samples. The relationship is inverse in that a higher perceived sense of control is associated with less stress and allostatic load.[33] This means that a better sense of control is linked to better cardiovascular functioning, lower measures of stress hormones, a lower heart rate, and less inflammation, leading to better overall health.[34] The effect of perceived sense on control on aggression will depend on the context. As we saw, social rank theory proposes that when individuals are confronted with a threat or perceived threat, they tend to show escalating behaviors towards subordinates and de-escalating behaviors towards superiors; that is, they will show more dominant behaviors towards those below them in the hierarchy and more submissive behaviors towards those above them. This hypothesis has been confirmed in humans in the workplace.[35] There is also a difference in how people interpret other people's facial expressions when they have a low sense of control. They may perceive neutral facial expressions as more threatening, which may trigger them to act aggressively.[36] Additionally, people with more perceived or experienced threats or histories of trauma may respond more aggressively.[37] This is common in younger children with histories of traumatic experiences who respond with aggression under perceived threats. They also tend to read the environment as threatening based on their previous experiences, even when it is not. Additionally, a threat or even *perceived* threat to one's social status can also trigger aggression. If the individual does not have alternative resources such as using verbal communication when threatened, they may show aggression with the purpose of increasing or maintaining their social status. The easiest example would be a toddler in a day care center whose toy has been taken away by another toddler, or a middle-school boy who has been publicly shamed and starts a fight to regain his honor.

Implications for practice and pediatric health

Why does all this matter? Considering social rank in mental health has implications for children in clinical practice, and also in settings like schools and the larger society.

In the clinical setting, measures of social status are not commonly used during mental health assessments. Yet, given the simplicity and accessibility of these measures, and their potential to capture overall stress, the associations of perceived social status with depression, suicidal thoughts and behaviors, and aggression along with other health conditions, consideration should be given to including them as part of the mental health visit. In general pediatric settings, the absence of psychiatric jargon in measures like the MacArthur's social status ladder could make it useful as a less stigmatizing assessment tool when full screening measures are rejected or not a possibility. Including and discussing issues of social rank during therapy sessions can potentially ease the guilt and improve the self-esteem of adolescents who have always lived in deprived environments from an early age and may have internalized their identity as of lower rank, or thought they or their families had a role in their relatively deprived socio-economic status. Younger children have a more egocentric view of the world. For that reason, they tend to think that the things that happen around them, good or bad, are caused by them. Being poor may be something they believe they or their families may have caused or deserve. These thoughts and feelings of responsibility for their situation may persist into their adolescent years. A way for them to understand system issues affecting their particular situation, and the universality of social rank differences and motivations for dominance and submission as a part of human nature, may help them free themselves of self-blame.

In addition to what has been said earlier about schools and social rank, there are other practical considerations related to status and aggression in schools. For example, in schools where there are high levels of violence, the beginning of the year is the most unstable as the students gage who is up or down in the social status ladder. To do that, some will test others and see their reactions. Fighting back or responding when being pushed or bullied, as opposed to letting it go and walking away, may be the only option to preserve yourself and your status, which in some of these schools may also mean preserving your physical integrity. Some students believe that not responding makes them look scared and weak. It makes them 'look easy' and they can become 'a target.' Schools should expect more of these exchanges at certain times, especially at the beginning of the school year or among students in younger or lower grades finding their place in new schools. This is important to keep in mind in large schools where the details of the interactions among students will be more difficult to track. Maintaining stability in groups may be a way to minimize the conflict while the groups establish hierarchies. Obviously, ways to assist those children and youth who feel at the bottom of the hierarchy will be important, especially when it comes to keeping them safe. Giving students alternatives to conflict resolution that does not involve physical violence is key. Schools should also consider assisting those children with histories of trauma who may be more reactive to threats.

Most importantly, while hierarchies are a part of the structure of our current human societies, or of our nature as primates, we have the ability to minimize the effects of these hierarchies on young people's health. For that, a cultural change is key. A society that assumes inequalities as part of its existence or even ignores them as one of the main causes of health disparities is missing the potential damage of these inequalities on youth. Finally, environmental interventions to improve environments in neighborhoods and communities and policies to decrease inequality will have the strongest effect by targeting larger populations. While social rank is a reality in social animals, and while as humans, we can expect status problems to appear and re-appear at all levels of wealth, we also have the ability to mitigate these effects not only by teaching coping skills, but also by creating fairer environments whenever possible, stimulating less damaging ways to deal with hierarchy differences, and becoming more aware of these dynamics. An example of culture change includes the changing views on obesity. Historically, as the obesity epidemic grew, obesity became stigmatized.[38] Obesity stigma grew in part due to an emphasis placed on the personal responsibility of people who were obese while deemphasizing socio-economic influences[39] that are out of the control of the individual and have an impact on obesity. This stigma negatively impacts physical and psychological health outcomes. Similar dynamics often take place with people in lower strata of society. Some of them are homeless, some are children of adults with little resources, and some are people with drug and alcohol addictions. The blame is placed on them as individuals while larger socio-economic factors that condition their situation are ignored. As youth grow up in societies with inequalities or they watch these inequalities from their smartphones in other parts of the world, it is key that we discuss them, and educate the population about their effects. In order to do that, the discussion should be not only about mental health interventions, but also about the public health policies that affect health.

In 2008, the Secretary of State for Health in the U.K. asked Professor Sir Marmot to chair a review to propose effective evidence-based strategies to reduce health inequalities. The final report, 'Fair Society Healthy Lives,' reaffirms that reducing health inequalities is a matter of social justice, that the existing social gradient in health results from social inequalities, and that 'action on health inequalities requires action across all the social determinants of health,' that actions need to be universal, and that these actions will benefit society in many ways.[40] The report also emphasizes that well-being, sustainability, and fair distribution of wealth, and not economic growth, are the most important measures of a country's success. Finally, the report explains that policy objectives should be led by central and local governments, national health services, and the private sector and community groups, and that decision-making should be shared with communities at the local level. Policy objectives to reduce health inequalities include giving every child the best possible start in life, enabling people of all ages to maximize their potential and have control over their lives, creating fair and good employment for all, ensuring a healthy standard of living for all, developing sustainable and healthy communities, and strengthening the role of disease prevention. Children have little control over their lives and it is up to the adults around them to ensure they grow in spaces that protect and promote their physical and mental health.

8 What teens have to say about status

In 2016, curious about the experiences of my patients with inequality, I interviewed adolescents from Baltimore City and its surrounding counties recruited at physician's offices and mental health clinics.[1] They shared their experiences with poverty, income inequality, relative deprivation, and perceived social status. At the time, the city of Baltimore, a potential hub of art, beauty, and achievement, was an enclave mostly known for its high poverty rates and high levels of community violence. It was, and is, often snubbed by the rest of the state, which has the highest average household income levels in the U.S., and by the rest of the country, that knew Baltimore as a city with one of the highest homicide rates.

The riches of Baltimore are undeniable. The city has been the home to writers such as Edgar Allan Poe and Scott Fitzgerald, the Peabody Institute, the Harbor, firstclass higher education and health institutions, and miles of fascinating architecture and cultures that blend with each other. Continued violence, social insults over decades, and during the pandemic, and a rapid process of gentrification have not made the disparities in health outcomes between neighborhoods any better. Baltimore is known for a century-long 'Black butterfly' resulting from federal policies in the early to mid-1900s that contributed to segregation and devaluation of housing prices of Black (and also Jewish) minorities, leading to today's difference in life expectancy of about 20 years between the wealthier (and generally Whiter) and the poorest (and overwhelmingly Black) neighborhoods within the city.

While Maryland is not the highest state in income inequality in the U.S., inequalities in Baltimore are palpable. One can walk from a block with housing worth nearing one million dollars to a neighboring block with homes valued around 20,000 USD in less than two minutes. Education funding is tied to property taxes, which means that schools in areas of low housing value continue to suffer from differences in education to this day. These differences cause people in both ends of the spectrum, those at the highest and those at the lowest socio-economic status to be highly aware of social inequalities. While many parents successfully segregate their families to their job, relatively safe neighborhoods, and private schools, it is nearly impossible to ignore these inequalities if you live here for some time. Every time one watches the news, reads a newspaper, goes on social media, or is a victim of crime themselves, the inequalities become more obvious. And while the rest of the state has largely managed to remain oblivious to these local disparities,

DOI: 10.4324/9781003535942-8

recent gentrification is moving minorities and lower-income groups to previously wealthier areas, making these inequalities more noticeable to all adults. However, at the time of our study, children attending some of the best public schools were already very aware of these differences in social status among students within the same city. To clarify, these differences among students were not those between a European child getting to travel to Poland with his family versus another one traveling to the French coast for the summer. The differences ranged from American children going hungry by the second week of the month when the family would run out of food stamps to children getting to travel abroad at least twice a year, while also being able to engage in many other expensive activities and afford many luxury goods.

Despite the racial, cultural, and income inequality differences between the U.S. and Sweden, the Swedish study mentioned in an earlier chapter and these interviews conducted in Baltimore show remarkably similar findings. These similarities suggest some universal, subjective social status mechanisms in adolescents across countries, at least in occidental culture. For example, in broad terms, our sample also talked about the complexities of status in schools, the respect students would get from others, the choice to participate or not in climbing the ladder of status, and the different dimensions of social status.

The adolescents interviewed were mostly Black, the majority were girls, and lived within the city limits, and their parents reported being of lower or middle household income. To summarize the findings, in order to gauge their position in the social ladder, the adolescents scanned their environments. They looked at the physical aspects of their environment, such as the state of their neighborhoods, and at the social aspects, such as the ability of their peers to participate in social life. They also used social comparisons to make estimations about their own status, and in order to make these comparisons they used different dimensions than those used by adults. For example, they compared themselves to others in a variety of facets, such as their personal values, popularity, physical appearance, and their family's financial status. Many felt a lack of control over their situation, and anxiety or discouragement about the future. However, they found the discussion about status helpful as it allowed them to understand external causes for their distress, instead of internalizing or blaming themselves or their families for their situation. As one of the adolescent girls shared, talking about status helped her think that it was neither her fault nor her mother's that they were struggling financially. Instead of feeling bad about it, she now believed that their situation of deprivation was a system issue that she could work towards fixing. This point has relevance in clinical settings where this discussion generally does not take place. Finally, adolescents used a series of coping strategies to manage feelings related to social status. The essence of these conversations is subsequently shown without identifying information to preserve confidentiality. In addition to answers from pre-prepared questions, the adolescents ranked themselves in the MacArthur subjective social status ladder, and then commented about the reasons for that particular ranking.

The innate impulse and the resistance to compare

In this group, there was little connection between the social comparisons made and race or family income. One would assume that Black adolescents who had potentially experienced racial discrimination, either directly or by hearing about it from the people they knew, and most certainly from family members who preceded them, would have compared to others more as they may have felt they belonged to a group that had traditionally been discriminated against and made feel lower in the social status ladder. We could assume the same about those adolescents from lower socio-economic status. But that was not always the case here. Social comparisons were universal. One freshman White girl of a middle-income class family attended a good secondary public school in the county, where the mean income is higher. Unlike in Europe, where the wealthier areas are concentrated in the inner city, in America, the wealthier have tended to live in suburban areas for decades, although this is changing with ongoing gentrification in many urban areas. This girl had good family support, and her basic needs were all covered. She had a long-term relationship with her neighbors and felt relaxed around them. Even with all these advantages, she felt pressure to keep appearances in school because people did not know her well and she thought they would judge her by the way she looked. Even though her close group of friends in school appeared to be of similar socio-economic status, she would compare herself to school peers by paying attention to, for example, the size of their homes.

Many adolescents tried not to engage in social comparisons, but these seemed inevitable. One boy mentioned that his brain made these comparisons 'subconsciously.' His insight into why he compared was exceptional as he admitted that as 'social creatures' we are always 'trying to be our best.' One wealthier teen denied making comparisons openly, but would often make them automatically during conversation, pointing that his family members were educated in the 'best universities' in the country or that they attended the 'best ranked schools.' Part of the resistance to compare or admit making comparisons was due to a distaste for seeming too ambitious or 'ungrateful' or even 'sound snobby,' if one was openly comparing him or herself to others on a positive light. While not common, some teens did not compare to others, not even celebrities. One of them shared that his religion taught him to accept things the way they are, and that included accepting his position in the social status ladder.

Physical environment

Assessments about one's status were made by gaging the environment. It was not usual for these adolescents to make observations about other people based on the size of their homes. For example, a young teenage boy who lived within city limits had a distinct lack of connection with his neighbors, but that did not stop him from making superficial assessments about his neighbors' status based on the homes they owned. Since many homes look the same in Baltimore, he did not feel of higher or lower status compared to his neighbors who all lived in same sized rowhomes. Another girl assessed neighborhoods based on location and type of home, differentiating those with 'big houses,' and those 'shady' areas with many 'trailers.'

Others had realized the home situation was more nuanced, and home size was not all that mattered. Instead, access to transportation and bus routes, or amenities such as a park, gave status. Additionally, the absence of 'shootings and killings' in a neighborhood, and someone's family not being in jail or doing drugs were signs of higher status.

Behaviors as status

The way people behaved contributed to their status. Behaviors such as how loudly people would talk or how much they argued, and whether they cursed and have physical outbursts were signs of status. An older teenage girl felt she was at the same financial status level as other people in her community who were 'on a budget,' but considered her family was of higher status because of the way they behaved. In an apparent dichotomy, she would blame people in her community for feeding existing stereotypes of low-income families by selling drugs and missing school, while at the same time, she recognized that her community needed more external investment that would give people a reason to go to school, because they would see a future ahead of them. There were times when her family could not provide for basic needs, such as clothes or shoes, and she perceived this as a failure of her parents. She was future-oriented. She could see her own future children ranking themsevelves higher 'in the ladder' and felt motivated to not be in the same situation when she grew up.

For other teens, their families' microculture of structure and organization in the midst of neighborhood chaos was a sign of higher status. For example, parents who had rules gave the adolescent a certain status because these rules created stability in the home, in comparison to other homes with no rules. One adolescent had the capacity to focus on the positive aspects of her situation (having a laptop, learning to help her mother in her job, having a 'wealth of love') even when her family did not have a lot of money. She would also rationalize and find reasons to devalue some of the goods other people owned. For example, a peer may have been given a car as a gift for his birthday, but his careless treatment of the car showed an undesirable behavior that damaged whatever social status he had gained by receiving the gift. She would compare herself with the Trumps and the Hiltons as points of reference, while also comparing herself with people who were very poor, which made her 'middle class.' She felt most comfortable surrounding herself with people who were just like her in every aspect to avoid conflict. Wealthier people also seemed more capable in her eyes, like Paris Hilton 'could also rap, who knew?' Sometimes, being different in very small ways, like owning an exotic pet, could be enough to make one feel special. This particular adolescent was a good example of the advantage human beings possess: their ability to modify their perspective to protect their mental well-being regardless of the environmental stressors. Much like Roberto Benigni's 1997 movie 'Life is Beautiful' in which a Jewish man is able to keep his son happy through the horrors of the Holocaust, some people are able to make the best out of very little, even when they socially compare to others, and even when living in relatively socially deprived environments.

Small actions in the parents' behaviors could be interpreted as caring. For example, a boy perceived his mom to be more involved than other parents because she exposed him to different types of music. However, while family was important, especially when they were accepting and supportive, teens were generally much more worried about their friends' than their family's perceptions. How they wanted to be perceived also varied. One could be concerned about being perceived as a good student, or good in sports, or popular, while others expressed wanting to be perceived as good or happy people, as personality mattered most to them.

Points of reference

To whom or what they compared to was essential to how socially comparing affected these adolescents. One immigrant girl from Central America, who had escaped poverty and a violent environment in her home country, had found a home with her extended family after being neglected by her own father. She felt socially rejected in school, did not have money for vacations, nor as many commodities as other people around her, but felt lucky and of higher social rank. She compared her current life to the life prior to immigration, when she had experienced deprivation to the point of not being able to buy school supplies or food, and being exposed to traumatic experiences. She felt safe in her current caring environment that was free of violence. Additionally, in her current situation, she was free of the social pressures with which she had grown up. For example, having to wear something new for Christmas did not matter in the U.S., but was important to maintain status in her home country.

Many adolescents would deny comparing themselves with their peers, but would happily admit to comparing themselves to celebrities, which was common and acceptable. These celebrities could be on TV, or social media sites like YouTube. The points of comparison could be material things, such as whether their houses, cars, and shoes were nicer, but also skills. One adolescent denied using social media because he believed nothing good would come out of him being mean to other people on it. It was surprising to hear that his assumption was that social media was an environment where people were 'mean' to each other. However, his perception was also understandable, as he had witnessed people writing 'go kill yourself' or 'get cancer' on social media sites. He also described concerns about the [lack of] security features, the wasted time on the social media platforms, and the fact that it was a 'comparison tool.' He did nonetheless admit to spending time on YouTube and comparing himself to people on social media, but clarified that he did it in a way that did not make him feel bad about himself.

In contraposition, a girl openly admitted to being on many social media sites, and comparing her looks to those of other people on TV, or the things she did with those her friends did. These comparisons were not done with intensity, nor appeared to affect her in a negative way. She tended to compare herself more with her friends on Instagram than with big celebrities. Because she wanted to be perceived as 'driven' and as someone who made a difference, she tended to compare herself with people who had the ability to change things. This girl was not atypical. Adolescent girls almost consistently made comparisons about their looks, but they would also compare on dimensions of things of their interest. For example, if they enjoyed editing videos, they would focus on the ability of others to create good online videos. These comparisons could be distressing. One adolescent admitted that even when she was aware that people on social media would tend to put their 'best side forward,' it was sometimes hard to remember that.

Unfortunately for humans, we have a negativity bias and a tendency to focus on the things we do not have or those we perceive as our weakness. Social media offers many opportunities to find those things we lack. We are all lacking in one way or another, and there are always better people than us in almost everything, if not all. It takes less than a minute to find that one person who is better than you at something online. For example, one girl shared that she thought her social life was not good, and interestingly, she would focus on how liked she was in comparison to her friends. Being liked is made very obvious on social media, as you literarily get more 'likes' and shares, or have more followers, when you are liked.

Other times, comparing onself to others did not make sense to the adolescent if the circumstances of the people they compared themselves with were very different. Understanding that everyone had their own particular circumstances to an extreme would render comparisons senseless. Conversely, if all things were generally equal or close to equal, seeing someone do well could be a motivator because it meant that the observer could also achieve the same thing. This is why representation is important. If you watch only White men playing tennis and winning titles, it will be harder for you to imagine winning titles in tennis as a young Black girl, but things change when another young Black girl, like Serena Williams, starts playing and winning titles. This is a double-edged sword, though, as seeing someone considered equal achieve things that you do not can also be demoralizing.

Another choice was to not use any point of reference to make comparisons that could be destructive, and just 'try your best,' which can translate into comparing your actual self to your old self. Finally, there are those comparisons that others impose on people. For example, a parent's favorite go-to is talking about the 'children who live in Africa' to point to their own children that others have worse living conditions. These comparisons can be invalidating, as the adolescent may be struggling even when living a more privileged life. Even if you do not like to compare, unfortunately, you will encounter parents, teachers, and friends who will compare you to other people. These other people can be your siblings or better-performing friends. One girl mentioned that comparing could be good to motivate her to save up money to improve her life, but that she hated 'when feelings were involved.' It would not be surprising to see children reacting negatively when their own parents compare them to other children in a way that makes them look bad, both explicitly or in more subtle ways, and even when done unintentionally.

Our ideas of other people's status

From thinking that having a minivan was a sign of an average-wealth family to thinking that average was having certain clothes, an iPhone, cable, and WIFI, or long hair (as hair was expensive for Black teens), adolescents' beliefs about what was the average reference point varied considerably. Some felt they were average or above average in their own community, but perceived the rest of the country (like 'Florida retirees') as much wealthier.

Others noted status differences within their own neighborhoods. One boy felt excluded from his own community as a private school mostly of White students was located in the middle of his all-Black neighborhood. He rationalized this feeling of exclusion saying he believed that an all-Black school was better for him anyway because he was under the impression that the staff knew how to prepare him well as a future Black man in this society.

Gaging what others think of the person was a way to assess one's own ranking in the social ladder. One adolescent said he ranked himself based on how other people responded to him. If people considered a person to be 'cool' or have many friends, that would place that person higher up in the social rank ladder.

Being able to engage in social life as a measure of status

When the adolescents assessed their environments, they also considered their access to opportunities to engage in social activities. One teen living with her brother and her single parent related that she had been in situations of real need, such as not having food, supplies for school, or money for field trips. During those times, she had felt compelled to find a job to be able to help, and when she was told that she could not get a job, she had felt helpless. She was upset that she could not participate in conversations about the field trip with her friends, and felt guilty about the times she had asked her mother for things they could not afford.

This drive to socially engage could be a problem for those living in violent neighborhoods as they could not safely engage outside of the home. In wealthier families, many adolescents feel overscheduled with little opportunity to freely socialize with peers and relax. In deprived areas of Baltimore, adolescents experienced the opposite: anxiety and demoralization due to a lack of opportunities for social engagement in the community.

In low-density, car-driven physical environments, or as the teens put it 'neighborhoods that were spread out,' activities existed for younger children (neighborhood pools), but there was a perceived lack of developmentally appropriate activities for teens to engage in, such as walkable movie theaters or shopping centers. When schools offered options for people of diverse background and interest, everyone could find their place, and the school was perceived as a better environment than other settings.

Some adolescents distinguished having one's 'needs' covered versus having their 'wants' satisfied. Not being able to socially participate and the uncertainty of not being able to do that in the future could keep them awake at night, or make them feel angry or sad.

Dimensions of comparison

Other teens had gone through a progression of comparing their family to other families' wealth by first noticing the differences in homes of friends they would visit when they were young, to later watching the cars they drove, or the clothes they wore. Many of the adolescents interviewed did not care about financial status. For example, one girl's biggest concern was not being able to keep up with the academic demands in school, including staying on as an honor roll student. She did not wish to be rich. She was aware of her family's financial struggles, but said she would have been satisfied with enough financial stability so as to not have to worry.

There was a general acceptance that people compared to each other constantly. One boy noticed comparisons being used to compete with others and make one-self 'look better' instead of these comparisons being neutral and not emotionally charged. Other comparisons were made within the immediate group of friends, and were not ill-intentioned and offensive, but meant to 'build each other up.' Comparisons could also be done at the academic level. As early as fifth grade, students were divided into different academic programs, some more advanced than others, and this objectively differentiated the students by ability. Being respected by peers could also be an area of pride and status.

Sometimes the value was placed by the environment. For example, some families valued basic needs they did not have, like money for basic goods. The same happened in school, where a culture of value of wealth, physical appearance, or skills in sports were sometimes placed over the value of getting good grades and being a good student. In those instances, a good student would feel of lower social rank in that school, even if they were the most successful academically. One of the girls ranked herself higher in the ladder when thinking about her grades, but said she was not high socially because she did not have friends and tended to be by herself in school, her family did not own a house, and they lived in a very deprived neighborhood. She felt her overall social status was low. She admitted to having low self-esteem and comparing frequently with others. While she admitted that getting good grades was something that gave her advantage over friends and school peers, she did not believe this was important to other people around her who focused more on how much money or possessions people owned. Since grades were not valued in her school, they did not give her as much status advantage as being wealthier would have given her.

Some teens were very clear about the various rankings, differentiating how they ranked in their school based on testing scores, grades, community involvement, and their family background, or they would compare their school versus others in the school district, and even the country. These students would make varied ranking assessments depending on the reference of comparison.

One student expressed frustration about the assumptions others made about her school. Based on the racial composition and lack of academic resources and opportunities for engagement, such as sports, she believed others perceived her school as less desirable. Even though the school was allegedly perceived as of lower rank, this adolescent ranked herself high as she was in the most advanced academic program at that school. Academic divisions designed by the school were a clear and easy way to rank oneself and others.

Being a good person and being good at certain things, such as being a good student or a good artist, could give a sense of pride and status. For example, one girl played several instruments and was good at painting. She identified with those activities and wanted to be judged by her skills and not the amount of money or commodities her financially comfortable family enjoyed. She would also tend to make comparisons with peers around that topic. This girl compared herself with one of her good friends in middle school, a good student and artist. When she engaged in upward comparisons in this dimension, she would feel 'down' as she thought she was 'not that good at things,' or may 'never be good' or 'the best at anything,' and similar cognitive distortions. Finally, those who were more social were also perceived as more popular, which makes one wonder about the status experience of people that are just simply more introverted.

School-based social comparisons

Noticing the socio-economic differences in diverse schools made some adolescents feel bad for others who were less fortunate. That is, comparing downward did not always result in improved mood. These comparisons also made people feel power-less. Adolescents were privy to these differences in the simplest ways. They knew that the less well-off would take the free school lunch instead of bringing lunch from home, would not attend field trips, could not buy new video games, or they simply looked 'down.' For others, comparing to people who were worse off would put pressure on them to try even harder, or make them feel guilty and undeserving.

School comparisons were perceived as being widespread, more than compari-sons outside of school, such as those done in one's neighborhood, likely because the neighborhood consisted of mostly adults whose opinions did not matter as much as those of school peers or teachers. Even though the purpose of school was to learn, there was a general acknowledgment that much of the focus was on appearances, grades, whether someone was wearing brand name shoes, wealth, how 'cool' one was, the neighborhood they lived in, and academic differences. Not being able to keep up with peers in academics made some teens 'feel dumb.' One student explained that at the beginning of the school year a teacher told a story about 'white collar' and 'blue collar' students. 'White collar' students were those who could do everything last minute and get 100s and the 'blue collar' students would have to work very hard to just get decent grades. This girl, who identified as a 'blue collar' student did not know that this is a workforce classification to differ-entiate higher paying non-manual jobs from lower-paying jobs. She believed this was just a way to describe the white-collar students as 'way smarter, more talented' and said the teacher had favorites who belonged to that category. However, she was able to have outlets like hobbies that decreased her stress and improved her mood when feeling down about her academic performance and her exclusion from this fabricated student classification. Comparing oneself to one's past self could be difficult if, for example, the student's academic experience in middle school was more successful than in high school, something not uncommon for many children in the Baltimore school system.

In the case of the youth who were more sensitive to judgment from others, it was unclear if the intensity of the social comparisons among students was real, or perceived. As one girl admitted, students in school were not necessarily overt about how they judged others, but 'you can kind of tell.' While she would overhear conversations about other people's shoes (some of which were customized and cost hundreds of dollars), it was not evident if that was a focus due to her own personal insecurities, or a reality that invaded most of the school life. Witnessing someone in school getting picked on for (for example) not changing clothes in three days could also make others aware of the need to be mindful about their own clothes to be not ridiculed or excluded. Close friends made them feel at ease and protected as they could 'just be themselves' in these trusted relationships, showing the power of acceptance and inclusion, and the benefits of social support.

While downward comparisons are thought to help with mood and self-assurance, they did not always help in this very unequal environment. As mentioned, comparisons could be distressing both when done upwards because they would cause someone to feel less popular, good-looking or wealthy than others, and also when done downwards because one could feel bad for others who were in a more disadvantaged position. One student thought it would be better if everyone was 'on the same level' but said that then people would not be unique. Some understood upward comparisons as a way of self-improvement. Many aspired to be NFL players, and having had local celebrities get to that level made that goal seem more attainable, but they were aware that 'it takes levels' for someone to get to be a celebrity.

Switching from public to private school and vice versa was a quick way to become aware of differences in social rank and the ways different populations navigated social status differences. The differences were related not just to financial wealth, but also to behaviors. Those who had navigated both private and public school environments gave insight on what these transitions meant regarding social status. One could feel of higher social status in public school and lower than others in private school. Competition in private schools could be even harder to navigate than in public schools, as in private schools everyone was 'rich and popular,' implying a narrower range of backgrounds that gave less opportunities to compare with others who were worse off from any vantage point.

Absolute deprivation

Some of the adolescents had experienced real deprivation such as not being able to buy food and having to ration the food so it 'could last.' Expectations such as having to have new shoes for Easter and Christmas could be a cause of stress for some families. Some adolescents felt trapped as they could not yet get a job and contribute to their family's finances, and did not want to make their parents feel they were not doing enough to provide for their families.

In desperate cases, parents would ask their children to sell drugs. The American mentality of individual responsibility was highly internalized by these adolescents. Some adolescents said they would just 'try better' if they found themselves in positions of deprivation, even while acknowledging feeling powerless. Those who experienced real deprivation would sometimes blame their parents, as the adoelscents could 'not understand' how their parentscould work '24/7' and not have enough money.

Feelings about status

Being in control over losing or gaining status can shield from negative feelings, and the prospects of losing status in the future can be bearable if the loss is by choice. For example, deciding to focus less on grades, and enjoying socializing and other non-academic activities, may decrease one's status as a student, but it may not be distressing if it is a conscious choice.

Most adolescents were very aware of differences in status in school, but some experienced these within their own families, like in the case of a girl whose parents were divorced, one parent being of higher and the other being of lower socio-economic status. For her, standing out from peers who were either lower or higher in socio-economic social was a source of shame.

As previously mentioned, people can compare themselves with others or with their past selves. Sometimes, other people's opinions's matter and other times, it is one's own aspirations or expectations of what should be accomplished what brings people's mood down. One of the adolescents felt that what she 'should be like' and what she had actually accomplished did not match, and that would bring up negative feelings, including thoughts about wanting to die.

On occasions, working hard on sports or academics was not enough to feel successful. One adolescent noted that wealthy and well-connected parents gave opportunities to their children that she could not have access to, such as meeting high-ranking politicians. However, not having the advantage of coming from a wealthy family could also be a motivator for some students to work harder in order to achieve the same goals as others around them. Regardless, the mountain seemed harder to climb when you were already at a disadvantage from the beginning. One clear and objective barrier to success was the inability to pay for college tuition.

The awareness of status differences among different people started early. One adolescent explained that she started becoming aware of social differences when she was six years old. She had a friend with a bigger home whose parents would always buy her what she wanted. At first, she thought they were just being nice, but as she grew older, she realized that they were rich. With time, she also understood that having connections was another powerful gift to which those of higher status had access.

Status and violence

One adolescent with a very mature view of social comparisons understood that by looking at someone superficially people could get a biased idea, as the observer would tend to focus on dimensions of the other person in which he or she stood lower in the social ladder by comparison. This very insightful expert in social comparisons shared that comparing himself to someone very different did not have as big an effect on him as comparing to someone similar. This phenomenon of comparing with more intensity to more equal ones is well-known. It is also an opportunity to do cognitive restructuring. If we feel bad about feeling lower than someone who is very similar to us, we can instead focus on the things that make us different from that person. For example, if you feel you should be doing as well in basketball as someone who you consider an equal or similar to you because maybe you are both tall, you could instead focus on how you and that person are different. The other person may have had more training, or have a more competitive personality, or may practice every day. All of those characteristics make you different from each other and would explain why the other person may be better at basketball. In that case, the thinking changes from 'I should be as good as that person' to 'we are different people with different skills.'

This phenomenon of comparison with people that are similar may have a role in inner city violence. This type of violence tends to be more common among people within the same social strata. Intuitively, we would expect more violence directed towards those of a higher socio-economic status. However, most of the killings by firearm in America happen between people within the same social strata (e.g., Black-to-Black homicides). This is in large part related to the territory turfs to sell drugs in a race away from poverty, and may also be due to fear of more institutional retaliation if you harm someone with more privilege. But the killing of successful Black young men who start out poor and 'make it out,' without any financial gain on the part of the perpetrator, nor a clear motive, suggests that there may be more to the story.

One person who 'made it out' in Baltimore was rapper 'Lor Scootta,' or Tyriece Travon Watson. He was killed in his car after a charity event for peace[2] around the time these interviews were conducted, and this murder was very much in some of the adolescents' minds. 'Scootta' was seen as loyal to the city and was giving back by buying school supplies, among other things. One adolescent in particular believed that jealousy and 'greed' were the causes of his death. She said that while drug-related territory turfs had a role, if it weren't the drugs 'it would be the phones, or the shoes, or watches, or designer belts...' 'Scootta' was not on the corner selling drugs; he had earned money with his job as a musician, and stayed connected to his community. One would think he would be an untouchable hero. Instead, he was killed. The person who killed him may have been less likely to kill a White successful man. But, Scootta was fair game.

The adolescents were clear about their impressions of these close connection between the deaths by firearm of successful young people in the community and the feelings of jealousy and greed of those who killed them. This was expressed clearly by a boy who said that if he could change something in the city, it would be the 'hate.' He said it was 'like crabs in a barrel' and that people would 'try to pull each other down' and not allow others to succeed; that jealousy was at the root of many of the killings because people wanted things other people had. Being famous and successful could put your life at danger.

Others tried to avoid comparisons with friends and even tried to differentiate themselves from them so as to create separation and prevent competition. Competition could end badly, as many had already witnessed. One teenager explained that comparing to other people could make people feel bad, causing them to 'act out' due to envy; the person could then engage in illegal activities, and even hurt others by trying to take things away from them. Instead, it was easier and safer to compare with people on social media or those with whom the teenager had short-lived interactions.

One adolescent believed people would encourage others to engage in drug consumption and dealings instead of helping them be better people. Surrounding yourself by people who wanted you to be successful and 'not leech off of you' was key to make it out without being boycotted. The culture mattered in status, and sometimes a change in culture was perceived as sorely needed, especially when it came to community violence, as people would sometimes 'brag' about shooting or selling drugs or 'banking' [several people attacking] instead of gloating about getting a job or taking care of their children. However, it was understood that socially comparing could also be a motivator to get a job and earn money, to improve oneself.

Looking ahead and resilience

Having 'humble beginnings' was not always seen as a negative thing. It could help you be resilient. One adolescent explained that he was on the debate team and they did not have a a coach, so more senior students had to teach the younger ones. The practices had to be canceled at times due to water breaks in the school building. His team would then have to compete with much more prepared groups. But being able to compete with those other teams with much less help was an accomplishment in itself. Some teens expressed feeling motivated to want to help their parents by giving them ideas on what to do or finding a job to help out. For some, having struggled with poverty gave them perspective and a desire to change the destiny of their own future families.

In conclusion, these adolescents had a lot to teach us about social comparisons and how to manage their assessment of their social status. Many avoided making social comparisons. This avoidance tended to happen when there was a fear that comparing to peers would bring up conflict. As if comparisons only implied envy, many of them refused to admit they were making them or tried to resist them. The ones that were successful in staying upbeat in the context of inequality and hierarchy differences would focus on dimensions of comparison that worked for them, and their self-esteem. There were some differences by class, with those in families lacking basic needs having aspirations to have those needs covered. In line with Maslow's hierarchy of needs,[3] if the adolescents belonged to families with financial needs, they would more frequently focus on and discuss issues related to housing, clothes, and safety, while others in wealthier families focused on self-esteem and actualization goals. All of them seemed to commonly be concerned about social support and belonginess. A successful strategy was to compare oneself not only in a different dimension but also with a different community. For example, one of the teens felt that when she compared herself to the community she lived in, she had better grades and more money, but when she compared herself to people in her school who were of higher status, this was not the case. In her case, being exposed to a diversity of environments helped her gain perspective.

9 The psychology of social rank

Social comparisons, dominance, and submission

Internal processes

We now know that adolescents' perception of their social status has more weight on health outcomes than objective or absolute socio-economic status, as the former captures part of what constitutes the social identity of the person and other causes of stress beyond one's socio-economic status. But to understand how to address these processes, one needs to understand what is really social rank and how it manifests in mental health.

There are various psychological mechanisms involved in social rank and domains of depression. Some of them have been discussed already and include sense of control, self-esteem, and social comparisons. We saw how a lower sense of control, or lower autonomy, was one of the ways in which perceived lower social status gets under people's skin and contributes to the health gradient. The concept of sense of control has been studied in the workplace environment in adults and to a lesser degree in other settings and in youth. By definition, adolescents are likely to have more or less autonomy depending on how much of it is given to them by their environment, but their sense of control may vary. There is evidence that some factors influence how much this sense of control results in depression in children and adolescents. For example, parental rejection,[1] academic achievement,[2] and maternal depressive symptoms[3] can influence the associations between low sense of control and depression. Sense of control is likely both a personality *trait* that is stable and inherent to the person and also a more malleable *state* of personality that shifts depending on the context and the age of the individual.[4] Of these two components of sense of control, the contextual, malleable component is probably the one that is most predictive of mental health problems such as depressive symptoms.[5]

We have also seen that self-esteem is connected to perceived social status and to social comparisons. People who make social comparisons will have better self-esteem if they perceive themselves to be better off than their comparison group. The frequency of upward social comparisons can have a negative impact on mood and anxiety, meaning that frequently comparing yourself to people who are better off can worsen your mood and cause your anxiety to rise.[6]

DOI: 10.4324/9781003535942-9

External factors: stress related to inequities

Being exposed to highly inequitable environments may lead to chronic stress and poor mental health. Stress is the product of a transaction between an individual's psychological and biological systems, and the environment surrounding that individual. The stress someone experiences depends on the person's cognitive appraisal or their understanding of how threatening the stressor is to them as well as their ability to cope with the stressor. Individuals will adopt certain copying styles depending on whether they believe they will have enough resources to be able to manage a certain stressor. They can adopt coping strategies that involve focusing on the positive aspects of their situation, using wishful thinking, or avoiding thinking about the stressor. These are *emotion-focused* coping strategies. When the individuals assess that they do have the resources to manage the situation, they use more *problem-focused* coping, and take the necessary steps to solve the problem.[7]

Transactional theory postulates that a behavior or strategy is never effective in every single situation an individual encounters. In fact, using the same coping strategy for every situation can be more harmful than beneficial.[8] That is why the coping mechanism used matters less than the individual's *coping flexibility*, or ability to modify the coping behavior depending on the stressor. This flexibility is considered to be key in coping with psychological distress as it allows the person to discontinue an ineffective coping strategy in order to use newer and more effective ones for the specific situation.

Being sensitive to feedback about the efficacy of one's coping strategies and able to adapt and engage in new alternative and more effective coping strategies has been associated with fewer depressive symptoms.[9] For example, imagine you are part of a track school team in which the coach always has you running in events that are not your forte. You may be a mid-distance runner, but you are made to run the 400-meter dash, for which you are too slow. You always lose, and realistically, your body is not built for that event, so you do not really understand the coach's decision. You are also a very competitive person who likes to win. You have two choices: continue to be upset about the fact that you are always going to be in an event in which you will lose, or use a growth-mindset and think about it as an opportunity to improve your speed for the time when you have a chance to run a longer distance. People who stay upbeat tend to take the second approach. They are flexible enough to refocus their thinking. People who are more likely to be or stay depressed tend to be less flexible in their choice of coping strategies than those less likely to be depressed. The more coping flexibility, the better the psychological functioning and health of the individual.

In the context of inequality, it is possible that youth who present a low perceived social status or sense of control in adolescence evolve to use coping strategies that may have worked for them to adapt to the stressful situation of relative deprivation and low social status they experienced. However, these coping strategies may not be effective to cope with situations they encounter as adults, or as the youth themselves navigate other environments that are not as stressful as the ones that required the coping strategies they initially used. Those adolescents with more cognitive flexibility may be able to adapt to different situations more easily. One example would be the culture of 'snitching' in some schools. The word 'snitch' becomes popular in some neighborhoods in the U.S. as a way to describe a resistance to inform police authorities about delinquent behavior in underserved and historically oppressed neighborhoods. It translates into prisons, and it is now often used in schools. In part, this behavior is a result of people expecting the responses from the authorities and institutions to be worse than the delinquent or mischievous behavior perpetrated by their peers. It is easy to understand the emergence of this behavior in communities where discrimination and oppression have been the norm for a long time. The first time I heard the word was in the sentence 'snitches get stiches' as I dwelled with some of my patients who would refuse to communicate bad or even dangerous peer behavior to school administrators. A child growing up in such school environment who then moves on to work as an adult in the healthcare setting, for example, where it is unacceptable to not report peer's bad behaviors as the health of patients is at stake, will have to make a leap in their thought process and view of the world to succeed in this new environment. More research is needed to better understand how one's ability to adjust one's coping strategy contributes to greater resilience in the face of economic deprivation or income inequality, and leads to better health outcomes. However, we already know that much of what a therapist does is guide the client in being able to see other perspectives, and helping them shift to using healthier coping strategies.

What has psychology taught us about social comparisons?

Festinger introduced the notion of a human drive to socially compare within our species.[10] We compare to understand our reality in the social world and maximize our inclusion in the group. Schachter expanded this theory to explain how social comparisons mediate the link between fear and affiliation, and implied that people tend to compare themselves with others more when experiencing uncertainty.[11] This experience of uncertainty is common in new environments, like when a young person moves to a new school or neighborhood. One may wonder why humans had to develop such sophisticated internal systems to adjust to hierachical environments and we did not just evolve to be all equal, since dominance causes stress. The reason that did not happen is that there may actually have been some evolutionary advantage to some people in groups being more dominant than others. Differences in dominance motivation may have been advantageous for the group as a whole, as they facilitate the acquisition of resources and maintenance of safety.[12] It is indeed difficult to imagine a successful and safe society in which everyone has a motivation to dominate. It would be a constant war. From an evolutionary perspective, this variety of dominance tendencies is plausible. As with any normal distribution of behaviors, there would be extremes. There would be people with extreme dominance motivation, and those with extreme submissive behavior, but the majority of people would fall somewhere in between and engage in more comparable dominant and submissive interactions. In situations of scarcity or inequality of resource distribution, the tendencies for dominant behaviors are amplified. For example, antisocial behaviors are more common in situations of disadvantage.

These theories assume that externalizing behaviors, and specifically, antisocial and psychopathic traits of personality, would be extreme forms of dominance motivation. Indeed, these disorder categories list many symptoms that are reminiscent of dominance features, including opposition to authority, aggression, disinhibition, decreased empathy, and power-seeking. It is impossible to separate the environment from all behaviors and mental health disorders, but even more so in the case of externalizing symptoms. Poverty, family dynamics, and influence from peers who do not follow social norms can have an impact on the risk for externalizing disorders.

Measures

One may think of dominance, and social rank and comparisons, as unimportant in mental health given that we usually do not openly discuss them in our daily clinical work. However, if we take a closer look, we will see that many of the existing scales we use measure dominance to some degree, and that there are other scales that measure it as a main and independent focus of evaluation.

An example is the Iowa-Netherlands Comparison Orientation Scale, which measures the tendency or orientation of an individual to make social comparisons, and it is considered a measure of concern for dominance. It examines how much people are tuned into cues of power, which is characteristic of people concerned with dominance motivation.[13] Beyond this scale, several personality traits related to dominance are embedded and measured in other scales. For example, the Multidimensional Personality Questionnaire has a social potency subscale and the Psychopathy Checklist-Revised Fearless Dominance, or Arrogant and Deceitful Interpersonal Style factor,[14] which have been associated with externalizing behaviors and with substance use.[15]

The dominance system

Social rank also has an emergence in psychopathology, or the study of mental disorders. As we have seen, humans are driven by dynamics of dominance. Johnson and colleagues call this tendency the dominance behavioral system, which encompasses biological, psychological, and behavioral components related to motivation and dominant and submissive behaviors. This system's goal is to control social and material resources, and is associated with clinical diagnoses.[16] As humans experience life, they assess their ability to achieve power and create internal working models that define their self-concept and guide them in strategies related to their goal of acquiring (or resisting) power for their own benefit.[17]

'Dominance motivation' is an individual's drive to pursue power and dominance. This motivation seems dichotomic, in that some people avoid and are uncomfortable with power while others strive for it. In reality, it is probably dynamic and context-dependent. Life goals of wealth accumulation, fame, and more sexual activity would be predicted by this type of dominance motivation.[18,19] Individuals will engage in dominant behavior to achieve power. Power is the ability to keep physical and/or social resources and distribute punishment to others. These dominance behaviors involve aggression and on the opposite end, avoidance of conflict and submission.

In non-human primates, dominant and submissive behaviors are based on dyadic interactions in which one member signals aggression and the other responds with submissive behaviors.[20] Humans, however, engage not only in competitive behaviors, but also in prosocial behaviors such as creating coalitions and befriending those in power, as well as being assertive, confident, and also aggressive in order to achieve dominance. This has been represented in two axes: a dominance/submissiveness and a warmth/hostility axis.[21] For example, high dominance and high hostility may involve taking resources and threatening others, intimidating, and being aggressive, whereas dominance and warmth would involve alliances, cooperation, and resource exchange, as well as engagement in socially-valued behaviors. Overall, prosocial strategies are more effective than aggression in acquiring and maintaining power.[22]

Most individuals can adapt their dominance motivation and behaviors to the context, as maintaining their power may depend on it. Humans have different levels of status in different settings. For example, a skilled recreational soccer player may have high status and receive recognition in the soccer field, but hold a job in which he has no autonomy. The same thing happens in adolescents. Some students ranking low in popularity at their school may hold a high degree of respect in their Jusitsu gym, or may be winning medals in gymnastics. A man could feel powerful with his children and wife at home, but not so much with his boss and colleagues at work. Or vice versa, a man or woman may have a very powerful position at their job, but not at home. However, some individuals are unable to shift across contexts and their always-dominant or always-submissive behaviors may be maladaptive. If the same man expects to be always dominant, he may encounter many difficulties in his job, or with his wife, depending on his boss' or his wife's reaction to his motivation for dominance.

Power, or lack of power, is linked not just to psychological but also to physiological outcomes. When individuals are powerful, they can access rewards, and their motivation and the behaviors to achieve those rewards increase.[23] This makes the powerful more likely to have positive emotions, confidence, expressivity, and more rapid cognitive processing, but also more impulsivity. They may also read into equivocal situations and think of those as sexual opportunities, and they may be more likely to violate social norms or be less sensitive, attentive, and compassionate towards others. Examples of this impulsivity abound amongst the powerful of our days. Meanwhile, those without power are more vulnerable and more reactive to threat when trying to reach rewards, often over-estimating other's perceived rejection. In other words, they may think they will be rejected when in reality, they are not even considered.

Because of the internalized ideas about dominance and subordinance, individuals experience emotions such as anger or shame when their power is threatened, and these emotions will translate into behaviors. For example, those experiencing shame or feeling inferior to others will show an avert gaze, or poor eye contact. The reactions will change depending on the individual's motivation for dominance. Some people are more motivated to hold positions of dominance, whereas others feel more comfortable and thrive in subordinate positions. The latter ones may even have a decline in performance when placed in positions of power.[24]

This dominance behavioral system is robust as it has been assessed through self-report measures (by asking people), observation (by watching them), and biological indices (by measuring their physiological markers). During observations, some children in ages as young as toddlerhood show a tendency to succeed in taking an object from a peer when faced with conflict.[25] This is all to say that some people will be primed with wanting to dominate others from an early age, while others will be more comfortable with submission. As contexts vary, so will the individual's predispositions to dominance.

Holding power

Humans can take almost any opportunity to dominate. For example, people can hold power when they are able to publicly shame others. Interviews by media figures that are focused on devaluing the interviewee as opposed to discussing the content and answers to the questions posed are a good example. The interviewer can decide to do an eye roll or change the tone, and if the spectator does not understand the topic at debate, this could be enough to put the interviewee in a position of less power. I invite anyone to see these dynamics in any or many of the YouTube channels or podcasts that have democratized 'professional' journalism. These interactions are so common that taking even a very small step back in any work meeting, family dinner, or friend gathering can provide plenty of information about who holds the power and what they do to keep it. Humans have become very subtle in the ways they hold power. What one does with this information is up to them, but at least, one can be aware and participate in these dynamics with open eyes.

Adolescents can be held in positions of less power when peers decide to share their personal information or confessions with others. Some may recall situations in which someone used information as power when they were teenagers. Maybe someone tried to get information from you, which you shared in confidence, and the next thing you see is this same information being disseminated to a larger group. Now imagine the same, but the sharing happens instantaneously and with hundreds, potentially millions of people. This is the case of sexting. The number of girls who send nude pictures to their boyfriends who then decide to share them with a few friends, in an escalation that leads to the pictures becoming 'viral,' is not insignificant. Or worse, the person with your picture decides to blackmail you into doing things you do not want to do in order to keep the pictures private.

It is not only the experience of having low power that matters, it is also the desire for power. Think about your school class. Some people were satisfied with their lives at the time, and others were very future-oriented and never felt what they had was enough. Our culture often talks about achievement as a goal, instead of a characteristic. In competitive societies, people may feel happy with their present selves and are often shamed for it. It is interesting that current trends about acceptance, well-being, and mindfulness are rejecting the idea of living in the future as the single right path for everyone, and instead make the focus the present. It is good to have options that allow a person to pursue this competitive drive, but it is also important to know that not everyone desires the same type of life. People are different.

Psychopathological presentations and social rank

Some authors have explained areas of psychopathology from the perspective of dominance. Narcissistic personality disorder is a presentation of self-centeredness and defensiveness towards signs of threat to one's self-esteem that leads to difficulties in interpersonal relationships. The Narcissistic Personality Inventory is a scale that includes exploitative behavior and leadership subscales related to dominance motivation, displaying the role of social rank dynamics in narcissism. Narcissistic people also tend to have a perception of their own power that is inflated and at odds with their real power. They are more prone to experience shame when their defense mechanisms fail to achieve power that preserves their self-esteem. An example would be a politician perceiving to have more power and admiration than the reality would suggest, losing an election and experiencing shame, and then proceeding to question the results of that election.

Another area of study between dominance and psychopathology is the one related to mania. Some authors have suggested there are similarities between symptoms of mania (i.e., grandiosity, hypersexual behavior) and dominance. However, for anyone who has witnessed people presenting the drastic changes in mood of the cycles of mania and depression in bipolar disorder, and the extreme symptoms which often involve psychosis, it would be difficult to imagine mania as a purely psychologically-driven power-seeking behavior, unless mania is understood as excessively heightened mood and not a symptom of bipolar disorder. People afflicted with bipolar disorder have little control over their symptoms. While they can manage to mitigate the symptoms to a certain degree by taking preventative measures, such as modifying their sleep pattern, the state entered when presenting these symptoms is not one in which the individual has much control. Some research has found that even in states of remission, individuals previously diagnosed with bipolar disorder reported very ambitious goals of fame and wealth, which have been associated with dominance motivation.[16] However, since there were no longitudinal studies on the topic, it would be difficult to conclude that these perceptions and goals are not related to the symptoms themselves. It could also be that people with more need for power may be more sensitive to changes in perceived power, and that these changes in perceived power could trigger mood changes, which may appear to others as depressive or hypomanic episodes. From a clinical perspective, though, true manic episodes are cyclic and episodic, responsive to pharmacological treatment, and too driven by internal versus external triggers for the explanation of dominance motivation as a driver of mania to be plausible.

In the case of depression, and given the current range of presentations that are considered depression, there is much more support for the role of dominance and power in both human and animal studies. I say 'current range of presentations' because the traditional clinical view of depression as a major depressive disorder, with symptoms of low mood or anhedonia and at least four other symptoms, including neurovegetative symptoms such as appetite and sleep problems, is different from a 'depressive disorder' or dysthymia, which require less symptoms and less acuity respectively, even though all are considered depression.

Several social theories of depression already mentioned involve forced subordination as a mechanism contributing to depression. In competitive situations, showing signs of defeat through submissive behaviors communicates to the dominant individual that there is acceptance of subordinate status by the defeated individual who no longer has an intention to continue the competition. These subordinate behaviors have a purpose. They reduce punishment, avoid more competition or aggression directed towards the defeated individual, and may even elicit sympathy and help from others. Theories of subordination in depression assume that while these behaviors are part of everyday life, what leads to depression is the lack of ability to escape or terminate the situation of submission. Depression is highly correlated with a subjective sense of subordination and feelings of inferiority in both clinical and non-clinical samples, as well as a tendency to experience shame.[26] In animals, social defeat can induce symptoms that correlate to the depressive symptoms experienced by humans, such as loss of sleep, weight, motivation, and interest in reward, and more social withdrawal. In childhood, experiences of shame, submissiveness, and subordination can be similar. Traumatic life events that could be experienced as defeat are major triggers for depression. Finally, the broader social context can also predict depression. For example, those living below the poverty line have almost four times the risk of depression than those in higher income brackets.[27]

Individuals who try to achieve high status tend to show more depressive symptoms. However, more recent studies have shown that what leads to depression is not as much an appetite to achieve exceptionally high or higher status than others, as it is the avoidance of submissive roles and inferiority. In other words, trying to avoid inferiority is more strongly associated with depression than being highly competitive.

Biologically, testosterone levels that are abnormally low are associated with mild depression in older adult men. These symptoms of depression respond to testosterone supplements in some studies. In fact, testosterone had been used as an antidepressant many decades ago.[28] One high-quality study, a randomized controlled trial, showed that citalopram, a selective-reuptake inhibitor commonly used to treat clinical depression, was associated with more dominance in interpersonal interactions.[29] You don't have to be depressed to show submission during interactions.[30] While it would feel more honest if we didn't, many of us interact in very different ways with our superiors than we do with those who we perceive as equal or lower in the social rank. Culture can affect these dynamics of power. In some cultures, superiors are to be respected and they hold immense power. European and American universities differ vastly in these power dynamics. Anyone with experiences in both settings will easily notice these differences. American professors are much more likely to be blamed for the shortcomings of the students in their system and expected to fill any knowledge gap with improved education techniques. Conversely, in Europe, the student may never even have a conversation with the professor outside of the classroom and is always expected to catch up with the work. If the student fails, it is seen as a failure of the student to keep up with the content delivered by the teacher, and not a failure of the teacher to teach.

Anxiety, in particular social anxiety, may also be related to dominance hierarchies. When people with social anxiety interact in groups, they tend to focus on avoiding rejection, are fearful of being excluded or humiliated by members with more social power, and may be more focused on social hierarchies in detriment to connectedness, and be more prone to social comparison. They may also be more sensitive to cues of dominance. For example, people with social anxiety are more sensitive to angry faces that cue threat compared to people with no social anxiety. Those with social anxiety disorder are also more prone to compare themselves to others negatively, report more shame, especially related to how they may be perceived socially, and engage in more submissive behaviors compared to controls with no anxiety. An experimental study with college students showed that losing in a competition that lasted 25 seconds increased anxiety levels, especially if the student was anxious at baseline. Those who present more motivation towards social dominance may also react more strongly to threats to their social power. However, as previously said, this may be due to a fear of inferiority more than a desire for superiority.[26]

Testosterone has also been studied in the context of anxiety for two reasons: because it enhances the function of the neurotransmitter gamma-aminobutyric acid (GABA) (a central nervous system inhibitor and a target of anxiolytic medications), and because in animals, the administration of testosterone reduces behaviors associated with threat-sensitivity. Testosterone levels diminish with age, with removal of the gonads, and in certain genetic variations, and this leads to threat sensitivity. The administration of testosterone reduces this threat sensitivity. However, the results in human studies are more mixed and no conclusions can be drawn at this time. What is clearer is the likely association between testosterone and the sensitivity to social threat. In an experimental study in which participants were designed to lose or win by a large margin in a competitive task, men with social anxiety presented a more abrupt decline in testosterone levels after losing, compared to controls, but these differences were not observed in women.[31]

Both anxiety and depression have been considered in the context of dominance. Yet, anxiety is related to dominance even when controlling for the effects of depression, while depression is no longer related to dominance when controlling for anxiety, suggesting that anxiety may hold a central role. Developmentally, children with anxiety have a higher risk of becoming adolescents and adults with depression. And biologically, chronic anxiety elevates stress hormones, which can lead to disease, including depression. Depression would rise in the context of entrapment, hopelessness, and defeat. Overall, there appears to be very good evidence for a role of dominant behavior in externalizing disorders, and somewhat in narcissism and mania, while depression and anxiety are more associated with submissive behaviors.

Dominance orientation could be considered a risk factor for psychopathology, the same way as we consider hereditability as predisposing individuals to certain disorders. Social factors that would lead to one versus another type of disorder would also need to be considered. For example, the same person with an orientation towards dominance may present more antisocial behaviors if experiencing a hostile environment with scarcity, narcissistic traits if growing in another more supportive and coddled environment, or more social anxiety and depression in the context of interpersonal stressors. There is also more research needed to understand how dominance motivation develops. Some research suggests that traumatic experiences in childhood may be associated with social comparison and dominance motivation in adulthood.

While one might think that the games of hierarchies start after the acquisition of language, a visit to a preschool program would suggest otherwise. Small children's power games may not be sophisticated enough in the eyes of an office worker used to a higher level of dominance disguised as office politics, but they also exist and are very alive in preschoolers. As early as eight months of age, infants engage in power struggles over toy possession. Usually, the most powerful are simply strong individuals who are bigger in body size. Children in preschool engage in games in which they reward the dominant peer as a way to ingratiate the one who holds the resources.[32]

Dominance motivation can even be reflected in the therapeutic relationship. For example, providing structured therapies and strict directives may trigger angry reactions and resistance in clients, and affect the therapeutic relationship. On the other hand, those who tend to be more submissive may re-enact these proclivities in the therapeutic relationship. Therapy can be used to help those with dominance motivation channel their impulses from aggression or negative reactions when their power is threatened into more prosocial ways, supporting their leadership through connectedness with others. Those with a tendency for subordinate behaviors may continue to present them as a strategy to avoid conflict in therapy. Therapy interventions that include small moments and experiences of mastery may help remove the client momentarily from the persistent experience of subordination and explore other ways to engage with the world.

Biology of dominance motivation

Biologically, natural (and not administered) testosterone seems to be associated with dominance motivation. Consistently and across settings like laboratories, college dorms, and prisons, those individuals with higher basal testosterone present more dominant behaviors. At the same time, individuals with low testosterone levels feel more comfortable maintaining a low-status position and experience more stress and discomfort when placed in higher-status positions.[16]

While high testosterone has also been associated with aggression, overall, this aggression seems mediated by dominance motivation. In other words, testosterone would not make someone aggressive per se, but would push that person to be more motivated to dominate others, which may or may not cause them to fight for that dominance with aggression. Interestingly, testosterone is also related to a greater self-perceived power, reward sensitivity, confidence, and social approach behaviors, including greater sexual activity and infidelity, and less sensitivity to threat and loss, all of which are likely to contribute to a lower quality of relationships with partners and children.[33]

Testosterone is also associated with externalizing behaviors and substance use. For example, a study found that boys presenting higher levels of testosterone at age 12 or 14 had higher likelihood of experiencing alcohol use at age 22 when they also presented dominance behaviors.[34] During puberty, the levels of testosterone in males increase much more than the levels in females. Girls and young adult women's levels are only one-third those of boys and young adult men. With age, the gap in testosterone between men and women narrows significantly. At the same time, testosterone levels could be increased in situations of power. Whether as cause or consequence, these changes in hormone levels explain to some degree the differences in depression and externalizing behaviors by sex.

Overall, the associations of power and testosterone are mixed, however, because these depend not only on sex and age, but also on the environment. Additionally, the studies on testosterone levels and dominance have mostly been conducted in adolescence, a time of rapid increase in testosterone levels due to puberty changes. The time when a person goes through puberty may also influence these processes, and those reaching puberty earlier may be more prone to present risky behaviors. As with everything in behavioral sciences, a dance between biology and the environment will be the key. For a boy with high testosterone levels, the difference between having deviant peers versus not could translate into presenting conduct disorder symptoms versus being a leader in a school club.

Testosterone also acts inhibiting cortisol and making it less reactive to stress. It works in conjunction with dopamine, amplifying the activity of the nucleus acumens, involved in reward. It is also associated with increases in serotonin function, which is decreased in situations of social defeat and is associated with depression and suicide. The opposite is true: an increase in serotonin function increases dominance behavior. As seen here, many dynamics in biology come together to determine rank predisposition and outcomes.

Dominance in social media comparisons

Many features of social media facilitate social comparisons. For that reason social comparisons have gained interest as a potential contributor to low mood in adolescents who use social media, and they deserve closer attention.[35] Yet, even before the advent of social media, decades of research exploring social comparisons have uncovered both the inevitability of social comparisons and the potential to modify them.

Social comparisons, social status, and depression may be associated through mechanisms that involve self-esteem. Social comparison orientation represents the inclination to compare one's skills or abilities with those of others. People with a greater tendency to compare to others may tend to evaluate themselves by using information about people who are similar to them both online and offline, trying to seek feedback and reassurance. However, this process of socially comparing may put them at risk for low mood, depending on how they make these comparisons. At the same time, depression and low self-esteem may also contribute to individuals searching for additional information about others. This leads to a feedback loop of social comparisons and lower mood, and possibly even depression. A tendency to make unfavorable social comparisons may not always be maladaptive as it could serve as a strategy of low gain and low risk, in which the individual has less to gain but also less to lose by not exposing themselves to competitive situations.[36] It is also possible that those who are able to maintain a high self-esteem do so by challenging themselves less or having a less diverse network of members, reducing the possibilities for social comparisons.[37]

Whether one makes social comparisons downward (with people who are worse off) versus upward (with those who are better off), social comparisons give social status information and affect mood. Research on social comparisons and social media use in adolescents is still nascent. However, individuals with a higher orientation towards social comparisons have been shown to relay lower self-esteem after comparing themselves with others on social media. After viewing social media, those with higher social comparison orientation are also more likely to make upward social comparisons.[38] Upward social comparisons are associated with depression.[39]

Comparing with others may be needed for individuals considered to be outside of the dominant group as they may be more sensitive to potential social threats. Consequently, there may be differences in the tendency to engage in social comparison depending on the social status of an individual within a group and when comparing to other groups. The reference groups of comparison may include close groups like friends and family, or comparisons at the societal level, and even across societies, as well as across time, and they may depend on the individual's personal characteristics.[40] Women who engage in frequent Facebook use report being more likely to compare themselves to others, and frequent Facebook use is associated with negative affect.[41] Likewise, high school students engaging in social media comparisons and feedback-seeking behaviors may form distorted perceptions of peers, which affects their self-esteem.[42]

There is no question that adolescents, as sponges with open eyes scanning the social world to understand it and fit in it, engage in these comparisons as part of the process of building their own identity, which also makes them more vulnerable to related mood changes. Socio-demographic factors such as socio-economic status,[43] sex at birth, race, and age combined with culture influence who people compare with and their self-esteem.[40] This combination of sex and age in the predisposition to make social comparisons and a cultural context that promotes these comparisons, makes adolescent girls particularly vulnerable to engage in these comparisons. The reader can take a journey through the ads and influencers that pop up in a teenage girl feed on Instagram or TikTok to know what makes them tick.

Social media companies, as any for-profit organization, have one goal: financial gain. Since users do not pay a fee to participate in them, the companies aim to keep users engaged for as long as possible so that the user spends more time seeing ads that provide revenue to these companies. The way to keep people engaged in social media sites is by offering material that is of their interest. For parents, one way to see what is in that social media-using child or teen's mind is watching the child scroll down their social media feed for only five minutes and seeing the content of that feed. Certainly, this is often much easier and more effective than trying to ask the confused adolescent what is in their mind and expecting that they will share any of their thoughts with the parent.

This is a time of increased social inequities. These are more obvious now that people can compare to others who are far away with the use of social media. Youth may not have the perspective, experience, and maturity to understand the breath of the lives people live, and may tend to overly focus on those that appear to be 'better lives' presented on social media sites; those of people who go viral, get more shares, and more ads. With a more globalized and technology-oriented environment, the understanding of these social network-based social comparisons is expanding and reviving the overall understanding of social comparisons, which had been studied for decades before the advent of social media.[44]

Systemic changes on social media platforms may be a way to help mitigate the effects of comparisons made on social media and preserve youth's mental health. For example, removing social media features that contribute to positive reinforcement, such as the 'like' button, may benefit youth by decreasing their social media use and their identification with a certain status based on the number of likes and shares.[45] Limiting ads and diversifying rather than continuing to feed narrow content that is interesting to the child, are other approaches to make it easier for the user to disengage. At the same time, we can use social media as a window to understand adolescents internal processes. After all, if social media companies are getting to understand our adolescents enough to sell them products, we as parents, teachers, and clinicians can also use the sites to understand how to best help adolescents navigate a very interesting, but tumultuous period of their lives.

Keeping children from experiencing social differences, whether on social media or in real life does not do them any service. Our modern societies have adopted a culture of fear of competition that keeps children believing they are all equal in order to protect their feelings and self-esteem. However, that leads to people being unable to accept differences. What we need is children who learn to continue working towards their own individual goals of self-improvement and self-acceptance, all while facing potential failure. Many studies have looked at how upward and downward social comparisons have different purposes and effects. We compare downwards to feel better about ourselves or present ourselves to others in good ways, but we compare upwards to motivate ourselves to be better. We may not want to get better at something and that is ok, we can then just continue to compare downwards. However, keeping children from comparing themselves with any point of reference that is higher in the social status ladder could delude them into thinking they are the best at everything and deprive them of reasons to motivate themselves to become better at things that matter to them, if that is what they wish to do. The high school success who only had opportunities to compare his soccer skills with peers in a less competitive environment may struggle when moving to college and not making the college team. Gaining perspective about the breath of competition is hard, but necessary.

The Netflix show 'Break Point' features the best tennis players in the world fighting to stay or keep their ranking position. Some players are fighting to get to the top ten, and others strive to be or stay as the number one. Others just want to remain within the top one hundred or be the best they can be. When I started watching, I believed I would learn all the skills necessary to be a better tennis player. I did not. In reality, the show is about the psychological processes and emotional turmoil these tennis players go through, which are not that different from those we, regular people, experience. The first-ranked tennis player in the U.S. is Taylor Fritz. Being first of a country is a laudable achievement, if you ask me. Yet, Fritz spends much of his time comparing himself with other players from around the world as his goal is to become first in the world. The first in the world will have to be able to maintain that position and accumulate more titles. All of the players featured, when they fail, question themselves and their value as tennis players. The drive to improve and remain on top is what makes them the greatest. We can certainly learn from them on how to recover and find a way to improve or compete at the highest level, if that is our motivation. If it is not, we will likely be spared of the pain of climbing the ladder. It is a choice we make. The key is knowing when to make that choice and how to make it, so that we are free to be who we are, the one who climbs to the top of the tree, the one who basks in the sun or eats a banana on a lower branch, and all the ones in between. All of them are, or should be, living beings worthy of good lives.

10 What to do

Examples of good use of status dynamics

What can adolescents do?

The interviews with adolescents give us some ideas about what helps them navigate the inevitable social hierarchies. Expanding opportunities for social comparison could give them perspective about the plight of other people in the world. However, sometimes, reducing opportunities for social comparison is better, especially when comparisons are made with curated depictions of a person or persona on social media sites. In-person interactions versus mostly virtual social connections help people see the reality of not just an unfiltered aspect of a person's looks or otherwise curated life, but also the nuances of other people's dimensions of status. A girl who compares with a friend's flawless physical presentation on social media will see her friend as more equal when her friend is not using social media 'filters' or when she confides on the effort she put forth to achieve her perfect look. This natural process becomes a challenge when the opportunities for real life interactions are reduced, and it is a good reason to encourage them.

Additionally, exercises to retrain the brain may have a role in reducing the distress caused by social comparisons. Some interventions and smartphone applications (or 'apps') have actually started to include *mindfulness exercises* on social comparisons. Mindfulness consists on raising awareness about one's own feelings, thoughts and behaviors, and emphasizes staying in the moment and being non-judgmental.[1] These exercises help the person be more aware of the type of social comparisons they engage in, and how these comparisons make them feel.

In addition to being aware, what if we taught children to be grateful very early in life? A simple way to be more grateful is by focusing on the positive rather than the negative things about ourselves and our environment through *gratitude exercises*. Humans have evolved to focus on and remember those things that are threatening in order to protect ourselves from danger. This process keeps us aware of threats to our life, our status, or both, as they are often linked. This orientation towards threat is helpful for survival, but can be harmful if we let it take over completely. We find emotional or mental comfort in attending to things that appear natural or brought in by inertia. But just like we may find more comfort in sitting on a sofa with a warm cup of coffee, but can teach our bodies through exercise to tolerate running a 5-kilometer race on a cold winter morning, which is good for our health,

DOI: 10.4324/9781003535942-10

we can also train our brains to focus on positive things. A psychologist from Duke University, Dr. Bryan Sexton, came up with an elegant and simple exercise that turned out to be effective in improving well-being. This simple exercise consists of training to focus one's attention on the positive things in our lives by asking the participants to think of three things that went well and the person's role in the positive outcome at the end of each day for at least two weeks.[2]

Another way to do this is by using *downward comparisons*, meaning that you try to compare yourself with people who are worse off than you. While I would discourage anyone to judge or laugh at someone who is worse off than them in any aspect, knowing that you are not alone in your despair can actually be helpful. This is why deep and meaningful connections are important; they allow people to know other people in their entirety, with their flaws and their potential. It is hard to know people fully on social media, where most tend to present the best version of themselves or amplify only those things that are most flattering. Because of the well-known potential for social media to expand opportunities for social comparisons, some studies are suggesting taking breaks from social media platforms. These studies are mostly focused on decreasing time spent on social media and improving wellness, and not necessarily on social comparisons, but they study a promising intervention that gives the young individual the mental space and the time to gain a broader perspective.

To lead healthier lives, we can also look at the lives of centenarians, or people living beyond 100 years of age. A significant number of people in the world are able to live past one century. While genetic predisposition is involved in how long a person lives, this only accounts for one-fifth of the explanation of a long life. The rest of it is environmental.[3] The *Blue Zones* study looked at places in the world with the highest numbers of centenarians and found that there were commonalities in certain groups across various geographical settings including faraway places like Sardinia, Italy, and Ikaria, Greece (in Europe), Japan (in Asia), Costa Rica (in Central America), and Loma Linda (in California, U.S.). People in these communities had in common that they moved naturally in their daily lives, walking to places instead of using cars, and doing manual activities like yard work with little help from machinery. They had a purpose, or a reason to wake up in the morning; and they had outlets or activities that allowed them to relax, be that napping or praying. They also had the habit of not eating until feeling completely full. Instead, they would only eat to 80% of their capacity, eating smaller meals as the day progressed, and avoiding eating later in the evening. This practice is very close to the fasting practices of some religions and the new dietary intermittent fasting craze. In these societies, meat was eaten in moderation, as the diets were mostly plant-based. They also moderated their alcohol intake and drank regularly as opposed to binging on alcohol. They tended to belong to a community, but prioritized their family, keeping parents and grandparents living nearby or in their home, which appears to also be good for the health of the children.[4] And they had a healthy tribe or a small group of friends with which they would engage in activities such as fishing together, like men do in Japan, or meeting for coffee, like women do in Spanish cities.

Hierarchies in group psychotherapy

The applications of dominance and submission extend to every type of interpersonal relationship. This includes the relationship between therapist and client, and also between clients in the setting of group therapy. James Kennedy and Roy Mackenzie discussed the evolution of relationships of dominance in therapeutic groups in 1986. They argued that social groups develop with a purpose and that there is an initial tendency to show submissive behaviors that favor the creation of cohesiveness, and a later tendency towards conflict or tension that promotes the establishment of stable hierarchies.[5] Understanding these dynamics can be helpful for therapy group leaders to maintain the group intact, or avoid its dissolution.

As we have seen, staying in a group benefits primates by providing protection, survival, or increased opportunities for reproduction. When groups begin to form, both animal and human primates display submissive behaviors to appease other members, often with body gestures like lowering one's body stature or avoiding eye contact. These submissive behaviors may not be enough to control potential conflict and maintain cohesion, and the intervention by third parties may be needed. For example, if a member in a group is being too aggressive or the conflict is becoming too intense so as to put group cohesion at danger, either a leader, or in their absence, another member of the group, or a third child in a group of friends, may intervene to keep the group intact. Flexible patterns that stimulate both cohesion and dominance to create group stability can also benefit therapeutic groups. Lieberman and colleagues described a U-shaped relationship between control and permissiveness of the leader of the group, in which both too much and too little control would create pathological groups. Groups that are too structured and authoritarian, and too disorganized or with too little structure would be problematic.[6] This approach is similar to the parenting styles in which authoritarian and permissive parenting also lead to relatively poorer outcomes than authoritative parenting, in which there is structure and limits, but also warmth and autonomy. Leaders who are so intrusive and confrontative that they force emotional interactions can contribute to group disintegration.

The engagement stage of group formation requires the individual to be accepted by the group, and to see some advantage to being in the group. In this first stage, there is a general positive emotional tone, and members try to find commonalities and avoid conflict. Among non-human primates, there are rituals, such as certain facial grimaces, mutual grooming, playing, and even mating, that inhibit conflict. Even among preschoolers, there is a period of calm before conflict starts to rise after the group is more established and aggression becomes more common. This period may last months, or a day. In psychotherapy groups, the themes that tend to arise in this first phase are about the similarities among the members. For example, the members will emphasize if they come from the same location, or if they have experienced similar stressors. After this initial stage, there is a new 'differentiation stage' in which competition and conflict arise to clarify group hierarchies and develop more stability in the system. During this stage, there is more anxiety and, unless there is conflict resolution, the continued competitiveness will lead to the dissolution of the group. Members will be more comfortable noting the differences among themselves. The group leader will need to moderate by allowing and accepting differences. Once the hierarchy is accepted, there is more stability and cooperation within the group.

These dynamics become evident when new members are introduced or leave the group, as there is more stress, and members will regress to more aggressive behaviors in order to set up new hierarchies. When loss of rank in a member leads to depression and avoidance of confrontation of superiors, other members may feel pity and protect the depressed individual to maintain the group intact. Members who are depressed may also show irritability towards lower-ranking individuals. This prevents them from falling to the bottom and disengaging from the group. Another aspect is scapegoating: the weakest individuals lose most in conflict situations and they may tend to act aggressively towards others of lower rank. Sometimes group members can unify by directing their aggression to the scapegoat. An example would be 'Bubbles' from 'The Wire.' Played by actor Andre Royo, 'Bubbles' is a weaker, less aggressive and assertive individual, who wanders between police informant and the hostile life of the streets of Baltimore, carrying a shopping cart. At times, he is robbed of the little money he makes with his sales by young people on the street, who are themselves of lower rank than the adults who dominate street life. 'Bubbles' medicates his agony with heroin. He is often beaten and bullied. He does not entirely belong to the group, and is much of the time on his own, except for when he cares for a boy whom he loves, but whom he treats harshly. 'Bubbles' is the scapegoat in the streets of Baltimore. Another example is the adult having a bad day at work and coming home to treat their partner or children badly. Called *displacement* in therapy, this is the process in which negative feelings are transferred to someone less threatening and lower in the social rank. Scapegoating also involves targeting a non-threatening, lower-ranking member with aggression when confronting another higher up in the ladder is riskier. In these situations, the leader of the group would need to take an active position. Finally, there is an action of inhibiting one's own cognitive abilities and behaviors when in the presence of a superior. When someone is clearly in charge, other potential leaders will back down and wait for their turn by acting as less intelligent or capable. In therapy, rotating the role of leader among the members of the group could be a method to help avoid this stagnation.

Dominance is also relevant in couple's therapy.[7] It is involved in understanding which member of the couple speaks more in a conversation, who introduces new topics of conversation, and who decides when the other person speaks and influences communication.[8] Again, as mentioned for group therapy, the therapist has a role in facilitating this interaction and in a way, affecting the dynamics of dominance by breaking up previous patterns. Dominance and submission have clinical and therapeutic implications. For instance, when one of the members of a couple in conflict presents depressive symptoms, the story the members tell each other can be contradictory. The depressed member may blame the other member of the couple for the struggles experienced. Understanding the power dynamics may help the therapist intervene and break this cycle, allowing the person with depression to maintain the relationship and receive support, and vice versa, instead of ending the relationship.

Motivational interviewing as an obliteration of status differences

Regarding individual therapy, Dr. William Miller, an expert in motivational interviewing (MI) suggests that dominance dynamics may have a role in the cross-cultural success of this type of therapy. MI is widely successful in treating substance use disorders across age groups, and supported as an approach to changing any type of addictive behavior, even those not related to substances.[9] Hundreds of scientific studies have proven its success in treating addictions. However, MI is more a philosophy or approach to interviewing than a detailed manually-based structured intervention. In MI, the therapist attempts to bring the patient or client from an early stage of behavior change in which the individual does not recognize the behavior as harmful and does not feel motivated (or feels ambivalent) to change it, to a stage of preparation or action, in which the individual is committed to changing the behavior. Words used to describe this type of intervention include collaborative, guiding, balancing listening and advice, respectful, and curious. Words like 'spirit' or the way of being with people, acceptance, compassion, and partnership have also been used to describe the interactions between therapist and client in MI, and denote a relationship process that stays away from directing or telling the patient what to do, or how to think or behave, and instead focuses on positioning oneself as a therapist at the same level as the client's, giving the client ownership and power to change the behavior. Any behavior change requires the person to want to change the behavior, so awakening the motivation in them is a big piece of the process of change. The power of MI is hard to understate. Its effectiveness is cross-cultural and cross-continental. There are published controlled trials from all over the world, suggesting it touches something innate to humans, regardless of language, location, political regime, and philosophy. Of course, that essential and innate human condition is status.

Even Miller admits there is no theory driving MI or a clear understanding of why it works. It arose from observing practice and then suggesting the ways in which it worked. In other words, with apologies to cooking experts: the secret recipe for the delicious dish of MI is not a written recipe to be implemented, or a study of chemical reactions that theoretically would make the dish taste good. It is closer to a learned experience after observing your grandmother work in the kitchen and spending the time training yourself to put that little extra in the dish that the book did not consider. While cooking is not my forte, I have seen enough cooks in my family to know that the 'spirit' in cooking involves a dynamic back and forth, and not just a unidirectional process. That 'magic' in MI, according to Miller, is a curtailed power dynamic or the effect of an absence of dominance.[9]

Miller describes *psychological reactance* as the resistance to change or to be compliant when given advice to change. This phenomenon had been noted by Carl Rogers, a humanistic psychologist and psychotherapy researcher known for the person-therapy approach. Rogers proposed that all humans have a reality or experience of the world, that the interaction with that environment and other individuals drives the structure of the 'self,' and that the best way to understand individuals is from the reference point of the individuals's themselves.[10] It is natural to resist changing our essence as humans. Relationships in therapy are inherently hierarchical, as the therapist may be perceived as being in a position of dominance. *Psychological reactance* would be a resistance to the imposition by a more dominant individual. This resistance likely functions unconsciously, and it may cause interventions such as punishment in addictions to be counterproductive to the goal of changing behaviors. Compliance in therapy would be seen as submission to the dominant individual, in this case, the therapist. In MI, the therapist gets to the same level as the client's, erasing the hierarchy of the therapeutic relationship. Unfortunately, psychotherapists and psychiatrists often label and grade their patients on whether they are being 'compliant' or not. Are they taking their medication? Are they doing their homework? Instead of using it as a label, 'compliance' could be seen as taking the temperature on how ready or close the patient is to changing a specific behavior.

The power struggles between adolescents and their parents are similar. Adolescents' reactions to being punished or to rigid parental rules can lead to more opposition and resistance than more leveled relationships. Essential to this reality is the approach suggested not only with toddlers and adolescents who present peak oppositionality in their development and resistance to direction, but also with children and adolescents with oppositional defiant disorder. This approach consists of finding a middle ground while keeping consistent rules, as suggested in Dr. Ross Greene's The Explosive Child.[11] Individuals' differences in personality traits like agreeableness will determine their resistance to change. Situational differences, such as being in a context where hierarchies are pronounced or competition is strong for power positions, may also affect psychological reactance.

The most valuable times in psychotherapy are those in which the client has a realization about a pattern of behavior in which he or she has engaged and that has long gone unnoticed or been ignored as a problem. Another key point is the moment the client experiences the dilemma of wanting to change that behavior but is unsure if he or she will be driving the change or if it is the therapist who will be driving it. In the latter instance, the client is much less likely to change that behavior. Therapists often talk about the need for the patient to be the one to come to the conclusion that they need to make a change. Any worthy therapy supervisor will tell you that you did a good job as a therapist when the client is the one who after many sessions realizes the need to change some pattern of behavior that you as a therapist had already noticed weeks before. The supervisor will say something like 'and she [the patient, and not the therapist] was the one who said it!' to which the supervisee will respond with a sense of pride, as walking along the client to that point of awareness is the biggest prize and recognition for a therapist.

These examples show that, in essence, therapy is abounding in dominance dynamics that play a prominent role in the patient's progress. Miller goes on to compare cross-cultural methods of resistance when humans have been faced with oppressive forces that have given rise to religions such as Buddhism and Christianity. More modern examples are the non-violent resistance movements of the 20th century led by Mahatma Gandhi and Martin Luther King. All of them intentionally placed themselves in situations in which they resisted without leaving the situation or trying to dominate their oppressors, but eventually the oppressor lost. They were also leaders that led by staying at the same level as the masses, and not above them.

Cognitive-behavioral therapy and social status

Cognitive-behavioral therapy techniques can also address social comparisons.[12] For example, just as we label feelings and become aware of behaviors during the initial stages of psychotherapy, taking a step back and recognizing and labeling the action of comparing (also called decentering and self-monitoring) may be useful. Other techniques include exploring the pros and cons of socially comparing, balancing upwards and downward comparisons, or making planned comparisons. An example of a planned comparison would be choosing to compare on one aspect or dimension (e.g., having more or less hair) with one every five people, as a way to increase awareness about the broad range of hair volumes in the world. This exercise would help the person realize that there is a balance of people who are better off and worse off than oneself in that aspect, which may give one some control.[13] The person may believe to be at the bottom of the ladder in a specific comparison dimension. For example, if the person is bold and comparing hair volume, doing a planned comparison may not be helpful. Alternatively, that person could choose to change the dimension of comparison. An example would be that of a child who has a good sense of humor, but does not excel in academics. We could ask the child to shift to comparing to more serious and less entertaining peers in order to regulate the child's mood. Obviously, we would also want that child to excel academically and not give up on learning, even if we are trying to help regulate the child's mood by finding other dimensions of comparison. Another exercise can involve playing around with making more or less comparisons and studying how that affects one's mood or performance, as it may motivate people to work on improving some aspects of themselves. Using distraction or shifting attention are other ways to gain control. Trying not to engage with one's thoughts is not usually a successful strategy to change thoughts; rather, shifting attention is preferable. In other words, telling yourself to stop thinking something does not always result in stopping those undesired thoughts. Focusing on something else is usually a more productive way of stopping unwanted thoughts. Being compassionate with oneself is another technique. One way to do this is by thinking about what you would say to yourself if you were your best friend. Understanding that socially comparing is an innate strategy to survive and that humans may be susceptible to cognitive distortions due to the stress or threat to their status can also give perspective and decrease angst when engaging in these social comparisons.

A third-wave or newer cognitive-behavioral type of therapy called acceptance and commitment therapy includes another aspect that may be valuable in social comparisons. In addition to including mindfulness practices and improving cognitive flexibiltiy, acceptance and commitment therapy focuses on the values the person holds and centers the therapy around those values.[14] Having a focus, or a goal in life, that may or may not be different from that of others around us, can help us avoid distractions when we see others who are better off in dimensions that are not the ones we value most. For example, some people may wish they could play tennis like Carlos Alcaraz or Iga Świątek, and feel sad when thinking that playing like them is not something they will ever be able to do. They could then be reminded of why they chose another professional path that they valued more. If you are a teacher, you probably valued educating the next generation of children; if you are a therapist, you may have valued assisting people in having better mental health; if you are an engineer, you likely valued contributing to the design and construction of public spaces for people. Reminding yourself of what you value may help you regulate your mood when you start engaging in comparisons with others that take very different paths in life.

Regardless of the therapy type, the style of the therapist seems to be the most important aspect of the success in therapy. Some therapists yield better clinical outcomes regardless of the therapy used. Getting to the level of the patient and minimizing social hierarchies as opposed to insisting on maintaining them at all cost, may be the ingredient that is missing for those therapists with little success.[15] The issues of dominance are understudied in therapy, but should be considered for both understanding therapeutic dynamics and addressing social comparisons.

Families and social status

Adolescents are at a time of transition towards more independence, but are nonetheless, still dependent, to a significant level, on their environments. Families, schools, and neighborhoods will have a role in mitigating the effects of social rank or using it to the advantage of the child or the teen.

The dynamics of status take place within families. These status dynamics are part of the relationships among siblings, among the adults, and between the adults and the children, and include immediate and extended family. But families these days also engage in status seeking and social comparisons with other families. One of the hardest things as a parent is trying to stay away from playing status games with your children. Many skeptics see today's parents encouraging their children to be successful and believe there is an attempt by parents to project their own unfulfilled dreams onto their children due to their own failure to achieve a desired status. While part of that may be true, I believe parents likely push their children out of anxiety about their ability to be successful in an uncertain world that is ever growing in complexity. Some parents are competitive by nature, but most are just trying to keep up so their children are not left behind. These decisions start early. Children are becoming experts in sports, playing instruments, or seriously engaging in other activities earlier and earlier, with significant added stress to in their lives at a very young age. There are also more obvious ways to ensure your children will keep their social status or go up on the social ladder. In the U.S., a way to do that is by helping children get the best or most reputable education possible. One example of this desire taken to the extreme is the college admission scandal. In 2019, a group of parents were found to have been involved in inflating their children's test scores and bribing colleges to ensure their children were admitted to highly-ranked colleges in California.[16] The pressures to attend highly-ranked schools in the U.S., and the amount of demands to stand out from other applicants drive students and parents to a point of absurdity in which everyone competes for a few college spots. The reality is that having a college education is already a ticket to a better life, and there are many universities providing a good education in the continent and abroad. Well-meaning financially comfortable families need to find a balance between a constant quest for higher status for their children and their wellbeing. At the same time, families without means to pay for college should not depend on a few available scholarships in order to afford sending their children to college. These scholarships will be for the best of the best at something, which again places the stress on the child and the family to compete for those few spots. More affordable college tuition would resolve some of these problems.

Social rank games not only manifest in and among families, but also in the broader environment, such as in their neighborhoods. As we heard from the adolescents themselves, how neighborhoods look, and how safe they are, give messages to adolescents about the status of the people who live in those neighborhoods and about their own status. However, the issue with neighborhoods is not only one of perception. There is the reality of the extent to which neighborhoods can limit or ensure social engagement. One example is that often older adolescents and young adults will be motivated to find a job and contribute to their families, but neighborhoods that are isolated with no transportation means make that impossible.

Using the right tools in schools, the complex case of uniforms

Schools have an incomparable role in navigating status and mitigating its effects in children. In addition to the child's own family and the social opportunities it provides, schools are a place where children and teens learn the most about navigating social structures. Creating spaces that encourage inclusion, or that emphasize the wholeness of a person and avoid unnecessary categorizations by a single dimension, are important.

Avoiding exclusion from groups can become the accepted culture in a building as early as in kindergarten and preschool.[17] Social rejection can feel to the brain as painful as physical pain, and some preschool programs teach children that everyone should be allowed to play and participate in new activities and groups. In schools, exclusion often happens by academic categories, such as advanced placement classes, and through separation by skill in varsity versus other sports teams. Some people thrive with competition and challenge, so the answer should not be to erase all opportunities for excellence. However, it is possible to minimize categories that are unnecessary and to value individuals for their own diverse skills, giving them opportunities to excel in some areas, instead of excluding them from any opportunity for self-growth. The trend to give trophies to everyone and rid schools of advanced placement courses is likely not the answer. The answer should be providing more varied opportunities for every child to engage and feel included in a group, be that high-level academic groups, history clubs, different sports, chess clubs, hair styling or singing clubs, and community involvement or advocacy groups. When I conduct clincial interviews with children and adolescents, every single one can idenfify an area of interest, or in which they perceive to have skills. Even when they are depressed, they can go back and identify an activity they used to be able to enjoy or do well. Everyone should have a place. It may be reading, and not an instrument, but it should not be hard to set up a book club in a school. In our original human societies, every member had a role. In communities with many centenarians, everyone finds a way to their life purpose. Understandably, schools have limited resources, so applying this philosophy can be a challenge without the appropriate support, but it should be an aspiration.

Schools have historically used uniforms as a way to level social hierarchies. It is unclear if the use of uniforms has an effect on academic outcomes. In fact, a review of studies published from the year 2000 to 2020 on uniforms in schools reported a lack of association between wearing uniforms and better academic outcomes.[18] However, other research of students across the world has found that wearing uniforms promoted an environment that encouraged academic achievement by helping students settle to do work.[19] Uniforms may also be helpful in maintaining classroom order and school security. Yet, other research suggests that the uniform could stiffly creativity, and be distracting and a cause of friction. One argument against uniforms is that many other factors contribute to classroom discipline and environment, such as class size, school funding, and the relationship with the teacher, which could be challenged by having to enforce school discipline related to the uniform. The opposing argument is that the uniform provides an opportunity for teachers and administrators to teach how to adjust to societal norms and school culture, and how to be a good citizen. This discussion is a painful reminder of the current debate over allowing or limiting the use of cellphones in schools. Limiting the use of cellphones seems a good idea, but some schools are afraid to enforce rules related to cellphones fearing increased conflict between teachers and students.

While there does not seem to be an impact of uniforms on academics, uniforms do seem to have an impact on health. For example, in Thailand and other countries where Dengue is endemic and clothing is treated with insecticide, only parents who could afford insecticide were able to provide their children with treated clothing, showing direct effects of socio-economic status on health. While physical activity may be restricted by uniforms, especially in girls, uniforms with a perfect balance of cost, durability, comfort, and design are probably yet to be accessed across the board. Beyond these direct effects on physical health, the effects on perceived social rank could be broader. We do know that uniforms reduce the pressure to wear expensive brands, or what is called 'competitive dressing,' and may efface socio-economic status differences.

Regardless of the data, anyone who has had to wear uniforms in school or whose children have worn uniforms will remember distinctly how nuanced middle and high schoolers can be about their attire, even with a uniform. Of course, like everything in health and in public health, nothing is perfect, and neither is the erasure of social inequalities by uniforms. Children and parents may have to worry less about the outfit, but differences in the price of the sweatshirts and the shoes they wear with said uniform, and how many times they can change the uniform, will still remain. For very poor students, the uniform can become another expense. These students may miss class when the uniform is dirty and the parents cannot afford to buy more than one uniform. Hence, while overall uniforms do have a role in decreasing major social discrepancies in schools, they should be provided by the system and not left to the parent's solvency.

The French government piloted a program in September of 2024 that mandated school uniforms with the purpose of reducing bullying and peer pressure, and minimizing inequalities among students. While the studies on the reduction of bullying by uniform-wearing show mixed results, minimizing inequities seems a smart approach in any school-based initiative. Supposedly having learned from others' poor decision-making, French municipalities are expected to share the cost with the state so that parents do not need to have any expenses related to the uniform, which is one of the criticisms of previous governments's initiatives related to uniforms. Students shared their dislike of the uniform design on TikTok. Others criticized it due to concerns about the imposition of secularist values at a time of mounting tensions in the context of an increasing number of immigrants affiliated with the religion of Islam, some of which support overt clothing requirements for women. But the French choosing to have their schools remain secular is a very French thing to do. France already locked the conversation when it banned long robes, headscarves, crosses, kippahs, and turbans in 2004.[20] Conversely, the U.S. has an ongoing debate about the balance between individual and religious rights, and the separation of state and church that often clash in the world of education.

French teachers are obviously aware that the uniform will not tackle social inequalities and that it may just be a patch. But the question here is, do uniforms help minimize the effects of social inequalities within the educational space? They probably do. They are not the solution for these larger social inequities, and they should not stop adults from working to reduce these inequities outside of the classroom, but they are part of the cocktail of things one can do to reduce unnecessary stress in the school setting. Furthermore, expecting schools to be the sole responsible institution for erasing socio-economic status differences among children is dangerous. It takes time to resolve unjust inequality, and waiting for it to be resolved would hinder any efforts to change things within the school setting. There is no harm in schools trying to do their part to make these differences less insufferable for children who have no control over their socio-economic status. Social rank will be evaluated in different ways and children will need to explore what they value and what dimensions of social rank they use to compare themselves with others for the benefit of their self-esteem; but children have no control over how poor or wealthy they grow up, and lessening the stress of those specific differences in schools should be the adults' responsibility.

Uniforms have also been seen as a form of communicating the school culture and values beyond those of the students. American researchers tend to point out a link between uniforms, generally associated with private education, and the intent to communicate the school's sense of rigor, discipline, and safety to the outside community. Sometimes the uniform increases the hierarchy signaling. Anyone growing up in the American public education system knows the connotations of being a freshman in school or in college, versus being a junior or a senior. Some grade schools use uniforms of different colors depending on the grade. This practice would make freshmen students very obvious, and be an example of an unnecessary practice that amplifies hierarchies without a purpose. If this differentiation has no apparent effect on academics, there is no reason to implement such practice. If the intent is to not 'lose' the students, then that school is likely to have bigger problems, like overcrowding.

Uniforms are also a method for students to internalize the values of society and a process to maintain the same power structures.[21] Cuban children, for example, receive one free uniform a year, supplied by the government with the colors of the Cuban flag reflecting the participation in the communist party. Obviously, we should not advocate for indoctrination in schools, but the reality is that we live in structures of power and within societies, and children may benefit from learning about the need to navigate these structures early on. Understanding the environments in which we live may actually give individuals more freedom, as we can then learn to engage with that environment in a way that is productive for all. Criticism has also ensued about the culturally-biased imposition of uniforms to the colonies by England, which initially adopted uniforms with the intent to minimize social class differences.

Regardless of the research and differences in opinion, uniforms are worn in most countries. Interestingly, higher-income countries mandate uniforms less frequently, and in the U.S., public school uniforms tend to be mandated more frequently in areas with higher compared to lower-poverty rates.[22] Despite the concerns of potential discrimination by enforcing uniform wearing, uniforms seem a much better way to ensure fairness than monitoring compliance with the schools' dress code. The school's dress code can be disrupted in infinite ways, as adolescents can get very creative. In the U.S., in particular, the strong culture of individualism and freedom of expression has traditionally made uniforms a pill hard to swallow. The acceptance of uniforms has increased over recent years, likely because of safety concerns. In short, while it is obvious that the use of uniforms does not lead to more socio-economic equality, they can help level the environment in the classroom, decrease stress over keeping up with others, and give the message that everyone is considered equal in the eyes of the school. Furthermore, they spare fights between teens demanding to keep up with the wealthier children in the classroom and parents of lower socio-economic strata who simply cannot afford to buy expensive clothes.

Navigating social media

Another example of the role schools can exert in buffering the stress of social rank is by teaching young citizens how to navigate the world of social media. As larger portions of our social life have transitioned to online relationships, knowing how to properly and safely navigate these social spaces is essential. Parents are often unaware of the rapid changes taking place in their children's online world. Schools already use interventions to teach children how to analyze media messages. These interventions include teaching self-awareness, by asking the student how the message makes him or her feel, or how one can interpret the message based on those emotions. Other aspects of media literacy being taught are self-management, or the actions one may take in response to the message; social awareness, or the understanding of who may be harmed or benefit from the message; relationship skills, or whether or not the source can be trusted; and responsible decision-making, or how one can participate productively in society after receiving the message.[23] Some schools are also responsibly and responsively introducing social media literacy in their health class. As opposed to traditional media, social media are interactive. Therefore, there are new aspects of social media use that need to be considered for health. These new aspects include the disclosures one makes about suicide, or plans to hurt others, the exposure to cyberbullying, how to identify and avoid spreading false news claims, and how to prevent overexposure and viral spread of violent images, among others.

One portion of this teaching needs to involve navigating social comparisons. The field of media literacy has long considered body image and eating disorders as aspects of mental health in which social comparisons have a role. Celebrities and thin magazine cover models like Kate Moss, and the rise of Instagram and other social media sites that are heavy on filtered and edited images, have raised concerns about their links with anorexia and other eating disorders in younger, more influenceable people. A certain degree of body dissatisfaction can be normal and exist without compromising health. Similarly, social comparisons and even feelings of envy are within the range of normality. The worry should be the emotional dysregulation and dysfunctional behaviors to which these may or may not lead, and not the innate tendencies we as humans have to compare to others. In other words, we cannot change our nature and desire to compare, but we can learn to change how we react to the comparisons, and how we navigate them in our modern world. Some researchers have tested brief interventions in people with low or high tendency to present disordered eating and have shown the benefits of media literacy for those who are vulnerable to suffer from these disorders.

The status of victimhood and mental health disorder

In one of the episodes of the latest seasons of the great social commentary that is the show *South Park*, Butters Stotch takes Stan Marsh to a company that exists exclusively to help people build a brand. The owner of the company has a computer where he enters some characteristics of the person who wants to be re-branded, and the computer generates an option with several words to describe the brand that the person is supposed to adopt in order to be successful. Every single brand has 'victim' as one of the words in the description. It seems as if at this time in history being a victim awards people a higher social status. Competition for victimization has led many to gain status by claiming more misfortunes than others. We now condemn people to a lower-status rank based on their morals or ethics, but also based on their political affiliation. This competition for victimhood can become a problem when the judgment about whose misery is worse and who has the higher moral standards becomes a group-based one. Naturally, you would judge some-one's ethics based on their individual specific behaviors. However, comparing peo-ple by race, or gender identity, and assuming that belonging to a specific group or another gives them higher morals and higher status than people belonging to other groups, can be problematic. Suddenly, we may find groups against groups, and nations against nations, all competing for sympathy. This is a point of conten-tion as some messages claiming that we are all racists by nature and support racist systems have recently been welcomed in the U.S. While it is true that there are systemic problems that sprung from policies implemented by the government, such as Red Lining Federal policies that segregated Black communities for decades, we cannot assume that any living White person today, which for the most part was not alive when those policies were implemented, is racist for belonging to the race of the 'oppressor.' Making assumptions about others based on external characteristics takes less cognitive effort than taking the time to understand all the layers of an individual. Instead, the goal ought to be to be aware of our personal biases and the existing structures of power. While we strive to make societies fairer, we also need to understand that blaming and assuming malintent on the part of individu-als belonging to the dominant group of the time only reinforces those structures. Another problem with these assumptions is that while creating more hierarchies, they also prevent open communication. As sensitivities run high, we are forced to walk on eggshells and ignore that everyone may have experienced their own share of imposed submission; if not because of their race, they do because of their age, or sex, or a multitude of other reasons people find to discriminate and dominate oth-ers. The same approach that claims to be comprehensive and accepting can end up excluding and pitting groups of people against each other. Humans are multi and not unidimensional and our identities are composed of many smaller identities. If before we meet someone and assess their status, we only focus on their race, we will be very unaware of all the other aspects that make up that individual. Social groups are not a monolith. Within each group, there are many types of people with different identities. Focusing on the *what* or the content of the differences among people, while ignoring the *how* or the processes of identifying and behaving around those differences seems counterproductive. In the U.S., differences by political party have become so profound that for many, knowing that someone belongs to a specific party will cause them to ignore every other aspect of that person. They will make assumptions based solely on party affiliation. This seems a very impoverish-ing way to live a life. One can miss opportunities to get to know decent people and learn to see the world from other perspectives.

Related to victimization is the idealization of the mental illness happening in social media. While mental health stigma continues to be a problem in many cir-cles and populations, groups in social media have taken it to the other extreme by idealizing mental illness and sometimes inflating symptoms to gain popularity. Many have gone online to talk about ADHD, depression, and even suicide. While the platforms can serve as effective means of health information dissemination, they are also open for anyone, trained or not, to comment and upload information on mental health disorders, often without depth of understanding. If you get more 'likes' by uploading your well-made video with catchy music about eating disorders on TikTok, you are reinforced and rewarded to post more videos, and sent to an algorithm of other videos that make your world online deeper, but smaller and centered around eating disorders and related commercial products. This can happen quickly. These powerful tools touch upon our own most basic instincts, the ones that reward us socially and increase our status, even if that status is being an influencer on eating disorder information. Some regulation in this area seems sensible to protect young minds.

In practicality, some steps may be needed to prevent status hierarchies from exploding on social media. These steps include raising awareness about healthy ways to use social media, about the effects of social comparisons on mood and behaviors, and about the benefits of managing feelings by changing the point of reference of comparison or focusing on being grateful.[24] With that purpose, and as mentioned, social media literacy interventions in schools and interventions in the clinical setting may be beneficial for young people. We should also consider including measures of social status, social comparison, and social inclusion when assessing the health of adolescents. Strategies used by emotionally mature individuals could be taught in therapeutic settings or by school counseling services to help navigate new and complex social contexts.[25] The goal of these strategies should not be to accept or acquiesce to societal inequalities but to help manage emotions and behaviors that can impact functioning. The developmentally appropriate early teen focus on celebrities may have morphed and become more intense with the constant access to social media celebrities or influencers through smartphones.[26] In these new context, parents and teachers should inquire about the responsible parties in accurate and healthy content sharing. Understanding these changes can provide policy-makers, educators, clinicians, and parents with the tools to better design and regulate these sites.

Resisting social status

In a way, it would be revolutionary to stop playing status games. It would certainly be a problem for some companies like the car or the beauty industries, as people would stop consuming as much. Resisting status games could be the biggest threat to all industries, but it would be as hard to fight as quitting alcohol for an alcoholic with beverages hidden in the basement or a person dieting with ice-creams waiting in the refrigerator. These industries are all based on status. This quest for status is not just about keeping up with the trends, or looking better than your co-workers or friends, or having more or as much as them, so that at least in some way, your status is maintained; it is also about securing your position in the group, belonging, staying relevant in society, being seen.

One can guess the values of a period by looking at what people aspired to purchase at each time in human history. Look at any American magazine from the

1950s, when marketing was very obvious and sometimes commercials filled up every page. In addition to cleaning products for women, cars for men, yard and house size, and furniture defined a family's status. At that time, middle class families were moving in mass to the suburbs and away from crowded cities, and the suburban house was a sign of status, along with all the things it contained. Marketing today is extremely subtle. We now get curated adds on our Facebook page, all appealing to our desire to be more beautiful, more in shape, wealthier, or to having fancier decorations as much as in the past. Societal values have changed slightly. Now status is gained by physical fitness as an epidemic of obesity invades the West, or by trips abroad as experiences, and not goods become signs of status. For children, status in the past was a toy or a video game marketed in commercials between breaks of your favorite show. The adds now sell ways of being. The cool kid, the artsy one, the sporty one will all lead a child to websites to buy the attire and preferred tools of that online celebrity, from the skateboard to the make up. But the essence remains. People will deny making social comparisons, just to go on to talk about the neighbors' new Tesla, or how someone else had lost weight and they wish they could lose it too. It is difficult not to make these comparisons, because this is how we learn to understand the world around us. It is part of our nature.

Is equality the key?

The elephant in the room is the question of equality. If we did away with all that consumption and those commercials, would we stop comparing? And the answer is, of course not. We could break the cycle of extreme empty productivity with the only goal to spend and enrich the companies. But, what would happen if we did not care anymore about the type of car we owned, or our prom dress? We would just find other ways to compare.

Many wonder at one point or another about their decision process in choosing their political affiliation. Some may have chosen a political orientation that favors communism or socialism, systems that in theory would make socio-economic status dynamics less extreme. But as mentioned earlier, socialist societies are not free of hierarchies. One may argue that these societies are not inherently flawed but more prone to fail due to external influences, like those that capitalist countries exert on them by isolating them financially. But to control for that potential factor, we can take a look at traditional societies or egalitarian community groups, as we saw with the *Tsimane*, and see that status and health differences remain in egalitarian societies.

Could we at least diminish the effects of these hierarchies on health? I think so. Sir Marmot[27] has already made recommendations for societies with a goal of fairness and equity. These recommendations included considering social status in policies and practices across settings (finances, neighborhoods, schools, housing,social and medical services), the organization in the workplace, the benefits of a balance in demands and control, and the need for a sense of reciprocity in all relationships. He also emphasized a need for reward that is not necessarily obtained by financial remuneration, but by career opportunities that give job security or paths to promotion, or other types of reward for a work well-done. These opportunities are chances for self-realization.

For children, safety guards are important. We have seen that individuals and small communities can mitigate the effects of social rank in young people's health. As children depend on the environments designed by adults, we should ensure these environments are fair. However, as all people will face challenges ahead, we should also encourage and promote resiliency. Social rank considerations should be more openly considered in clinical settings, the education system, and social media. There is work to be done, and small, easy steps can be implemented to protect children, while also teaching and training them to navigate a world of inevitable hierarchies.

Our future

As it is obvious from this book, I have a personal concern with power structures. I worry about my patients growing up in deprived environments of limited access to healthy foods or heat in the winter. Structural social differences, too obvious to ignore in a country with vast inequities like the U.S., are evident. But beyond these cases of absolute deprivation, which are unjust and in need of repair, differences in status will remain. Social dominance exists because as humans, we are designed to live in groups. We may delude ourselves into thinking that we could live alone, which technically, and on account of technology, we indeed can. But a human without a social group is like a fish without water. The fish may survive in those conditions, but only for a very short period of time. The same will happen with a child who withdraws from the world. Sooner or later, depression and anxiety will materialize. Humans do not thrive in isolation.

The youth mental health crisis has been blamed on the lenient ways in which parents are raising their children and on helicopter parenting, on the economic pressures on newer generations and on their privilege, on stigma, college tuition, the pandemic, social media, the fragmentation of the nuclear family, discrimination, immigration, climate change, gun violence, chemicals, and even vaccines and antidepressants, among many other factors. When trying to understand why young people have been struggling with their mental health for the last couple of decades, we have found reasons in a multitude of social changes. In doing so, we have also ignored a factor that encompasses many: the human quest for status.

The pursuit of status means different things for different people. For some, gaining status entails having basic needs covered. Many of the people exposed to stress and violence work in underground economies without protection or rights. They are abused by people who own them and prosecuted by the law. These jobs are a lifeline, a way to pay for a place to stay, or for food, in the midst of wealth and comfort. Underneath is the reality of a system in which many people do not have enough to sustain themselves with dignity. A good society would rid humans of these inter-individual differences by addressing all basic needs. In a way, European countries strive to be like that. However, in these societies, social rank differences still exist, and people still compare themselves to others to keep or improve their social status. At the end of the day, those who are more capable or skilled will gain access to more partners who will ensure the reproduction and survival of their genes. There is not much we can or would want to do about this. As a modern society we are not going to force people to partner with people they do not like, just to level out the genetic playing field. But as humans, we can make the choice to strive to ensure a dignified life for every fellow human being in this competitive world, especially when it comes to children. Humans have the right to live with dignity, purpose, and some sense of stability and security. If anything, societies need to ensure all children are nurtured and provided with the fundamental tools to live with dignity.

There are many challenges facing humanity: climate change, animal species at risk due to our abuse of the planet, the need to understand sickness and suffering, caring for those who are not able to care for themselves, preventing wars and respecting all cultures, small and big, salvaging languages that are at risk of disappearing, and creating economies that serve all people and not just those few at the very top. We will experience those challenges for many decades, and we need people working to resolve them. There is simply too much work to be done. That work needs to be appropriately remunerated so that everyone can live with dignity. Good jobs would address many of the problems we face due to income inequality, including health disparities, violence, and substance use problems. Maybe not in their totality, but in significant ways.

However, even then, we will need to come to terms with the fact that humans are primates and will always strive to compete for resources, and that mitigating the effects on health will not change the fact that we are designed to live our lives needing to balance competition and group belonging. Knowing this should not make our futures grim. It should be a chance for us to be aware of our motives and decide what to do with them, as individuals and as societies. It is also a chance to guide children in less confusing ways, by acknowledging their human nature, and at the same time, giving them the tools to become happy, and contributing members of society.

References

Chapter 1

1. Mortensen AN, Smith B, Ellis JD. The social organization of honey bees. *EDIS*. 2015;2015(9):1–4.
2. Shimoji H, Abe MS, Tsuji K, Masuda N. Global network structure of dominance hierarchy of ant workers. *Journal of the Royal Society Interface*. 2014;11:20140599.
3. Atrooz F, Alkadhi KA, Salim S. Understanding stress: insights from rodent models. *Current Research in Neurobiology*. 2021;2:100013.
4. Maier SF, Seligman MEP. Learned helplessness at fifty: insights from neuroscience. *Psychological Review*. 2016;123(4):349–367.
5. Sapolsky RM. Social status and health in humans and other animals. *Annual Review of Anthropology*. 2004;33(1):393–418.
6. Shively CA, Day SM. Social inequalities in health in nonhuman primates. *Neurobiology of Stress*. 2015;1(C):156–163.
7. Abbott DH, Saltzman W, Schultz-Darken NJ, et al. Adaptations to subordinate status in female marmoset monkeys. *Comparative Biochemistry and Physiology. Part C: Comparative Pharmacology and Toxicology*. 1998;119(3):261–274.
8. Greene RW. *The explosive child: a new approach for understanding and parenting easily frustrated, chronically inflexible children*. Sixth edition. HarperCollins; 2021.
9. Booth A, Shelley G, Mazur A, et al. Testosterone, and winning and losing in human competition. *Hormones and Behavior*. 1989;23(4):556–571.
10. Abbott DH, Keverne EB, Bercovitch FB, et al. Are subordinates always stressed? A comparative analysis of rank differences in cortisol levels among primates. *Hormones and Behavior*. 2003;43(1):67–82.
11. Sherman GD, Lee JJ, Cuddy AJC, et al. Leadership is associated with lower levels of stress. *Proceedings of the National Academy of Sciences - PNAS*. 2012;109(44):17903–17907.
12. Gianaros PJ, Manuck SB. Neurobiological pathways linking socioeconomic position and health. *Psychosomatic Medicine*. 2010;72(5):450–461.
13. Noonan M, Sallet J, Mars R, et al. A neural circuit covarying with social hierarchy in macaques. *PLoS Biology*. 2014;12(9):e1001940.
14. Koski JE, Xie H, Olson IR. Understanding social hierarchies: the neural and psychological foundations of status perception. *Social Neuroscience*. 2015;10(5):527–550.
15. Moors A, De Houwer J. Automatic processing of dominance and submissiveness. *Experimental Psychology*. 2005;52(4):296–302.
16. Deaner RO, Khera AV, Platt ML. Monkeys pay per view: adaptive valuation of social images by Rhesus Macaques. *Current Biology*. 2005;15(6):543–548.

17. Cheng JT, Tracy JL, Foulsham T, et al. Two ways to the top: evidence that dominance and prestige are distinct yet viable avenues to social rank and influence. *Journal of Personality and Social Psychology.* 2013;104(1):103–125.
18. Beck A. Cognitive therapy a 30-year retrospective. *American Psychologist.* 1991;46(4): 368–375.
19. West P, Sweeting H, Young R. Transition matters: pupils' experiences of the primary-secondary school transition in the West of Scotland and consequences for well-being and attainment. *Research Papers in Education.* 2010;25(1):21–50.
20. Mitra R, Sapolsky RM. Acute corticosterone treatment is sufficient to induce anxiety and amygdaloid dendritic hypertrophy. *Proceedings of the National Academy of Sciences.* 2008;105(14):5573–5578.
21. Felitti VJ, Anda RF, Nordenberg D, et al. Relationship of childhood abuse and household dysfunction to many of the leading causes of death in adults: the adverse childhood experiences (ACE) study. *American Journal of Preventive Medicine.* 1998;14(4):245–258.

Chapter 2

1. Deaton A. *The great escape.* Princeton University Press; 2013.
2. Erdal D, Whiten A, Boehm C, et al. On human egalitarianism: an evolutionary product of Machiavellian status escalation? *Current Anthropology.* 1994;35(2):175–183.
3. Boserup E. *The conditions of agricultural growth.* First edition. Routledge; 1965.
4. Whiten A, Erdal D. The human socio-cognitive niche and its evolutionary origins. *Philosophical Transactions of the Royal Society B* 2012;367(1599):2119–2129.
5. Tooby J, DeVore I. The reconstruction of hominid behavioral evolution through strategic modeling. In: Kinzey WG, ed. *The Evolution of Human Behavior: Primate Models,* SUNY Press, Albany, NY; 1987.
6. Avis J, Harris PL. Belief-desire reasoning among Baka children: evidence for a universal conception of mind. *Child Development.* 1991;62(3):460–467.
7. Knauft BM, Abler TS, Betzig L, Boehm C, Dentan R, Kiefer TM, et al. Violence and sociality in human evolution [and comments and replies]. *Current Anthropology.* 1991;32(4):391–428.
8. Marlowe FW. The mating system of Foragers in the standard cross-cultural sample. *Cross-Cultural Research: The Journal of Comparative Social Science.* 2003;37(3): 282–306.
9. Pew Research Center. Available at: https://www.pewresearch.org/short-reads/2016/04/ 19/5-ways-americans-and-europeans-are-different/.
10. Ames KM. On the evolution of the human capacity for inequality and/or Egalitarianism. In: Price TD., Feinman GM, ed. *Pathways to power. Fundamental issues in archaeology.* Springer; 2010:15–44.
11. Wiessner P. Hunting, healing, and hxaro exchange: a long-term perspective on !Kung (Ju/'hoansi) large-game hunting. *Evolution and Human Behavior.* 2002;23(6):407–436.
12. Gavrilets S, Duenez-Guzman EA, Vose MD. Dynamics of alliance formation and the Egalitarian revolution. *PLOS ONE.* 2008;3(10):e3293–e3293.
13. Zink CF, Tong Y, Chen Q, Bassett DS, Stein JL, Meyer-Lindenberg A. Know your place: neural processing of social hierarchy in humans. Neuron. 2008;58(2):273–283.
14. Boyd R, Richerson PJ. Culture and the evolution of human cooperation. *Philosophical Transactions of the Royal Society B.* 2009;364(1533):3281–3288.
15. Bowles S, Smith E, Borgerhoff Mulder M. The emergence and persistence of inequality in premodern societies: Introduction to the special section. *Current Anthropology.* 2010;51(1):7–17.

16. Gamble C. Palaeolithic society and the release from proximity: a network approach to intimate relations. *World Archaeology.* 1998;29(3):426–449.

17. Lieberman DE. Speculations about the selective basis for modern human craniofacial form. *Evolutionary Anthropology.* 2008;17(1):55–68.

18. Boehm C. Hierarchy in the Forest: The Evolution of Egalitarian Behavior. Copyright Date: 1999. Published by: Harvard University Press.

19. Lee R. Is there a foraging mode of production? *Canadian Journal of Anthropology.* 1981;2(1):13–19.

20. Woodburn J. *Egalitarian Societie*, vol. 17. Royal Anthropological Institute of Great Britain and Ireland; 1982.

21. Smith E, Hill K, Marlowe F, et al. Wealth transmission and inequality among hunter-gatherers. *Current Anthropology.* 2010;51(1):19–34.

22. Kelly R. *The foraging spectrum: diversity in hunter-gatherer lifeways.* Smithsonian Institution Press; 1995.

23. Gurven M, Borgerhoff Mulder M, Hooper PL, Kaplan H, Quinlan R, Sear R, et al. Domestication alone does not lead to inequality. *Current Anthropology.* 2010;51(1):49–64.

24. Hawkes K, O'Connell JF, Blurton Jones NG. Hadza meat sharing. *Evolution and Human Behavior.* 2001;22(2):113–142.

25. Alvard M, Gillespie A. *Good Lamalera whale hunters accrue reproductive benefits.* Research in Economic Anthropology. In: Socioeconomic Aspects of Human Behavioral Ecology. Emerald Group Publishing Limited; 2004. pp. 225–247.

26. Cashdan EA. Egalitarianism among hunters and gatherers. *EA Cashdan. American Anthropologist.* 1980;82(1):116–120.

27. Kohler TA, Smith ME, Bogaard A, et al. Greater post-Neolithic wealth disparities in Eurasia than in North America and Mesoamerica. 2017;551(7682):619–622. [published correction appears in Nature. 2018;555(7694):126].

28. Alfani G. Inequality in history: a long-run view. *Journal of Economic Surveys.* 2024:1–21.

29. World Inequality Database. https://wid.world/. Updated 2023.

Chapter 3

1. Marmot M. *The status syndrome.* 1. American edition. Times Books; 2004. https://www.loc.gov/catdir/description/hol053/2004040529.html.

2. Wilkinson RG. Income inequality and population health: a review and explanation of the evidence. *Social Science & Medicine.* 2006;62:1768–1784.

3. Deaton A. Health, inequality, and economic development. *Journal of Economic Literature.* 2003;41(1):113–158.

4. Cohen S, Janicki-Deverts D, Chen E, et al. Childhood socioeconomic status and adult health. *Annals of the New York Academy of Sciences.* 2010;1186(1):37–55.

5. Offenhauer P. Women in Islamic societies: a selected review of social scientific literature. Federal Research Division, Library of Congress under an Interagency Agreement with the Office of the Director of National Intelligence/National Intelligence Council (ODNI/ADDNIA/NIC) and Central Intelligence Agency/Directorate of Science & Technology. Federal Research Division Library of Congress Washington, D.C.; 2005.

6. Allen JR, Felbab-Brown V. The fate of women's rights in Afghanistan. https://www.brookings.edu/articles/the-fate-of-womens-rights-in-afghanistan/. Updated 2020. Accessed June 25, 2024.

7. Yerkes RM, Dodson JD. The relation of strength of stimulus to rapidity of habit-formation. *Journal of Comparative Neurology and Psychology.* 1908;18(5):459–482.

8. Sapolsky RM. Social status and health in humans and other animals. *Annual Review of Anthropology.* 2004;33(1):393–418.

9. McCune J. Immunotherapy to treat cancer. *Clinical Pharmacology and Therapeutics.* 2016;100(3):198–203.

10. Kawachi I, Kennedy BP. Socioeconomic determinants of health: health and social cohesion: why care about income inequality? *BMJ.* 1997;314(7086):1037.

11. Seligman ME, Maier SF. Failure to escape traumatic shock. *Journal of Experimental Psychology.* 1967;74(1):1–9.

12. Kaplan H, Thompson RC, Trumble BC, et al. Coronary atherosclerosis in indigenous South American Tsimane: a cross-sectional cohort study. *The Lancet (British edition).* 2017;389(10080):1730–1739.

13. Cole SW. Social regulation of human gene expression: mechanisms and implications for public health. *American Journal of Public Health (1971).* 2013;103(S1):S84–S92.

14. Adler NE, Epel ES, Castellazzo G, Ickovics JR. Relationship of subjective and objective social status with psychological and physiological functioning. *Health Psychology.* 2000;19(6):586–592.

15. Singh-Manoux A, Marmot M, Adler N. Does subjective social status predict health and change in health status better than objective status? *Psychosomatic Medicine.* 2005;67(6):855–861.

16. Goodman E, Huang B, Schafer-Kalkhoff T, et al. Perceived socioeconomic status: a new type of identity that influences adolescents' self-rated health. *Journal of Adolescent Health.* 2007;41(5):479–487.

17. Goodman E, Adler NE, Daniels SR, et al. Impact of objective and subjective social status on obesity in a biracial cohort of adolescents. *Obesity.* 2003;11(8):1018–1026.

18. Mclaughlin KA, Costello EJ, Leblanc W, et al. Socioeconomic status and adolescent mental disorders. *American Journal of Public Health.* 2012;102(9):1742–1750.

19. Vidal C, Latkin C. Perceived family and individual social status and its association with depression and suicidality in an adolescent clinical sample. *Journal of Community Psychology.* 2020;48(8):2504–2516.

20. Galobardes B, Lynch JW, Smith GD. Is the association between childhood socioeconomic circumstances and cause-specific mortality established? Update of a systematic review. *Journal of Epidemiology & Community Health.* 2008;62(5):387–390.

21. Pollitt RA, Rose KM, Kaufman JS. Evaluating the evidence for models of life course socioeconomic factors and cardiovascular outcomes: a systematic review. *BMC Public Health.* 2005;5(1):7–7.

22. Banasr M, Valentine GW, Li X, Gourley SL, Taylor JR, Duman RS. Chronic unpredictable stress decreases cell proliferation in the cerebral cortex of the adult rat. *Biological Psychiatry.* 2007;62(5):496–504.

Chapter 4

1. Erikson EH. *Childhood and society.* Vintage Digital; 2014.

2. Tanti C, Stukas AA, Halloran MJ, et al. Social identity change: shifts in social identity during adolescence. *Journal of Adolescence.* 2011;34(3):555–567.

3. Cooley CH. *Human nature and the social order.* First edition. Routledge; 2017.

4. Sebastian C, Viding E, Williams KD, et al. Social brain development and the affective consequences of ostracism in adolescence. *Brain and Cognition.* 2010;72(1):134–145.

5. Goodman E, Huang B, Schafer-Kalkhoff T, Adler NE. Perceived socioeconomic status: a new type of identity that influences adolescents' self-rated health. *Journal of Adolescent Health.* 2007;41(5):479–487.

6. Destin M, Rheinschmidt-Same M, Richeson JA. Status-based identity. *Perspectives on Psychological Science.* 2017;12(2):270–289.

7. Rowley SJ, Burchinal MR, Roberts JE, et al. Racial identity, social context, and race-related social cognition in African Americans during middle childhood. *Developmental Psychology.* 2008;44(6):1537–1546.

8. Rosenberg M, Pearlin LI. Social class and self-esteem among children and adults. *American Journal of Sociology.* 1978;84(1):53–77.

9. Sweeting H, Hunt K. Adolescent socio-economic and school-based social status, health and well-being. *Social Science & Medicine.* 2014;121:39–47.

10. Thomsen L, Frankenhuis WE, Ingold-Smith M, et al. Big and mighty: preverbal infants mentally represent social dominance. *Science.* 2011;331(6016):477–480.

11. Mascaro O, Csibra G. Representation of stable social dominance relations by human infants. *Proceedings of the National Academy of Sciences.* 2012;109(18):6862–6867.

12. Charafeddine R, Mercier H, Clément F, et al. Children's allocation of resources in social dominance situations. *Developmental Psychology.* 2016;52(11):1843–1857.

13. Strayer FF, Trudel M. Developmental changes in the nature and function of social dominance among young children. *Ethology and Sociobiology.* 1984;5(4):279–295.

14. Heck IA, Shutts K, Kinzler KD. Children's thinking about group-based social hierarchies. *Trends in Cognitive Sciences.* 2022;26(7):593–606.

15. Lansu TAM, Cillessen AHN, Karremans JC. Adolescents' selective visual attention for high-status peers: the role of perceiver status and gender. *Child Development.* 2014;85(2):421–428.

16. Zettergren P, Bergman LR, Wångby M. Girls' stable peer status and their adulthood adjustment: a longitudinal study from age 10 to age 43. *International Journal of Behavioral Development.* 2006;30(4):315–325.

17. Cillessen AHN, Rose AJ. Understanding popularity in the peer system. *Current Directions in Psychological Science.* 2005;14(2):102–105.

18. LaFontana KM, Cillessen AHN. Developmental changes in the priority of perceived status in childhood and adolescence. *Social Development.* 2010;19(1):130–147.

19. Lansu TAM, Cillessen AHN. Peer status in emerging adulthood. *Journal of Adolescent Research.* 2012;27(1):132–150.

20. de Bruyn EH, Cillessen AHN. Popularity in early adolescence: prosocial and antisocial subtypes. *Journal of Adolescent Research.* 2006;21(6):607–627.

21. Pellegrini AD, Bartini M. Dominance in early adolescent boys: affiliative and aggressive dimensions and possible functions. *Merrill-Palmer Quarterly.* 2001;47(1):142–163.

22. La Freniere P, Charlesworth W. Dominance, attention, and affiliation in a preschool group: a nine-month longitudinal study. In: Smith P, Rutland A (ed.), *Childhood social development.* SAGE Publications Ltd; 2014:III11. 584 pages.

23. Bolling DZ, Pitskel NB, Deen B, et al. Development of neural systems for processing social exclusion from childhood to adolescence. *Developmental Science.* 2011;14(6):1431–1444.

24. Koski JE, Xie H, Olson IR. Understanding social hierarchies: the neural and psychological foundations of status perception. *Social Neuroscience.* 2015;10(5):527–550.

25. Joffer J, Randell E, Öhman A, et al. Playing the complex game of social status in school - a qualitative study. *Global Health Action.* 2020;13(1):1819689.

26. Galinsky AD, Magee JC, Inesi ME, et al. Power and perspectives not taken. *Psychological Science.* 2006;17(12):1068–1074.
27. Gruenfeld DH, Inesi ME, Magee JC, et al. Power and the objectification of social targets. *Journal of Personality and Social Psychology.* 2008;95(1):111–127.
28. Woolley HT. Agnes: a dominant personality in the making. *The Pedagogical Seminary and Journal of Genetic Psychology.* 1925;32:569–598.
29. Jack LM. An experimental study of ascendant behavior in preschool children. University of Iowa Studies. *Child Welfare.* 1934; 9:7–65.
30. Page, ML. The modification of ascendant behavior in preschool children. University of Iowa Studies. *Child Welfare.* 1936;12:69.
31. Hawley PH, Bower AR. Social hierarchies. In: Zeigler-Hill V, Shackelford TK, ed. *The SAGE handbook of personality and individual differences: volume III: applications of personality and individual differences.* SAGE Publications Ltd; 2018.
32. Maslow AH. *A theory of human motivation.* General Press; 2019.
33. Volk AA, Dane AV, Al-Jbouri E. Is adolescent bullying an evolutionary adaptation? A 10-year review. *Educational Psychology Review.* 2022;34(4):2351–2378.

Chapter 5

1. Easterlin RA, McVey LA, Switek M, et al. The happiness-income paradox revisited. Proc Natl Acad Sci USA. 2010;107(52):22463–22468.
2. Becchetti L, Conzo G. Avoiding a "despair death crisis" in Europe: the drivers of human (un)sustainability. *International Review of Economics.* 2021;68(4):485–526.
3. Khalil EL. Solving the income-happiness paradox. *International Review of Economics.* 2022;69(3):433–463.
4. Kahneman D, Deaton A. *High income improves evaluation of life but not emotional well-being,* vol. 107. National Academy of Sciences; 2010.
5. Giambra LM. Daydreaming characteristics across the life-span: age differences and seven to twenty year longitudinal changes. In: Kunzendorf RG, Wallace B, ed. *Individual differences in conscious experience.* John Benjamins Publishing Company; 2000:147–206.
6. Urry HL, Gross JJ. Emotion regulation in older age. *Current Directions in Psychological Science,* 2010;19(6):352–357.
7. Cowen T. The new heroes and role models. The Free Library. 2000;32(1):30–36. Available at: https://www.thefreelibrary.com/THE NEW HEROES AND ROLE MODELS.-a062162015
8. Min S. 86% of young Americans want to become a social media influencer. 2019. Available at: https://www.cbsnews.com/news/social-media-influencers-86-of-young-americans-want-to-become-one/
9. Zandt F. What do U.S. teens want to be when they grow up? https://www.statista.com/chart/31014/most-popular-future-jobs-with-united-states-teenagers/. Updated 2023.
10. Chasan A. Why are the Academy Awards called the Oscars? Learn the nickname's origins. 2024. Available at: https://www.cbsnews.com/news/why-we-call-the-oscars-the-oscars/
11. Fraser BP, Brown WJ. Media, celebrities, and social influence: identification with Elvis Presley. *Mass Communication & Society.* 2002;5(2):183–206.
12. Kosenko KA, Binder AR, Hurley R. Celebrity influence and identification: a test of the Angelina effect. *Journal Health Communication.* 2016;21(3):318–326.

13. Paluck EL. Reducing intergroup prejudice and conflict using the media. *Journal of Personality and Social Psychology*. 2009;96(3):574–587.

14. Population Media Center. https://www.populationmedia.org/storytelling/projects. Updated 2024.

15. Walling MA. Suicide contagion. *Current Trauma Reports*. 2021;7(4):103–114.

16. Festinger L. A theory of social comparison processes. *Human Relations*. 1954;7(2): 117–140.

17. Vidal C, Lhaksampa T, Miller L, et al. Social media use and depression in adolescents: a scoping review. *International Review of Psychiatry*. 2020;32(3):235–253. doi:10. 1080/09540261.2020.1720623.

18. Nesi JPM. Using social media for social comparison and feedback-seeking: gender and popularity moderate associations with depressive symptoms. Journal of Abnormal Child Psychology. 2015;43(8):1427–1438.

19. Ho SS, Lee EWJ, Liao Y. Social network sites, friends, and celebrities: the roles of social comparison and celebrity involvement in adolescents' body image dissatisfaction. Social Media + Society. 2016;2(3):205630511666421.

20. Twenge J. M. (2020). Increases in Depression, Self-Harm, and Suicide Among U.S. Adolescents After 2012 and Links to Technology Use: Possible Mechanisms. *Psychiatric research and clinical practice*, 2(1), 19–25.

21. Vidal C, Sussman C. Problematic Social Media Use or Social Media Addiction in Pediatric Populations. Pediatric Clinics of North America. 2024; in press.

22. Pew Research Center, August 2022, Teens, Social Media and Technology 2022.

23. Vidal C, Philippe FL, Geoffroy MC, et al. The role of social media use and associated risk and protective behaviors on depression in youth adults: a longitudinal and network perspective. *International Journal of Mental Health and Addiction*. Advance online publication. 2024. https://doi.org/10.1007/s11469-024-01313-0

24. Potter WJ. Guidelines for media literacy interventions in the digital age. *Medijska istraživanja*. 2014;20(2):5.

25. Jeong S, Cho H, Hwang Y. Media literacy interventions: a meta-analytic review. *Journal of communication*. 2012;62(3):454–472.

26. Coughlin JW, Kalodner C. Media literacy as a prevention intervention for college women at low- or high-risk for eating disorders. *Body Image.*2006;3(1):35–43.

27. Frey J, Black KJ, Malaty IA. TikTok Tourette's: are we witnessing a rise in functional tic-like behavior driven by adolescent social media use? *Psychology Research and Behavior Management*. 2022;15:3575–3585.

28. Yeung A, Ng E, Abi-Jaoude E. TikTok and attention-deficit/hyperactivity disorder: a cross-sectional study of social media content quality. *Canadian Journal of Psychiatry*. 2022;67(12):899–906.

29. Carraturo F, Di Perna T, Giannicola V, et al. Envy, social comparison, and depression on social networking sites: a systematic review. *European Journal of Education and Psychology*. 2023;13(2):364–376.

Chapter 6

1. United Nations. Universal Declaration of Human Rights. Available at: https://www.un.org/en/about-us/universal-declaration-of-human-rights

2. Huynh BQ, Chin ET, Kiang MV. Estimated childhood lead exposure from drinking water in Chicago. *JAMA Pediatrics*. 2024;178(5):473–479.

3. Taylor RL, Cooper SR, Jackson JJ. Assessment of neighborhood poverty, cognitive function, and prefrontal and hippocampal volumes in children. *JAMA Network Open.* 2020;3(11):e2023774.

4. Whitehead TL, Peterson J, Kaljee L. The "Hustle": socioeconomic deprivation, urban drug trafficking, and low-income, African-American male gender identity. *Pediatrics (Evanston).* 1994;93(6 Pt 2):1050–1054.

5. Floyd LJ, Alexandre PK, Hedden SL, et al. Adolescent drug dealing and race/ethnicity: a population-based study of the differential impact of substance use on involvement in drug trade. *The American Journal of Drug and Alcohol Abuse.* 2010;36(2):87–91.

6. Uggen C. Crime and the great recession. A great recession brief. 2012.

7. Baumer EP, Wolff KT. Evaluating contemporary crime drop(s) in America, New York City, and many other places. In: Rosenfeld R, Terry K, Chauhan P (eds.), *Understanding New York's crime drop*, vol. 1. First edition. Routledge; 2020:5–38.

8. De Courson B, Nettle D. Why do inequality and deprivation produce high crime and low trust? *Scientific Reports.* 2021;11(1):1937.

9. Cingano F. *Trends in income inequality and its impact on economic growth*, vol. 163. OECD Publishing; 2014.

10. Institute for Research on Poverty. Connections among poverty, incarceration, and inequality. Fast Focus Research/Policy Brief No. 48-2020. 2020.

11. Wright DJ, Montiel LM. Divided they fall: hardship in America's cities and suburbs. 2007.

12. Lopez E, Boxerman B. Crime trends in U.S. cities: year-end 2023 update. 2024. Available at: https://counciloncj.org/crime-trends-in-u-s-cities-year-end-2023-update/#:~:text=Looking%20at%20other%20violent%20offenses,violence%20incidents%20each%20rose%202%25

13. National Insurance Crime Bureau. Auto thefts surge in 2020 according to new NICB report. 2021.

14. Guo X, Egan V, Zhang J. Sense of control and adolescents' aggression: the role of aggressive cues. *PsyCh Journal.* 2016;5(4):263–274.

15. Fournier M, Moskowitz D, Zuroff D. Social rank strategies in hierarchical relationships. *Journal of Personality and Social Psychology.* 2002;83(2):425–433.

16. Greitemeyer T, Sagioglou C. Subjective socioeconomic status causes aggression: a test of the theory of social deprivation. *Journal of Personality and Social Psychology.* 2016;111(2):178–194.

17. Hall CW. Self-reported aggression and the perception of anger in facial expression photos. *The Journal of Psychology: Interdisciplinary and Applied.* 2006;140(3):255–267.

18. Sullivan D, Landau MJ, Rothschild ZK. An existential function of enemyship. *Journal of Personality and Social Psychology.* 2010;98(3):434–449.

19. Kuntz L. A year of record-high suicide rates. *The Psychiatric Times.* 2024;41(4):COV.

20. Swanson JW, Easter MM, Alanis-Hirsch K, et al. Criminal justice and suicide outcomes with Indiana's risk-based gun seizure law. *The Journal of the American Academy of Psychiatry and the Law.* 2019;47(2):188–197.

21. Small Arms Survey. https://www.smallarmssurvey.org/.

22. Kong Y, Zhang J. Access to farming pesticides and risk for suicide in Chinese rural young people. *Psychiatry Research.* 2010;179(2):217–221.

23. The Washington Post. World suicide rates by country. https://www.washingtonpost.com/wp-srv/world/suiciderate.html. Updated 2005. Accessed June 27, 2024.

24. Case A, Deaton A. Rising morbidity and mortality in midlife among white non-Hispanic Americans in the 21st century. *Proceedings of the National Academy of Sciences.* 2015;112(49):15078–15083.

25. Beseran E, Pericàs JM, Cash-Gibson L, et al. Deaths of despair: a scoping review on the social determinants of drug overdose, alcohol-related liver disease and suicide. *International Journal of Environmental Research and Public Health.* 2022;19(19):12395.

26. Faux J. NAFTA's impact on U.S. workers. 2013.

27. China and the WTO: Interview with Mauro Guillen (edited transcript).

28. Case A, Deaton A. Mortality and morbidity in the 21st century. *Brookings Papers on Economic Activity.* 2017;2017(1):397–443.

29. Zeglin RJ, Niemela DRM, Baynard CW. Deaths of despair in Florida. *Health Education & Behavior.* 2019;46(2):329–339.

30. Golberstein E, Gonzales G, Meara E. How do economic downturns affect the mental health of children? Evidence from the National Health Interview Survey. *Health Economics.* 2019;28(8):955–970.

31. Jayashankar A, Murphy A. High inflation disproportionately hurts low-income households. Federal Reserve Bank of Dallas Web site. https://www.dallasfed.org/research/ economics/2023/0110. Updated 2023. Accessed June 30, 2024.

32. United Nations News. Global food prices rose 'sharply' during 2021. 6 January 2022. https://news.un.org/en/story/2022/01/1109212

33. Currie J, Tekin E. Is there a link between foreclosure and health? *American Economic Journal. Economic Policy.* 2015;7(1):63–94.

34. Gassman-Pines A, Ananat EO, Gibson-Davis CM. Effects of statewide job losses on adolescent suicide-related behaviors. *American Journal of Public Health.* 2014;104(10): 1964–1970.

35. Charles KK, DeCicca P. Local labor market fluctuations and health: is there a connection and for whom? *Journal of Health Economics.* 2008;27(6):1532–1550.

36. Hoynes HW, Miller DL, Schaller J. Who suffers during recessions? *Journal of Economic Perspectives.* 2012;26(3):27–47.

37. Rajkumar RP. The association between nation-level social and economic indices and suicide rates: a pilot study. *Frontiers in Sociology.* 2023;8:1123284.

38. Er ST, Demir E, Sari E. Suicide and economic uncertainty: new findings in a global setting. *SSM - Population Health.* 2023;22:101387.

39. Dückers MLA, Witteveen AB, Bisson JI, et al. The association between disaster vulnerability and post-disaster psychosocial service delivery across Europe. *Administration and Policy in Mental Health.* 2017;44(4):470–479.

40. Hofstede G. Dimensionalizing cultures: the Hofstede model in context. *Online Readings in Psychology and Culture.* 2011;2(1).

41. Forbes India. The top 10 largest economies in the world in 2024. 2024.

42. Confronting Poverty Discussion Guide. https://confrontingpoverty.org/wp-content/ uploads/2021/10/CP_Discussion-Guide_All_2020.pdf. 2024.

43. Agerbo E, Mortensen P, Eriksson T, Qin P. Risk of suicide in relation to income level in people admitted to hospital with mental illness: nested case-control study/commentary: suicide and income--is the risk greater in rich people who develop serious mental illness? *BMJ. British Medical Journal (International ed.).* 2001;322(7282):334.

44. Lester D. The role of shame in suicide. *Suicide & Life-Threatening Behavior.* 1997;27(4):352–361.

45. Daly MC, Wilson DJ, Johnson NJ. Relative status and well-being: evidence from U.S. suicide deaths. *The Review of Economics and Statistics.* 2013;95(5):1480–1500.

46. Ruhm CJ. Are recessions good for your health? *Journal of Economics.* 2000;115(2): 617–650.

47. Helliwell JF. Well-being and social capital: does suicide pose a puzzle? *Social Indicators Research.* 2007;81(3):455–496.

48. Rayo L, Becker G. Evolutionary efficiency and happiness. *The Journal of Political Economy.* 2007;115(2):302–337.
49. Klein Teeselink B, Zauberman G. The Anna Karenina income effect: well-being inequality decreases with income. *Journal of Economic Behavior & Organization.* 2023;212: 501–513.
50. Jachimowicz JM, Frey EL, Matz SC, Jeronimus BF, Galinsky AD. The sharp spikes of poverty: financial scarcity is related to higher levels of distress intensity in daily life. *Social Psychological & Personality Science.* 2022;13(8):1187–1198.
51. MacKerron G, Powdthavee N. Predicting emotional volatility using 41,000 participants in the United Kingdom. 2022. Available at: https://arxiv.org/abs/2205.07742
52. Tikkanen R, Abrams M. U.S. health care from a global perspective, 2019: higher spending, worse outcomes? *Policy File.* 2020.

Chapter 7

1. Wasserman D, Cheng Q, Jiang G. Global suicide rates among young people aged 15-19. *World Psychiatry.* 2005;4(2):114–120.
2. Mojtabai R, Olfson M, Han B. National trends in the prevalence and treatment of depression in adolescents and young adults. *Pediatrics.* 2016;138(6):1.
3. Miron O, Yu K, Wilf-Miron R, et al. Suicide rates among adolescents and young adults in the United States, 2000-2017. *JAMA: the journal of the American Medical Association.* 2019;321(23):2362–2364.
4. Blease CR. Too many friends, too few likes? Evolutionary psychology and Facebook depression. *Review of General Psychology.* 2015;19(1):1–13.
5. Price J, Sloman L, Gardner R, et al. The social competition hypothesis of depression. *British Journal of Psychiatry.* 1994;164(3):309–315.
6. Allen NB, Badcock PBT. The social risk hypothesis of depressed mood. *Psychological Bulletin.* 2003;129(6):887–913.
7. Joiner TE. *Why people die by suicide.* First edition. Harvard University Press; 2005.
8. Klonsky ED, May AM. The three-step theory (3ST): a new theory of suicide rooted in the "ideation-to-action" framework. *International Journal of Cognitive Therapy.* 2015;8(2):114–129.
9. O'Connor RC, Kirtley OJ. The integrated motivational–volitional model of suicidal behaviour. *Philosophical Transactions of the Royal Society B.* 2018;373(1754):20170268.
10. Wetherall K, Robb KA, O'Connor RC. Social rank theory of depression: a systematic review of self-perceptions of social rank and their relationship with depressive symptoms and suicide risk. *Journal of Affective Disorders.* 2019;246:300–319.
11. Johnson J, Gooding PA, Wood AM, et al. Resilience as positive coping appraisals: testing the schematic appraisals model of suicide (SAMS). *Behaviour Research and Therapy.* 2010;48(3):179–186.
12. Hawton K, Saunders KE, O'Connor RC. Self-harm and suicide in adolescents. *The Lancet (British edition).* 2012;379(9834):2373–2382.
13. Zhang J, Wieczorek WF, Conwell Y, et al. Psychological strains and youth suicide in rural China. *Social Science & Medicine.* 2011;72(12):2003–2010.
14. American Psychological Association. Socioeconomic status. https://www.apa.org/topics/socioeconomic-status. Updated on 15 Nov 2023.
15. Adler NE, Epel ES, Castellazzo G, et al. Relationship of subjective and objective social status with psychological and physiological functioning. *Health Psychology.* 2000;19(6):586–592.

16. Mclaughlin KA, Costello EJ, Leblanc W, et al. Socioeconomic status and adolescent mental disorders. *American Journal of Public Health.* 2012;102(9):1742–1750.

17. Goodman E, Huang B, Schafer-Kalkhoff T, et al. Perceived socioeconomic status: a new type of identity which influences adolescents'. *Self Rated Health.* 2007;41(5):479–487.

18. Rosenberg M, Pearlin LI. Social class and self-esteem among children and adults. *American Journal of Sociology.* 1978;84(1):53–77.

19. Vidal C, Latkin C. Perceived family and individual social status and its association with depression and suicidality in an adolescent clinical sample. *Journal of Community Psychology.* 2020;48(8):2504–2516.

20. Vidal C, Jun H, Latkin C. The effects of social rank and neighborhood and school environment on adolescent depression and suicidal ideation: a structural equation modeling approach. *Child Psychiatry & Human Development.* 2023;54(5):1425–1437. doi:10.1007/s10578-022-01347-2.

21. Jeon G, Ha Y, Choi E. Effects of objective and subjective socioeconomic status on self-rated health, depressive symptoms, and suicidal ideation in adolescents. *Child Indicators Research.* 2013;6(3):479–492.

22. Rideout V, Peebles A, Mann S, Robb MB. Common sense census: media use by tweens and teens, 2021. San Francisco, CA: Common Sense; 2022.

23. Niu G, Luo Y, Sun X, et al. Qzone use and depression among Chinese adolescents: a moderated mediation model. *Journal of Affective Disorders.* 2018;231:58–62.

24. Nesi JPM. Using social media for social comparison and feedback-seeking: gender and popularity moderate associations with depressive symptoms. *Journal of Abnormal Child Psychology.* 2015;43(8):1427–1438.

25. Steers M, Wickham R, Acitelli L. Seeing everyone else's highlight reels: how Facebook usage is linked to depressive symptoms. *Journal of Social and Clinical Psychology.* 2014;33(8):701–731.

26. Turner BJ, Hu C, Villa JP, Nock MK. Oppositional defiant disorder and conduct disorder. In: Scott KM, de Jonge P, Stein DJ, Kessler RC., (eds.), *Mental Disorders Around the World: Facts and Figures from the WHO World Mental Health Surveys.* Cambridge University Press; 2017. pp. 209–222.

27. Georgiev AV, Klimczuk ACE, Traficonte DM, et al. When violence pays: a cost-benefit analysis of aggressive behavior in animals and humans. *Evolutionary Psychology.* 2013;11(3):678–699.

28. Tuvblad C, Raine A, Zheng M, et al. Genetic and environmental stability differs in reactive and proactive aggression. *Aggressive Behavior.* 2009;35(6):437–452.

29. Tremblay RE. Developmental origins of disruptive behaviour problems: the 'original sin' hypothesis, epigenetics and their consequences for prevention. *Journal of Child Psychology and Psychiatry.* 2010;51(4):341–367.

30. Buchmann A, Hohmann S, Brandeis D, Banaschewski T, Poustka L. Aggression in children and adolescents. *Current Topics in Behavioral Neurosciences.* 2014;17.

31. Chen B, Zuo Y, Zhao Y. The relationship between subjective social class and aggression: a serial mediation model. *Personality and Individual Differences.* 2018;131:174–179.

32. Guo X, Egan V, Zhang J. Sense of control and adolescents' aggression: the role of aggressive cues. *PsyCh Journal.* 2016;5(4):263–274.

33. Cohen S, Gianaros PJ, Manuck SB. A stage model of stress and disease. *Perspectives on Psychological Science.* 2016;11(4):456–463.

34. Seeman M, Stein Merkin S, Karlamangla A, et al. Social status and biological dysregulation: the "status syndrome" and allostatic load. *Social Science & Medicine.* 2014;118:143–151.

35. Fournier M, Moskowitz D, Zuroff D. Social rank strategies in hierarchical relationships. *Journal of Personality and Social Psychology.* 2002;83(2):425–433.
36. Hall CW. Self-reported aggression and the perception of anger in facial expression photos. *The Journal of Psychology.* 2006;140(3):255–267.
37. Sullivan D, Landau MJ, Rothschild ZK. An existential function of enemyship. *Journal of Personality and Social Psychology.* 2010;98(3):434–449.
38. Puhl RM, Heuer CA. Obesity stigma: important considerations for public health. *American Journal of Public Health.* 2010;100(6):1019–1028.
39. Finkelstein EA, Ruhm CJ, Kosa KM. Economic causes and consequences of obesity. *Annual Review of Public Health.* 2005;26(1):239–257.
40. The Marmot Review. *Fair society, healthy lives.* The Marmot Review; 2010.

Chapter 8

1. Vidal C, Wissow LS. Adolescents' social comparisons, subjective social status, and coping to maintain well-being: a qualitative study. *Journal of Applied Social Science.* 2023;17(2):291–301. doi:10.1177/19367244221140306.
2. Baltimore rapper Lor Scoota, By Vivian Kuo C. killed. https://www.cnn.com/2016/06/27/us/lor-scoota-tyriece-travon-watson-killed/index.html. Updated 2016.
3. Maslow AH. *A theory of human motivation.* General Press; 2019.

Chapter 9

1. Magaro MM, Weisz JR. Perceived control mediates the relation between parental rejection and youth depression. *Journal of Abnormal Child Psychology.* 2006;34(6):863–872.
2. Moe A. Perceived control mediates the relations between depressive symptoms and academic achievement in adolescence. *The Spanish Journal of Psychology.* 2015;18:E70.
3. River LM, Borelli JL, Vazquez LC, et al. Learning helplessness in the family: maternal agency and the intergenerational transmission of depressive symptoms. *Journal of Family Psychology.* 2018;32(8):1109–1119.
4. Wolfle LM, List JH. Temporal stability in the effects of college attendance on locus of control, 1972-1992. *Structural Equation Modeling.* 2004;11(2):244–260.
5. Keeton CP, Perry-Jenkins M, Sayer AG. Sense of control predicts depressive and anxious symptoms across the transition to parenthood. *Journal of Family Psychology.* 2008;22(2):212–221.
6. Butzer B, Kuiper NA. Relationships between the frequency of social comparisons and self-concept clarity, intolerance of uncertainty, anxiety, and depression. *Personality and Individual Differences.* 2006;41(1):167–176.
7. Folkman S, Lazarus RS. Stress processes and depressive symptomatology. *Journal of Abnormal Psychology (1965).* 1986;95(2):107–113.
8. Bonanno GA, Burton CL. Regulatory flexibility: an individual differences perspective on coping and emotion regulation. *Perspectives on Psychological Science.* 2013;8(6):591–612.
9. Kato T. Coping with stress, executive functions, and depressive symptoms: focusing on flexible responses to stress. *Journal of Clinical Medicine.* 2021;10(14):3122.
10. Festinger L. A theory of social comparison processes. *Human Relations.* 1954;7(2):117–140.
11. Schachter S. *The psychology of affiliation: experimental studies of the sources of gregariousness.* Stanford University Press; 1959.

12. Price J, Sloman L, Gardner R, et al. The social competition hypothesis of depression. *British Journal of Psychiatry.* 1994;164(3):309–315.

13. Gibbons, F. X., & Buunk, B. P. (1999). *Iowa-Netherlands Comparison Orientation Measure (INCOM)* [Database record]. APA PsycTests.

14. Tellegen A, Waller NG. Exploring personality through test construction: development of the multidimensional personality questionnaire. In: Boyle GJ, Matthews G, Saklofske DH, (eds.), *The SAGE handbook of personality theory and assessment: volume 2 — personality measurement and testing.* SAGE Publications Inc.; 2008. pp. 261–292.

15. Patrick CJ, Hicks BM, Krueger RF, et al. Relations between psychopathy facets and externalizing in a criminal offender sample. *Journal of Personality Disorders.* 2005;19(4):339–356.

16. Johnson SL, Leedom LJ, Muhtadie L. The dominance behavioral system and psychopathology: evidence from self-report, observational, and biological studies. *Psychological Bulletin.* 2012;138(4):692–743.

17. Zuroff DC, Fournier MA, Patall EA, et al. Steps toward an evolutionary personality psychology. *Canadian Psychology = Psychologie Canadienne.* 2010;51(1):58–66.

18. Duriez B, Vansteenkiste M, Soenens B, et al. The social costs of extrinsic relative to intrinsic goal pursuits: their relation with social dominance and racial and ethnic prejudice. *Journal of Personality.* 2007;75(4):757–782.

19. Schultheiss OC, Wirth MM. Biopsychological aspects of motivation. In: Heckhausen J, Heckhausen H (eds.), *Motivation and action.* 3rd ed. New York: Cambridge University Press; 2018:407–451.

20. Dunbar RIM. *Primate social systems.* First published edition. Comstock Public Schools; 1988.

21. Wiggins JS. A psychological taxonomy of trait-descriptive terms: the interpersonal domain. *Journal of Personality and Social Psychology.* 1979;37(3):395–412.

22. de Waal FB, Aureli F, Judge PG. Coping with crowding. *Scientific American.* 2000;282(5):76–81.

23. Keltner D, Gruenfeld DH, Anderson C. Power, approach, and inhibition. *Psychological Review.* 2003;110(2):265–284.

24. Josephs RA, Sellers JG, Newman ML, Mehta PH. The mismatch effect: When testosterone and status are at odds. *Journal of Personality and Social Psychology.* 2006;90(6): 999–1013.

25. Boyce WT. Social stratification, health, and violence in the very young. *Annals of the New York Academy of Sciences.* 2004;1036(1):47–68.

26. Gilbert P, McEwan K, Bellew R, Bellew R, Mills A, Gale C. The dark side of competition: how competitive behaviour and striving to avoid inferiority are linked to depression, anxiety, stress and self-harm. *Psychology and Psychotherapy.* 2009;82(2):123–136.

27. Kessler RC, Berglund P, Demler O, et al. The epidemiology of major depressive disorder: results from the National Comorbidity Survey Replication (NCS-R). *JAMA: The Journal of the American Medical Association.* 2003;289(23):3095–3105.

28. Danziger L, Schroeder H, Unger A. Androgen therapy for involutional melancholia. *The Journal of Nervous and Mental Disease.* 1944;100(5):521.

29. TSE WS, BOND AJ. Serotonergic intervention affects both social dominance and affiliative behaviour. *Psychopharmacology (Berl).* 2002;161(3):324–330.

30. Fournier M, Moskowitz D, Zuroff D. Social rank strategies in hierarchical relationships. *Journal of Personality and Social Pscy<ology.* 2002;83(2):425–433.

31. Maner JK, Miller SL, Schmidt NB, et al. Submitting to defeat: social anxiety, dominance threat, and decrements in testosterone. *Psychological Science.* 2008;19(8):764–768.

32. Thomsen L. The developmental origins of social hierarchy: how infants and young children mentally represent and respond to power and status. *Current Opinion in Psychology*. 2020;33:201–208.
33. Archer J. Testosterone and human aggression: an evaluation of the challenge hypothesis. *Neuroscience and Biobehavioral Reviews*. 2006;30(3):319–345.
34. Tarter RE, Kirisci L, Kirillova GP, et al. Social dominance mediates the association of testosterone and neurobehavioral disinhibition with risk for substance use disorder. *Psychology of Addictive Behaviors*. 2007;21(4):462–468.
35. Steers M, Wickham R, Acitelli L. Seeing everyone else's highlight reels: how Facebook usage is linked to depressive symptoms. *Journal of Social and Clinical Psychology*. 2014;33(8):701–731.
36. Vogel EA, Rose JP, Okdie BM, et al. Who compares and despairs? The effect of social comparison orientation on social media use and its outcomes. *Personality and Individual Differences*. 2015;86:249–256.
37. Cast AD, Burke PJ. A theory of self-esteem. *Social Forces*. 2002;80(3):1041–1068.
38. Wang J, Wang H, Gaskin J, Hawk S. The mediating roles of upward social comparison and self-esteem and the moderating role of social comparison orientation in the association between social networking site usage and subjective well-being. *Frontiers in psychology*. 2017;8:771.
39. Bäzner E, Brömer P, Hammelstein P, et al. Current and former depression and their relationship to the effects of social comparison processes. Results of an internet based study. *Journal of Affective Disorders*. 2006;93(1–3):97–103.
40. Gugushvili A. Which socio-economic comparison groups do individuals choose and why? *European Societies*. 2021;23(4):437–463.
41. Bonfanti RC, Coco GL, Ruggieri S. Social comparison on Facebook and its effect on an individual's well-being. In: *Social media in the 21st century: perspectives, influences and effects on well-being*. Nova Science Publishers, Incorporated; 2021.
42. Nesi J, Prinstein MJ. Using social media for social comparison and feedback-seeking: gender and popularity moderate associations with depressive symptoms. *Journal of Abnormal Child Psychology*. 2015;43(8):1427–1438.
43. Twenge JM, Campbell WK. Self-esteem and socioeconomic status: a meta-analytic review. *Personality and Social Psychology Review*. 2002;6(1):59–71.
44. Wolff LS, Subramanian SV, Acevedo-Garcia D, et al. Compared to whom? Subjective social status, self-rated health, and referent group sensitivity in a diverse US sample. *Social Science & Medicine*. 2010;70(12):2019–2028. doi:10.1016/j.socscimed.2010.02.033.
45. Marengo D, Montag C, Sindermann C, et al. Examining the links between active Facebook use, received likes, self-esteem and happiness: a study using objective social media data. *Telematics and Informatics*. 2021;58:101523.

Chapter 10

1. The Mindfulness Project. Comparing ourselves with others. https://www.londonmindful.com/blog/comparing-ourselves-with-others/. Updated 2022.
2. Sexton JB, Adair KC. Forty-five good things: a prospective pilot study of the Three Good Things well-being intervention in the USA for healthcare worker emotional exhaustion, depression, work-life balance and happiness. *BMJ Open*. 2019;9(3):e022695.
3. Christensen K, Bathum L, Christiansen L. Biological indicators and genetic information in Danish twin and oldest-old surveys. In: Weinstein MVJ, Wachter KW, ed. *National*

Research Council (US) Committee on advances in collecting and utilizing biological indicators and genetic information in social science surveys. National Academies Press (US); 2008. Available at: https://portal.findresearcher.sdu.dk/da/publications/459002f0-c1ff-11dd-a428-000ea68e967b

4. Lessons from the Blue Zones®. Roundtable on population health improvement. Board on Population Health and Public Health Practice. Business engagement in building healthy communities: workshop summary. 2015.

5. Kennedy JL, MacKenzie KR. Dominance hierarchies in psychotherapy groups. *British Journal of Psychiatry.* 1986;148(6):625–631.

6. Lieberman MA. Up the right mountain, down the wrong path theory development for people-changing groups. *The Journal of Applied Behavioral Science.* 1974;10(2): 166–174.

7. Vall B, Seikkula J, Laitila A, et al. Dominance and dialogue in couple therapy for psychological intimate partner violence. *Contemporary Family Therapy.* 2016;38(2):223–232.

8. Artigas Miralles L, Vilaregut Puigdesens A, Feixas Viaplana G, et al. Dialogue and dominance in couple therapy for depression: exploring therapists' responses in creating collaborative moments. *Family Process.* 2020;59(3):1080–1093.

9. Miller WR, Moyers TB. The forest and the trees: relational and specific factors in addiction treatment. *Addiction (Abingdon, England).* 2015;110(3):401–413. doi:10.1111/add.12693.

10. Rogers CR. *Counseling and psychotherapy.* Houghton Mifflin; 1942.

11. Greene RW. *The explosive child: a new approach for understanding and parenting easily frustrated, chronically inflexible children.* Sixth edition. HarperCollins; 2021.

12. Psychology Tools. Social comparison. https://www.psychologytools.com/resource/social-comparison/. Updated 2024.

13. Fairburn CG. Eating disorders: the transdiagnostic view and the cognitive behavioral theory. In: *Cognitive behavior therapy and eating disorders.* Guilford Press; 2008:7–22.

14. Acceptance & commitment therapy. Association for Contextual Behavioral Science. Available at: https://contextualscience.org/act

15. Miller WR, Moyers TB. The forest and the trees: relational and specific factors in addiction treatment. *Addiction.* 2015;110(3):401–413.

16. Richer AD; Binkley C. TV stars and coaches charged in college bribery scheme. *AP Worldstream.* Mar 12, 2019. Accessed June 30, 2024. https://search.proquest.com/docview/2190168073.

17. Harrist AW, Bradley KD. "You can't say you can't play": intervening in the process of social exclusion in the kindergarten classroom. *Early Childhood Research Quarterly.* 2003;18(2):185–205.

18. Reidy J. Reviewing school uniform through a public health lens: evidence about the impacts of school uniform on education and health. *Public Health Reviews.* 2021;42:1604212.

19. Baumann C, Krskova H. School discipline, school uniforms and academic performance. *International Journal of Educational Management.* 2016;30(6):1003–1029.

20. France 24. France to try out school uniforms in bid to reduce bullying and inequality. *France 24.* January 8, 2024. https://search.proquest.com/docview/2911082301.

21. Meadmore D, Symes C. Keeping up appearances: uniform policy for school diversity? *British Journal of Educational Studies.* 1997;45(2):174–186.

22. Oppenheimer M. *The downsides of school uniforms*; 2018. The New Yorker. Available at: https://www.newyorker.com/culture/culture-desk/the-unquestioned-goodness-of-school-uniforms.

23. Rogow F. Sharing media literacy approaches with parents and families. In: Donohue C, ed. *Family engagement in the digital age.* Routledge; 2017:217–232.
24. Nicuță EG, Constantin T. Take nothing for granted: downward social comparison and counterfactual thinking increase adolescents' state gratitude for the little things in life. *Journal of Happiness Studies.* 2021;22(8):3543–3570.
25. Urry HL, Gross JJ. Emotion regulation in older age. *Current Directions in Psychological Science.* 2010;19(6):352–357.
26. Raviv A, Bar-Tal D, Ravi A, et al. Adolescent idolization of pop singers: causes, expressions, and reliance. *Journal of Youth and Adolescence.* 1996;25(5):631–650.
27. The Marmot Review. *Fair society, healthy lives.* The Marmot Review; 2010.

Index

acceptance and commitment therapy 135–136

Adler, N.E. 41, 91

adolescence: absolute deprivation 110–111; aggression in 78; and child development 49, 93, 134; deaths by opioids 80; depression in 70, 88, 97, 115; interviews 129; popularity in 47–49, 52; social comparisons in 67, 69, 96–97, 103, 111–113; social hierarchies 129; social media among 36, 69–71, 105; social rank 91, 94, 97; social status 44–45, 47, 49–50, 54–55, 67, 96, 107, 116, 136–137; socio-economic status measures 91, 103; stress among 92; suicide rates among 36, 83, 93

Adverse Childhood Experiences (ACE) study 14

aggression: in adolescence 78; in children 46; and counter-aggression 46; dominance 11; experiencing *vs.* witnessing 2; levels of 5, 10, 78, 98; physical 49; and popularity 49; relational 47, 49; and social status 78, 97–99; testosterone levels 124–125; verbal 1, 98; victims of 4

Alcaraz, Carlos 136

Ames, K.M. 20

Anna Karenina principle 87

attention deficit hyperactivity disorder (ADHD) 3, 71, 97, 142

Avis, J. 17

Baron-Cohen, Sasha 17

Baron-Cohen, Simon 17

Blue Zones study 130

Boehm, C. 21

Bush, George H.W. 80

Case, A. 79

celebrity(ies): Angelina Jolie effect 65; birth of 63–66; death by suicide 65–66; Edutainment 65; Hollywood 63, 69; online 144; Papageno effect 66; rise of social media 63–64, 105, 143; social comparisons 63, 68, 69, 103, 105; values and behavior 64–65

child development 34; and adolescents 49, 93, 134; aggression 46; depression 5, 115; and economic downturns 83–84; and health 37–39, 42–43; hierarchies 45–46; mental health services 84; physical and social environments 43; popularity 47; poverty 43, 85; sensitive periods 43; social comparisons 66–67, 124; social media 2, 28, 36, 47; social status 47–49, 52; socio-economic status 42–43; status and dominance dynamics 47, 57; using right tools in schools 137–140

chronic stress 13–14, 116

clinical depression 61, 122

Clinton, Bill 80

cognitive-behavioral therapy (CBT) 12, 41, 135–136

competitive dressing 138

conduct disorder (CD) 97, 125

Cooley, C.H. 44

coping flexibility 116

corticosteroids 4

cortisol 5–6, 8, 13, 35, 40, 42

counter-aggression 46

counter dominance 19, 21–22

COVID-19 pandemic: effects of 78; lockdowns 38; recessions 82, 86; social media 38

cumulative disadvantage process 81

and its contributors 78–79; linked to social support 36; lower rates 85; public 65; rates and income inequality 84; risk for 86; schematic appraisals model 90; social media among adolescents 36; and social rank 85–86; socio-economic status 86; youth 36, 65
Świątek, Iga 136

testosterone levels 4, 6, 10, 11, 122–125
Thatcher, Margaret 27
threat of loss 84
three-step theory 89
TikTok 66, 71, 126, 139, 143
toddlers 46, 66, 98, 120, 134
Tolstoy, Leo 87
Tooby, J. 16
transactional theory 116
trauma 7–8, 13–14, 33, 35, 78–79, 93, 98–99, 105, 122, 124

Ukraine, war in 28

verbal aggression 1, 98
victimhood, status of 141–143
vulnerability paradox 84

well-being: and income 86–87; mental 60, 104; relative income theory 62; and social rank 94; subjective 54, 59, 86
Werther Effect 65
Whitehall studies 31–32
Whiten A. 15, 16, 20
Wilkinson, R.G. 33, 41
Woodburn, J. 23, 24
Wooley, Helen 57

Yerkes-Dodson Law 34
youth: Black 73; with emotional disorders 70–71; mental health crisis 31, 69, 88, 127, 145–146; popularity 48; social status 11–13, 115; suicide 36, 65–66, 80
YouTube 64, 105, 120

For Product Safety Concerns and Information please contact our EU
representative GPSR@taylorandfrancis.com
Taylor & Francis Verlag GmbH, Kaufingerstraße 24, 80331 München, Germany

9 781032 880341